Monograph 43
# THE AMERICAN ETHNOLOGICAL SOCIETY

*June Helm, Editor*

# PIONEERS

contributions by

Jacob Gruber

Nancy Oestreich Lurie

Ross Parmenter

Ronald P. Rohner

# of AMERICAN ANTHROPOLOGY

## *THE USES OF BIOGRAPHY*

edited by June Helm MacNeish

UNIVERSITY OF WASHINGTON PRESS

*SEATTLE*               *LONDON*

2458H

# PREFACE

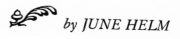 *by JUNE HELM*

The title of this volume is anticipatory. As Jacob Gruber points out in the first essay, anthropologists have scarcely begun to explore the uses of biography in charting the development and nature of their discipline. This is the more surprising in that in their professional roles anthropologists have commonly dealt with small societies, wherein the life history serves as one kind of distillation of the life-ways of the group. Nor have anthropologists been insensitive to the role that individual character may play in modulating and directing the conduct of life in the little community.

In these essays, as anthropologists appear and reappear in different contexts and stances, we are reminded how like the little community the social body of anthropologists has been, and — with perhaps greater subdivision into interactional and intellectual *barrios*, each with its patron saints — it remains so today.

Anthropologists have long been accustomed to analyze and argue the role of various intellectual ideologies in the development of the discipline. The many assessments of Boas as scientist, impressing his intellectual purview upon a generation of anthropologists, are proof enough of that. But Ross Parmenter's account of Nuttall's dealings with Boas and other American and Mexican colleagues presents a slice of the politics of anthropology, a dimension which has seldom explicitly been held up to scrutiny by the profession. Drawn to his study of the Boas-Nuttall correspondence by avocation, Parmenter has escaped the inhibitions of professional convention in his choice of subject and treatment.

Nancy O. Lurie's study of the women pioneers in American anthropology shows those stalwarts modestly casting themselves in the role of *woman*-anthropologist, but in the field and the study soon transcending that role to become simply anthropologists. In many of their professional judgements they were unable to move far from the norms and premises of their time and culture and profession. Evolution and Progress were to them not subjects of inquiry but first principles. Their sentiments, their moral and intellectual commitments are instructive samplers of the world view of the educated nineteenth-century American.

In charting the span and content of Boas' field work on the Northwest Coast, Ronald Rohner has met a felt need in the study of the history of anthropology — the need for an explication of "the facts" behind the pious acceptance of Boas as the intellectual father of systematic field work in American anthropology. However, in Boas' letters from the field, as edited by Rohner, are to be found more than "the facts": in and between the lines can be read something of the role played by the temper of the man in the shaping of the scientist.

Like any other human group woven together in common interest and activity, anthropologists have their folklore, their myths and culture heroes. For how many novice anthropologists has the tale of Frank Cushing's commitment to the sacred secrets of the kiva served the Malinowskian function of the myth — to safeguard and enforce one's personal anthropological morality? His humanist, or simply human, heritage enjoins the anthropologist to attempt empathy with the persons behind the masks, be they the masks of demi-gods or of professionally "interchangeable functionaries." Further, it is the hallmark of cultural anthropology as a science that penetration into the meanings and motives that underlie behavior is held to be necessary for the full understanding of any human group. The anthropologist, then, properly cannot ignore the natures of the actors — his professional ancestors, his peers, and himself — who create his system of action.

# CONTENTS

# ILLUSTRATIONS

*following page 82*

# PIONEERS
## OF AMERICAN ANTHROPOLOGY

# IN SEARCH OF EXPERIENCE:

## Biography as an Instrument
## for the History of Anthropology

 *by JACOB GRUBER*

*Jacob Gruber is professor of anthropology and chairman of the department of anthropology at Temple University, Philadelphia, Pennsylvania.*

*This is a revised version of a paper delivered at the Conference on the History of Anthropology, April 13–14, 1962. The Conference was sponsored by the Social Science Research Council of New York.*

A relatively minor, although interesting, phenomenon of the late nineteenth-century literary scene was the almost deadening regularity with which individuals of varying degrees of importance were immortalized by multi-volumed collections of their letters. These collections, which now clutter the shelves of the booksellers, passed for biography. Often rigidly edited by a relative of the deceased, accomplishing a familial duty of sanctification, or by a friend or student, discharging his obligation to speak only well of the dead, these parodies of life stand today as memorials to the earnestness, the overt seriousness, the press for goodness which was one, sometimes over-exaggerated, feature of the intellectual climate of the period.

Almost tragic in the spirit and the point of view that motivated these kinds of biographical treatment was their assumption of a definition of the role of the individual in history which was already changing, and changing so radically that the seriousness and reverence of the biographical intent is turned to humor and bathos. Personal memoirs of this type extoll the belief that history is but the instrument of individual action, that men make history, all of history, and that great men make great history. For the biographer who writes — or merely edits — in this vein, his subject — whose importance is already assumed — stands at the vortex of the historical events with which he deals and has real effect upon the outcome of these events.[1]

From the tremendous sociocultural changes occurring during

the middle half of the century, however, a new view of history was emerging which was to subordinate the actions of the individual to abstract forces — historical, sociological or what have you — and to destroy the entire concept of individual greatness and historical will upon which the biographical tradition of the nineteenth century had been built. "Social scientists" crowded to construct a mechanics through which forces analogous to those binding physical particles together could be defined for human particles, and they invoked concepts of historical force, tradition, etc., to provide the power which made human societies go. Within this context we can see emphases upon the concepts of society, culture, and race emerging as active agents for the production of continuing human behavior.

In *War and Peace*, written during this period of ideological change, Tolstoy describes not only the physical battlefields of the Russian landscape, but as significantly, the intellectual conflict between these opposing ideas with respect to man and his place in history. For at the same time that the new men of biology were concerned with man's place in nature, their sociological analogues were defining his place in society. On the one hand Tolstoy mocks the myth that great men direct history:

> In historical events (where the actions of men are the subject of observation) the first and most primitive approximation [of historical cause] was the will of the gods, and after that, the will of those who stood in the most prominent position — the heroes of history. But we need only penetrate [as Tolstoy took great pains to do] to the essence of any historic event — which lies in the activity of the general mass of men who take part in it — to be convinced that the will of the historic hero does not control the actions of the mass but is itself continually controlled. . . . There is, and can be, no cause of an historical event except the one cause of all causes. But there are laws directing events. . . . The discovery of these laws is only possible when we have quite abandoned the attempt to find the cause in the will of some

one man, just as the discovery of the laws of the motion of the planets was possible only when men abandoned the conception of the fixity of the earth.[2]

But, as Isaiah Berlin has suggested,[3] Tolstoy, although seeking some universal law of history, some overriding explanatory principle or force, was contemptuous of the easy explanations fetched up to supplant man as the principal agent of history. In a period during which man contested with something called historical force to explain his presence and his future, Tolstoy's genius enabled him to reduce the new high-sounding explanatory abstractions to verbal rubble. He possessed, as few did during that period of scientific optimism and secular determinism, an intuitive understanding of the multiple forces of accident and design, of persons and people, that together weave the fabric of the human moment. The light of this understanding illuminates *War and Peace*; and this light, for Tolstoy, enshadowed the overly simple systems of historical explanation whether made by theologian, philosopher, scholar, scientist, or revolutionary.

Some intellectual historian of the future undoubtedly will seek to describe as dispassionate process what we may call "the life and death of the great man theory of history." And certainly the one-sided emphasis of Tolstoy's historical analysis — with its destruction of the hero and the heroic — will be seen to have played its role in shifting responsibility for human events from the individual to "history." Whatever the specifics of this process, however, by the first decades of this century, man had become not the maker of history, but its pawn. The new biography showed man at his foolishly worst — pitiful in the illusion of his historical value. And by the 1930's, as John Garraty notes, biography made of man either a personality — more aptly a character — removed from the historical stream or an historical channel through whom the charge of history flowed, a vessel for the containment of history rather than the wine itself. Even those who, for one reason or another, sought to see history in terms of particular men, wrote a kind of intellectual biography whose focus was upon formally expressed ideas — whose values emerged on the basis of hindsight — and their place in the intellectual milieu of the period. Ideas were kinds of cultural objects — and their analysis was the objective of "intellectual biography."

Against these admittedly polar views of man and/or biography, we may set another. Stemming from a more sophisticated understanding of the man-culture-society problem, it represents a synthesis of the Tolstoyan extremes, a synthesis that in effect makes Tolstoy's paradox irrelevant except for historical purposes. Biography of this sort neither sets the individual against the sociological currents of his time nor does it seek alone its historical explanations in the reification of those abstractions we call historical forces. Such biography, ideally, can demonstrate the ways in which a single individual enacts the changing system that is his culture — whatever the extent of the system and whatever the extent of his involvement. In this way, biography may be seen not as an historical document but as a human document valuable for cultural reconstruction; neither the meticulous marshalling of the minutiae surrounding a life nor the intuitive grasp of the romance of character; but the visualization of an individual against the backdrop of his time; the reconstruction of an historical period, a culture, through analysis of the behavior of the individuals who enacted it and who were involved in it. This biography is based upon the premise of a synthesis of culture and person, a synthesis so vital for the definition of either that to separate them does violence to both. This synthesis is analogous to that which, on a biological level, exists between the organism and its particular environment — the biosphere — which leads to a definition of either in terms of its relation to the other.

Within the history of science, the nature of the subject matter and the emphasis upon the impersonal method (the necessity of replication, objectivity, extrahuman sources of observation, community consensus of observers) through which scientific content is achieved, has tended to obscure the role of the individual and the irrational in scientific invention.[4] In his Bampton Lectures delivered at Columbia University, several years ago, Joel Hildebrand, a distinguished chemist, noted that there are

> two aspects of science; one may be designated content, the other enterprise. The one is, as the dictionary says, "classified knowledge"; the other is the ways in which scientists work and think. The one is the way we write up our results, in papers and books, in the passive voice, giving the impression that we start with precise measurements and proceed by strict logical steps to incontrovertible conclusions. The other is the way we really do it — starting with hunches, making guesses (most of which prove to be wild), making many mistakes, going off on blind roads before hitting on one that seems to be going in the right direction. That is science in the making.[5]

Biographical treatment in the history of science too often defines the science in the first of Hildebrand's terms — a definition that, of course, determines the treatment to be afforded the subject. To understand the history of a science through biography, however, we must stress the wandering process of the search — with its blind turnings, its mistakes and accidents — rather than the formal aspects of the achievements.

The value of recent Darwinian scholarship — and particularly that of Loren Eiseley — not only for the history of science but also for the broader range of intellectual history, is that the idea of organic evolution itself need no longer be extolled. It is now possible to concentrate on the particulars of the process of the origins of the *Origin* without being accused of theological conservatism if one finds that Darwin may have been mortal. For a century we have been subjected to the myth of a Darwin, meditating in isolation, poring over his journal and his barnacles, and suddenly, while reading Malthus, seized with the inspiration of natural selection. Much more perceptive, however, and probably much more in accord with the normal process of the generation of ideas, is Eiseley's tracing out of the readings and the particular influences that had gone into Darwin's mind to emerge, at times in an altered form, within the limits of his system.[6] Such descriptions of the personal operations of the scientist — operations which involve both sociological and intellectual processes — constitute the description of science in the making.

It comes as something of a surprise to see that anthropologists have virtually ignored biography as a means of understanding their own intellectual origins. This surprise is reasonable when one considers the extent to which anthropologists have made use of biography as an instrument of ethnography. Not only is much of the traditional methodology of ethnography based upon the premise that culture achieves its operational unity — if not its reality — through the interpretation and behavior of a normally functioning participant — the informant — but anthropologists have used the biographically oriented life history as an important source not only of culture content but also of the understanding of the dynamic or operational aspect of culture. In these biographies, the individual was neither regarded as a unique and separate entity to be understood in his separateness nor as a mouthpiece for the expression of his culture. Rather he was seen as a mediator through whom the culture took on form as well as substance. This form of "ethnographic biography" can be as meaningful in the construction of the behavioral system — the form and substance — of an institution, such as that of science, as it can in that of a total culture.

Despite the general recognition of these values in the biographical form however, those few biographies of anthropologists qua anthropologists, with a possible exception, tell us little more of the nature of the field itself and the process of its growth than can be gleaned from even a cursory examination of the better-known writings of the subject. We expect little more of the obituary, for here we have the force of tradition directing the well-chosen words of the author; we expect the obituaries to be devoid of the fragments of a life's experiences that show the dead to have been alive, to have lived through history so that he touched and was touched by it. The rule, apparently, in writing a good obituary is to write it in such a manner that only those who knew the subject well can see his image there. But the few more ambitious biographies attempt little more; and, except for a somewhat more expanded treatment of the institutional role played by their respective subjects, accomplish only what they attempt.

In making an assessment of this sort, I have restricted myself to the past century, a period within which I believe the history of anthropology as a self-conscious discipline may be confined. Certainly, arguments can be raised against such a restriction. It seems to me, however, that anthropology emerged as a discipline, with goals (and eventually methods) clearly distinguished from existing fields only as the consequence of two separate but related events which occurred almost simultaneously at the close of the 1850's.

One was the discovery of the unquestioned association of human artifacts with the bones of an extinct "antediluvial" fauna at Brixham Cave in 1858; the revolution occasioned by this demonstration of man's previously rejected antiquity threw man back into a previously inconceivable past. This new dimension of man's existence made necessary a reconstruction of cultures which, now extinct, were available for study only through the "fossils" they had left.[7] The remarkable use which first Georges Cuvier in France and then Richard Owen in England had made of comparative anatomy for the reconstruction of fossil faunal forms provided a ready-made model for the reconstruction of these prehistoric cultures through the development and use of a comparative ethnography.

The second event was, of course, the publication of Darwin's *Origin of Species* in 1859, which provided a new direction for the studies of man's nature and variety that had, for half a century, been pursued either as ethnology or as the natural history of man. Darwin's evolution through natural selection provided a new meaning for man's physical nature as well as a theoretical system within which to view his "ethnological" or racial differences around which so many controversies had developed.[8] The subsequent emphasis upon or recognition of the fact that unlike other organic species, man varies along two different and independent paths — the physical and the "cultural" — made possible an increasing awareness of the unique nature of the latter, a uniqueness which was to provide the center around which an entire set of anthropological interests — theoretical, methodological, and controversial — were to revolve for almost a century.

Certainly there were anthropological interests and enterprises prior to the early 1860's. In addition to an increasing number of students devoted to the description of the racial varieties and linguistic stocks of the human species, several societies were organized to serve as the focus for both the collection and distribution of pertinent data. The Society of the Observers of Man (*Societé des observateurs de l'homme*) was established in Paris in 1800 "to stimulate studies on the natural history of man" and "to form a foundation and a direction for the researches of travellers," whose reports would feed the meetings of the Society.[9] This attempt to organize researches into the natural history of man lasted only a few years; but the Ethnological Society of Paris was founded in 1839, followed by the Ethnological Society of New York in 1842 (predecessor of the present American Ethnological Society), and the Ethnological Society of London in 1844. And following the lead of the French, the British Association for the Advancement of Science, at the urging of James Cowles Prichard whose paper "On the Extinction of Some Varieties of the Human Race" was read at the 1839 meetings, appointed a small committee to draft a "set of queries to be addressed to those who may travel or reside in parts of the globe inhabited by threatened races." This report appeared in 1841 as a small pamphlet of a dozen pages listing 89 questions covering such areas as physical characters, language, buildings and monuments, works of art, domestic animals, government and laws, geography and statistics, social relations, and religious superstitions.[10]

All of these studies of man however may be encompassed within a general rubric of the natural history of man, an approach, essentially descriptive, designed to define the limits of variability that characterized the species — a species whose unity (in Europe) was generally assumed and whose permanency was accepted. Valuable as the work of these "proto-anthropologists" was, it lacked any distinction in point of view. It was one branch of natural history.

With the founding of the Anthropological Society of London in 1863, Thomas Bendyshe was able to write a long and detailed "History of Anthropology" as one of its first published memoirs in 1863. But both he and his associates in the new society recognized that the intellectual changes of the preceding few years had significantly altered the course of man's interest in himself and from that alteration there had emerged a *science* of anthropology. Bendyshe wrote his history as much to point the new way to the future as to honor the past.

The rise of anthropology into a science has necessarily been very slow [he noted] but the gradual steps by which, at last, it has arrived at recognition and become a systematic study, are of great interest. I propose to trace this progress from the earliest times, and to show how anthropology — which, at its onset, was embarrassed with speculations on the origin of all things — has gradually become disentangled from the smaller sciences, which have been carved out of it, and through which still lies the path to some of the generalizations, by means of which alone it can be carried to perfection, until at last it stands no risk of being confounded with any other department of knowledge, excepting that of ethnology, — the essential difference between which and itself is becoming more clearly understood every day.[11]

The innocence of the arrogance with which Bendyshe and his colleagues, particularly James Hunt, the Society's president, carried on their battle for recognition, is some kind of testimony not only to the importance but also to the novelty of the anthropology they espoused.

Whatever interests there were prior to the middle of the last century in what we might today define as anthropological pursuits, they derived from a spirit and from a definition of man and his place in the universe quite different from that which gave rise to the anthropology we know. For the world of which man was the center and in which he existed apart from the rest of organic creation was split asunder by the intellectual events of the 1850's and the early 1860's — and the old conception of man that provided significance to the work of the Blumenbachs, the Herders, the Catlins, the Lathams, and their noble kind was gone forever in the unified nature of a new world.

Perhaps this very recency of anthropology's beginnings accounts for the limited use of biography to reconstruct its past. The heroic age is still too near; the ties to the heroes still too close. After all, E. B. Tylor lived well into the twentieth century; and Alfred Haddon and Franz Boas died almost yesterday. The feeling of recency provides no real scope for historical movement; and the almost familial ties which still exist between the generations inhibit any but the most self-conscious of biographical treatments. As we know from too many examples, a biography of a parent by his child reveals more of the latter than of the former.

But has not the tradition of the disinvolvement of the anthropological observer also inhibited historically useful biographic treatments? The anthropologist has invested a tremendous amount of psychic capital in an image of himself as the almost faceless observer, sympathetic but never empathetic, within a group but never of a group, a recorder of events but scarcely a participant in them. The nature of the role that the anthropologist has created for himself inevitably makes for an air of diffidence about the nature of or the importance of his own activities as a person in the events of which he is a part. It was impossible for me to read Robert Lowie's professedly autobiographic account of his anthropology without feeling on almost every page his inability or his unwillingness to treat himself biographically, that is, in any other way except as an interchangeable functionary. And perhaps it is significant in this respect that Ruth Benedict found something of a personal refuge in the form of her poetic pseudonym, Anne Singleton.

Events, both conceptual and historical, have altered the situation; and in that alteration anthropology has attained a degree of maturity which permits it to speak of its past in something other than purely descriptive or adulatory terms. The Second World War provided the break between the present and the past that was necessary for the construction of some perspective of history.[12] The historical line has been stretched so that it is somewhat easier to disentangle the present from the past. Perhaps even more importantly, we have followed the pendulum as it has come to trace the greater role of the individual in the operation of his sociocultural systems; and we have come to realize the significance of the anthropologist as person as well as functionary in the operations he performs.[13]

Whatever the reasons, however, in the small amount of the history of anthropology that has been written, biography is poorly represented. Only Lewis Henry Morgan has been subjected to a reasonably full study; but until the spirited advocacy of Bernhard Stern and Leslie White, he was barely recognized as a person of importance to anthropology.[14] Moreover he, like his contemporary John Wesley Powell,[15] is already an *historical* figure who belongs as much to "American Civilization" as he does to anthropology. Of the others who have played more active and more direct roles in the development of anthropology as a discipline, we have only an occasional memoir. R. R. Marett's object was an assessment of Tylor's contributions to the social sciences;[16] and A. Hingston Quiggin's sketch of Haddon is excellent as a sketch, but deserves expansion for value as an historical document.[17]

American anthropologists have not fared better. Judging from the series of which it was a part, Melville Herskovits' memoir of Franz Boas was meant to be an adulatory description of a "great man" and his work;[18] and that is what it is. Lowie's posthumously published reminiscences are sadly uninformative.[19] Only Margaret Mead's memorial to Ruth Benedict — perhaps because the author was intimately associated with the situations she describes — provides, in the form of biography and only as biography can, views of subject and events as part of an historical process.[20] The success of this book lies in Dr. Mead's ability to evoke the spirit of the period through the juxtaposition of both important and unimportant events — a juxtaposition that can be made only if later evaluations are avoided. In addition, both Boas and Malinowski have been the subject of recent joint memoirs.[21] These, however, are intended primarily as assessments of the contributions and impact of important figures. As Raymond Firth notes for the Malinowski volume, "the essays as a set do give a synoptic view of the main strength and weakness of Malinowski's contribution and its modern relevance." [22] The Boas volume, published two years later, has a similar function. Both, however, are joint efforts; they are the views of different observers standing at different vantage points. As such they present fragmented rather than unified pictures of their subjects. Each contains the stuff of which biography is made; [23] but they are of greater value for the history of ideas than for a history of anthropology.

If these biographies are, in the main, unsatisfactory for the history of a scientific discipline, what do they lack, what might they contain? Let me suggest at least two areas in which I think biographic emphasis can illumine anthropological history in particular or the history of science in general.

There would be, I think, little disagreement among professional anthropologists concerning the importance of field work as both an initiatory experience and a continuing source of intellectual fertility. It was Tylor's journeys in Mexico with Henry Christy, the remarkable amateur, that turned him at the age of twenty-four to his lifelong interest in and study of culture as a human phenomenon; it was Boas' winter with the Eskimo, at the same age of twenty-four, that turned him from physical geography to anthropology; and there is almost a mystic quality about Morgan's need for the field, a quality that is not lessened by the tragic loss of his daughters associated with his last great and unsuccessful field trip in 1862 to Fort Benton.

What is it in the field that commits a man to anthropology and to the particular concepts — not always capable of verbalization — that make up the anthropological universe? What are these elements of culture shock, of the necessity for research improvisation, of humanism blended with science, of cultural variability beyond the capacity of vicarious experience — what is this complex we call field experience which is so effective and affecting that it drives some to suicide, some to decay, but most to the continuation of the anthropological enterprise? The important — almost nourishing — effect of the laboratory and the solution of its problems upon the scientist is implicitly recognized in every discussion of either the nature of science, its history or the problems associated with the training of scientists. In *The Search*, his novel of the rise, and eventual translation, of a physicist, C. P. Snow describes the culmination of the laboratory experience, the moment of discovery:

> I was carried beyond pleasure. . . . It was further [than previous delights] from myself. My own triumph and delight and success were there, but they seemed insignificant beside this tranquil ecstasy. It was as though I had looked for a truth outside myself, and finding it had become for a moment part of the truth I sought; as though all the world, the atoms and the stars, were wonderfully clear and close to me, and I to them, so that we were part of a lucidity more tremendous than any mystery. I had never known that such a moment could exist.[24]

The involvement of the person in the field and its effect upon him is of central biographical concern for a reconstruction of anthropological history; few areas in which the individual operates are of greater importance. If the field is vital in shaping the anthropologist, anthropology must have derived, must derive, its direction at least in part from its individual effects. It is during his experiences in the field that the individual anthropologist forges his methods and tempers his concepts. It is the sense — perhaps the security — of his field experience that forms the backdrop against which the systematic presentation of his results is projected. Is it also not this same involvement in the whole of a human culture that tempts the anthropologist to move easily from his data to those generalizations upon whose holism and universalism rests some of the uniqueness of anthropology among the social sciences? The anthropological literature contains sometimes valuable accounts and descriptions of native informants.[25] For providing an understanding of the process of anthropology, these accounts have value; but they contain little concerning the meaningful experiences of the field worker himself. I have no doubt that such material forms sizable parts of the field journals, that they are recounted in the correspondence, and that they are scattered through the unedited and unarranged field notes. They may be discussed among friends, in those moments when the mental guards are down; some may be embroidered into the illustrative and, I suspect, partly legendary tales that a teacher tells his students. But rarely do we see them as part of a life — either of the anthropologist or of anthropology. Here, among the various experiences in the field, lie uncollected and unexploited data basic to intellectual biography, data whose value for an understanding of the history of anthropology cannot, I think, be overstated.

Intellectual activity is a kind of constant and continuing discourse. By whatever process, ideas are developed, and communicated. One of the tenets of the institution of science is that communication is a necessary part of the process of science — a communication that provides the raw materials for further intellection. The Philosophical Transactions of the Royal Society of London — as those of many other early scientific societies — began as letters, i.e. communications, sent from one investigator to others through the secretary of the society; and still, scientific articles are often referred to as communications.

Without exploring at any length the nature of the communication process or its implications for intellectual activity, I wish to suggest the importance of personal interaction as a significant factor in the development of science. And it is this interactional aspect of science — both on a personal and an ideational level

— that furnishes another fruitful source for historically relevant biography.

Of especial value are the studies of these interactional levels during the formative periods of a particular discipline. These formative periods are characterized by rapid conceptual experimentation and expansion. New ideas are constantly brought forward for testing as a response to the new intellectual ecological niches that are opened through either ideological or technological invention.

Thus the intellectual breakthrough which resulted in the rise of anthropology during the 1860's stimulated a period of intense activity during that decade. It was followed by a relatively stable and quiescent period during the last quarter of the century. This activity, it is scarcely necessary to add, was that of individuals, each of whom had ideas which he wished to express and impress. To the extent that such ideas were assumed to be in conflict, to that extent did conflict exist between their adherents, a conflict often characterized as much by the personalities involved as by the ideas expressed. Thus, in what I consider to be the important events of the 1860's during which the direction of English anthropology was being set for a generation, at least as significant as the assumed differences in the ideas with reference to man were the personal differences between James Hunt and Thomas Huxley. The letters extant concerning this conflict — which was eventually resolved through the amalgamation of the Anthropological Society of London with the Ethnological Society — indicate that Huxley, who was rapidly assuming the role of prophet of the New Science, could not personally trust Hunt and thus was unwilling to cooperate with him on any level. Of course Hunt and his supporters felt the same way about Huxley. The conflict — essentially a personal one — was resolved only after the sudden death of Hunt.

Such interactional determinants of anthropology — or any

other science — are a constant source of direction. Often un-
charitably referred to as "politics," the informal, often nondi-
rective communications between persons involved in the matters
and operation of the discipline give rise to at least the temporary
form that the discipline will have; the stability of that form
will depend upon the particular characteristics — influence,
power, etc. — of its adherents. While, of course, conflict and
controversy are often the more dramatically revealed aspects
of this interaction, these need not always be present. When
Huxley and eight of his friends set up the informally organized
x-Club* in London in 1864, they established a small group that
had a tremendous effect upon the direction science was to take
and the image it was to construct for the last half of the nineteenth century. In somewhat similar fashion, "schools" of anthropology influence the history of the field as much by virtue
of the characteristics of the adherents as by the validity of the
doctrines.

It seems to me that examination of personal relations, whether
they are featured by conflict or not, is a function of biographical
analysis; for to describe the conflict or growth of ideas without
describing the personal medium within which they grow is to
deprive them of their human character. It is the failure, too, to
interpret intellectual conflicts in terms of their "human" participants that makes it difficult not only to sense the problem
but also to understand the relevance of the tactics and argu-

*The x-Club was an informal supper group organized in 1864 to
provide the opportunity for several close friends in the scientific community of London to meet together on the Thursdays of the Royal
Society meetings. The membership consisted of nine persons: Huxley;
Hirst, a mathematician; Frankland, a chemist; Tyndall, the physicist;
Spottiswoode, a printer and mathematician; George Busk, the anato-
mist; John Lubbock; Herbert Spencer; and J. D. Hooker, the botanist.
This very influential group in the "politics" of English science persisted until 1893, by which time death and the infirmities of old age
among the members had made meetings impossible.

ments used. This attempt to objectify and depersonalize the idea leads to the dreariness of much that passes for intellectual biography. If we extoll only the idea, must we not subscribe to a view that great ideas have necessarily been put forth by great men? And if we do, must we not describe them *only* in terms of their greatness? To follow such a view, we must, I think, believe that an idea makes the man rather than the reverse. The charm, and perhaps real value, of Margaret Mead's *An Anthropologist at Work* is that we see Ruth Benedict *being* an anthropologist. Her ideas emerge, her role takes form, her associates live — and we see a moment in the history of anthropology exposed: it is a moment in the life of anthropologists.

In summary, biography as an instrument for either a more general intellectual history or as a means for reconstructing a particular stream within that history should answer a series of related questions within an historical rather than a particular frame of reference. What, for example, were the pressures within the existing intellectual system and the direction of thought that resulted? What were the movements and/or ideas already expressed — "in the wind" so to speak — to which the biographic subject did or did not respond? With what phases of his intellectual universe was he able — or unable — to communicate effectively? What were the impediments or spurs — personal, ideological, sociological — to communication? What was the individual's reaction to these various sources of experiences to which he was subject? What kind of synthesis or interpretation was he able to create as his adaptation to the intellectual pressures surrounding him? To write biography with these questions in mind is to attempt the reconstruction of a universe now gone, but one in which a man lived, of which he was a part, from which he drew his intellectual nourishment and to which he contributed direction. However we limit that universe, for the solution of the historical problems it is necessary to delineate the dimensions that contain it.

I feel that in most instances it is not possible to write or think this kind of biography with a central hero around whom the biographer groups his data. The growth of science represents a constant process of selection from a multiverse of ideas or systematic modifications; this selection is made in terms of particular expositors of one expression or another. It is only hindsight, the "ultimate victory" in a given period of one position over another, that permits us to see one position as "naturally" more valid than another. Thus in viewing the difficulties which Boucher de Perthes encountered during the 1840's and 1850's in establishing his thesis of the antediluvial quality of his *haches de silex*, we are, on the basis of later events, too quick to apply the easy label of "bigot" or "conservative" to his adversaries without recognizing that, at least in terms of a newly emerged scientific canon, the skepticism directed toward Boucher de Perthes was deserved; that, in a sense, while his critics were wrong for the right reasons, he was right for the wrong ones.

As an attempt to achieve a view of history in the making while maintaining the necessary vantage point of the present, a comparative biography appears to me to possess considerable promise, a comparative biography in which the subjects are chosen so as to illustrate somewhat differing positions with reference to the accomplishment of the same goal. Currently I am engaged in what I hope will be a somewhat enlightening analysis of certain nineteenth-century developments in natural science through a comparative biography of Richard Owen and Thomas Huxley. Both of these men were leaders within the scientific community — formal and informal — during the century; both were active in the biological sciences; both were active in the politics of science; they were contemporaries; and they were bitter antagonists who not only disagreed with one another on almost every issue, but who, for the last third of their lives, did not speak to one another. Behind the personal antagonism, there lay, at least as a partial cause, a deep-seated difference as to a basic *weltanschauung* that directed their respective particular activities as scientists. Nor were their differences idiosyncratic; for each represented a major intellectual current of the century. It was the conflict between these currents that produced the mental rip-tide that eventually transformed the ideological coastline. In extolling Huxley as a hero in nineteenth-century natural science without doing full justice to his dragons, we miss the significance of his victory as one event in the process that is the history of science. The conflict, however, assumes proportion as well as a degree of personal reality when seen through the continuing relations of two of its major participants.

Similarly, within the more restricted field of anthropology, comparative biographies have utility in sharpening the ideological disputes — sometimes scarcely realized by the participants — out of which succeeding stages of a field emerge. Because of the emphasis upon the Boasian basis of American anthropology, we often ignore the fact that prior to the coming of Boas a methodologically and conceptually distinct anthropology had developed in America — an anthropology that was concerned to a large extent with Indian origins and relations and that drew heavily upon archaeology and linguistics.[26] While a biography of Boas would be valuable in its own right — and I am certain one will soon be written — for the history of anthropology a comparative biography of Boas, Holmes, and Putnam would, I suspect, have even greater value. Or what about a composite study of Lowie, Kroeber, and Goldenweiser — all of whom had much the same background, but each of whom represents a somewhat different path followed by American anthropology in this century. Or, perhaps, a joint biography of Haddon and Boas, or Radcliffe-Brown and Malinowski.

The intent of these biographies is not to list the differences and similarities of the subjects. It is, rather, to illustrate — again always from the vantage point of the present — the haziness of an existing intellectual moment through which particular individuals grope for what they hope will be a future certainty; and which, if they are successful, their successors make into a certainty. On behalf of intellectual history, we must attempt that which is surely impossible: the recreation of an entire mental state that no longer exists; not only must we recreate it, but for purposes of our understanding we must consciously enact it. For anthropologists more than for any other group, the necessity and value of these recreations should need no justification. Nor should the use of the personal document and life history in such a task call for apology on behalf of the writer.

The important matter is the ethnographic one: the collection of materials. This, of course, is essentially a practical problem; but its solution precedes any of the more difficult problems of historical reconstruction. While published works provide much that is valuable for understanding the intellectual dimensions of a period as well as the particular, though formal, role of the writer, we must recognize that the published article is always written for posterity, that too often it contains a certainty and finish that mask the significant processes which went into its construction. Dependence upon works written to be published shows us only part of a man; they are the landmarks of an intellectual life.

Much more important — and, of course, much more difficult to come by — are the informal and fugitive products — letters, journals, and impressions. From these we can glimpse a science in the making. How much more do we know of Columbia's anthropology in the twenties from Margaret Mead's informal account of her induction into formal anthropology than may be gleaned in reading the literature of the period![27] How much we can learn of the "politics" of the 1860's through reading the almost daily exchange of letters among those who saw a discipline emerging! How meaningful is Malinowski's explanation (in a letter to Firth as student) for his much criticized lack of synoptic work on the Trobrianders![20] Not only do these fugitive works, written within a personal context, enable us to relive the almost day-to-day happenings of anthropology in the making, but they fill in the troublesome gaps in history that are often subject to speculative interpretations long after the event and in the absence of the unique spirit of the moment.

If we, or our successors, are to write the history of anthropology, we must seek the materials for the history of anthropologists; for in writing the biographies of anthropologists we can also write the biography of the discipline they made. To do either or both, it is necessary to find some method to preserve the documents — personal and professional — that are the sole remnants of that which becomes history. There is no one who has attempted to collect the miscellaneous manuscript material that makes history who is not conscious of the rapid destruction to which these materials are subject. I venture to suggest that scarcely a month goes by that does not see the loss of some collection of manuscript materials of significance to the history of science.

Toward the preservation of materials of anthropological interest, two steps can be taken immediately:

1. It is necessary that unpublished manuscripts relating to the history of archaeology and anthropology be located and a preliminary catalogue constructed. Such a listing should include not only collections such as the Tylor manuscripts in the Pitt-Rivers Museum of Oxford University or the Boas collection in the American Philosophical Society, but also, and perhaps more importantly, those that remain in private hands. So far, only the Library of the American Philosophical Society has made any attempt at all to develop a collection of anthropological source material — and this by virtue of the society's

possession of the Boas, Sapir, and Speck collections to supplement its excellent collection relating to early attempts to study the American Indian.

2. An attempt should be made to reduce the oral tradition of anthropology to some more permanent form. With the changes the twentieth century has wrought in the communication patterns between individuals, there is a smaller and smaller body of manuscript materials available in which are recorded the everyday events of history. We need to collect the reminiscences and the informal experiences of those who have participated in the history of the field, recorded in sufficient detail that those who follow us and who are separated from the events with which we are familiar can make historical sense out of that which we will to them. This recording process requires that the anthropologist at some point in his career — or perhaps at several points in his career — become the informant for future students of his own culture. I realize that the self-conscious recounting for posterity may in itself distort the record; even in a distorted form, however, such a record would be invaluable for the reconstruction of history.

Anthropology, like the other sciences, has become historically minded so recently, so conscious of its own past, that we must raise first the foundation upon which a meaningful history can be built. Among the materials significant for the firmness of that foundation are those stemming from and relating to the operations of anthropologists themselves. In the study of men, we must realize the importance of the men who study.

# WOMEN IN EARLY AMERICAN ANTHROPOLOGY

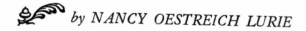 *by NANCY OESTREICH LURIE*

*Nancy Oestreich Lurie is associate professor of anthropology at the University of Wisconsin at Milwaukee. This paper, embodying some new data, was originally prepared for a Conference on the History of Anthropology, sponsored by the Social Science Research Council, April 13–14, 1962, in New York.*

In choosing to write about a select group in a relatively new discipline, it is necessary to set the ground rules regarding period, persons, and problem. The problem, in the form of many engaging questions to be answered, emerged from the data which at first were collected somewhat at random. As to period and persons, the limitations are these: "early" begins with the first woman to take her place among her male contemporaries in helping to establish a recognized discipline of anthropology and ends with the termination in death of the careers of women born prior to 1885. The roster thus includes Erminnie Smith, Alice Fletcher, Matilda Stevenson, Zelia Nuttall, Frances Densmore, and Elsie Clews Parsons. The year 1885 was chosen as a significant one because it marked the founding of the Women's Anthropological Society, while the entire period under discussion reaches from the era of largely self-trained scholars who often financed their own researches to the now established arrangements of graduate training leading to the Ph.D. degree and the earning of one's living as an anthropologist. The problem is to examine and assess the early role and achievements of women in American anthropology. The following pages will concentrate on those women who attained significant professional recognition in anthropology. I have excluded, reluctantly but necessarily for purposes of comparison, that early company of women active almost entirely in the fields of folklore and classical archeology because their work is not in the main line of historical development of the discipline of anthropology as we know it today in the United States.

Before research was actually begun, a number of ideas were entertained concerning women as a group worth special attention in the history of anthropology. First, there was the somewhat sentimental motivation to rescue from obscurity women who must have been remarkable personalities if only as pioneer spirits. Second, there was the hope of excitement: militant feminism on the march doing battle for women's rights in science. Finally, there was curiosity about any definable role of women in anthropology. As it turned out, early women have been relegated to no more obscurity than have many of their male contemporaries who were also remarkable pioneer spirits. That they were unusual, given the social position of women in the late nineteenth and early twentieth centuries, is reflected in their lives, and a great deal of charming folklore attaches to their memories whenever their names are mentioned.[1] Although women in Washington, D.C. banded together in their own society for a few years as a reaction to exclusion from male discussions in that city, no woman in anthropology has ever had the struggle of an Elizabeth Blackwell in medicine[2] or a Myra Colby Bradwell in law.[3] In the United States, a generally more tolerant view has been taken toward women in the sciences than in the professions. This may be due in part to the tremendous influence in the second half of the nineteenth century of Louis Agassiz who popularized science and welcomed women to his public lectures and later to his classes at Penikese Island.[4] By the time Erminnie Adele Smith delivered the earliest recorded anthropological paper by a woman before a learned society in the United States, the 1879 meeting of the American Association for the Advancement of Science, three women had already presented papers before this group in chemistry and natural history the preceding year. Furthermore, women were listed as members of the A.A.A.S. as early as 1869.

Even the strong feminist inclinations of Elsie Clews Parsons antedated her introduction to anthropology and became progressively less urgent as she bent her efforts to anthropological research. The sense of struggle for equal acceptance and recognition which has been observed among women anthropologists since the writer joined their sometimes petulant ranks seems to be related to the increasing professionalism of the discipline.

For many years the anthropological field was open and there was a need for as many earnest researchers as would be willing to devote themselves to the task of rescuing from oblivion the data that seemed to be rapidly disappearing. Apparently, women did not become so acutely aware of contesting with men until the 1930's when, complicated by the fact of a national depression, the number of trained anthropologists threatened to exceed the number of salaried positions available in teaching and research. Although this circumstance is now changing, some bitterness unquestionably remains. The purpose of this paper is not to discuss the professional and economic fortunes of contemporary women anthropologists; however, the situation of the last several academic generations stands in contrast to that of the very early years of anthropology.

Doubtless, the first women anthropologists encountered the general difficulties of scholarly women whose ambitions seemed presumptuous — if not actually laughable — to many of their male contemporaries.[5] However, not only was acceptance relatively amicable, the more perceptive men in anthropology viewed the participation of women as peculiarly enriching to the new science of anthropology, specifically in ethnology.

It is generally known that Franz Boas recognized the particular contributions women could make to anthropology and welcomed women students who were willing to prove themselves capable of the standards of scholarship he exacted. Considerably earlier, however, no less a person than Edward B. Tylor admonished his male colleagues not to look askance at women who sought to share their intellectual interests. Tylor had made a tour of the far west where he visited James and Matilda Stevenson at Zuñi. In an address before the Anthropological Society of Washington in 1884 he commented of this couple:

> And one thing I particularly noticed was this, that to get at the confidence of the tribe, the man of the house, though he can do a great deal, cannot do it all. If his wife sympathizes with his work, and is able to do it, really half the work of investigation seems to fall to her, so much is to be learned through the women of the tribe which the men will not readily disclose. The experience seemed to me a lesson to anthropologists not to sound the "bull-roarer," and warn the ladies off from their proceedings, but rather to avail themselves thankfully of their help.[6]

Tylor obviously saw women's work in terms of a team of husband and wife, although by 1884 at least two women, Erminnie Smith and Alice Cunningham Fletcher, had engaged in field work on their own. Nevertheless, the Stevensons do appear to have been harbingers of a series of famous anthropological teams. One has the impression, although it has not been checked out quantitatively, that in other disciplines a Sidney and Beatrice Webb or a Charles and Mary Beard are exceptions and not the commonplace such pairs are in anthropology. Even when a wife does not have formal training in the discipline, she often becomes an "anthropologist by marriage" in contrast to spouses in even such related fields as sociology, psychology and economics, to say nothing of the natural and physical sciences.

However, "the ladies" freely interpreted on the Tylorian view and concluded that women as a group could obtain information complementary to that of men as a group. Furthermore, from the beginning there were lone investigators among the women who, like male anthropologists, collected all the data they could obtain. They did not depend heavily upon their roles as men or women, but upon the novelty value of the interested stranger, a role all field workers exploit to some extent as an acceptable excuse for concerning themselves with topics inappropriate to their sex or age among members of the group investigated.

Tylor had addressed a mixed audience, but the actual membership of the Anthropological Society of Washington was exclusively male. It would appear that the exclusion was not so much conscious as automatic, and reflected the usual organization of such groups in the national capital. The society was founded in 1879 by a small group of men who inserted a notice in a local newspaper announcing a meeting open to persons interested in forming an anthropological society. As far as records show, no women put in an appearance, nor, in the next few years, did it seem to have occurred to women to request membership in the group. Largely owing to the efforts of Matilda Stevenson, they simply started their own association.[7]

Unfortunately, little information is available concerning the Women's Anthropological Society, which remained active for about fourteen years, 1885–1899. Unless otherwise noted, all references to the group in the present discussion derive from a small pamphlet, "The Organization and Constitution of the Women's Anthropological Society," privately printed in Washington, D.C., in 1885. The admonition that women would have to demonstrate real sincerity and ability in order to be accepted as anthropologists may have underlain some of the serious determination implied in the pamphlet. The Women's Anthropological Society was to be no pink tea gathering of talkative ladies, refreshments were not to be served at meetings, and no paper was to exceed thirty minutes unless by special permission of the board of directors. The determination is also made explicit in such words as these:

This organization has for its object: first, to open to women new fields for systematic investigation; second, to invite their cooperation in the development of the science of anthropology.

In view of the intellectual future that appeared to be opening to women by 1885, the society invited:

> . . . all who are clear in thought, logical in mental processes, exact in expression, and earnest in the search for truth, to make contributions of ascertained and properly related facts, and thus aid in the solution of the mighty problems that make up the humanity wide science of Anthropology.

The women set forth their definition of the fields and organization of anthropology according to an outline suggested to them by Otis T. Mason. It includes terms such as "anthropogeny" and "hexicology," with the disciplines of sociology and psychology blithely subsumed as but subfields of anthropology. However, in various guises we see the now familiar physical anthropology, archeology, linguistics, ethnography and ethnology, and, of course, a strong orientation toward cultural evolution as not one theoretical approach but the very and only nature of the universe to be explored ever more fully and understood by specialized studies under the various categories listed in the outline.

The group did not imagine themselves as innovators in anthropology, but as contributors of special information which would enrich a defined discipline. They appeared willing to tackle almost anything, but they emphasized the special work they could do as women. For example, without really explaining how it was to be done except through "tact" and "scholarship," they pointed out that only women would be able to obtain really intimate information on life in the harem or the zenana. Yet, they did "not exhort [women] to *leave* their present life-conditions, but to *master* them." Study among faraway peoples was desirable, but, they asked rhetorically, "What state, what town, what household is destitute of choicest materials for our work?"

Though burning with scholarly zeal, so completely did they adopt ideas current in their day of ineffable spiritual differences between men and women that their flowing nineteenth century prose requires some twentieth century translating. *Man* means all humankind distinguished from animals, but *woman* means simply the female of the human species, *viz*: "The highly organized religious nature of woman gives her special adaptation for the study of the sublime *differentia*, by reason of which man, alone, sins, sacrifices, worships."

These women clearly accepted their role as women. Problems of "career *vs.* marriage" and complaints about disadvantages and discrimination attendant upon being a woman were to come later. Seeing themselves as capable of making special contributions to anthropology because they were women, and subscribing to views of their day that the infancy of the individual reflects the infancy of mankind, they engaged in further rhetorical questioning. In the "earliest unfoldings of thought, language, and belief, who can collect so valuable materials as can mothers?" For those unable to fulfill their expected destiny as wives and mothers, "every day of a teacher's life is a revelation." Their numbers must have included some bona fide early "career women," since they also mentioned the unique contributions physicians might make to anthropology.

Recognizing that women had long performed special services in works of charity and other endeavors of Christian benevolence, they chose to stress the need to understand social problems if such problems ever were to be alleviated. Thus they sought to analyze as well as to break bread with the "needy brother" in order that they might "chant in noble unison, 'I count *nothing* that affects humanity foreign to myself!'"

According to the pamphlet, the first president was Matilda Stevenson; vice presidents and board of directors were not yet chosen at the time of printing, and the other officers — Mrs. Emma Louise Hitchcock, Miss Sarah A. Scull, and Mrs. Mary

Parke Foster — did not achieve any great fame as anthropologists.

In 1893 a joint meeting was held with the Anthropological Society of Washington, and Zelia Nuttall delivered the principal address, "The Mexican Calendar System." Otis T. Mason, president of the men's group, presided, and Mrs. Nuttall was introduced by Alice Fletcher, president of the women's group. A second joint meeting held April 9, 1895, was a symposium on folklore and among the participants were Dr. Washington Mathews, Miss Elizabeth Boyant Johnston, and Col. Weston Flint. (If anthropological history takes little notice of Miss Johnston, it deals an equally fleeting fame to Colonel Flint.) Two more joint meetings were held in 1895 and at least one more in 1896. Likewise, in 1896, a joint meeting of all the scientific societies of Washington was conducted, and from this beginning the Washington Academy of Sciences was formed in 1898. In that same year, the Anthropological Society of Washington extended an invitation of membership to the Women's Anthropological Society. On January 3, 1899, forty-nine women were received into the Anthropological Society of Washington, presumably disbanding their own organization at that time since this is the last we hear of it. Their acceptance into the group was obviously complete, and by 1903 the president of the Anthropological Society of Washington was a woman, Alice Fletcher.[8]

Some curious circumstances seem to have contributed to the eventual merging of the two societies. The joint meeting of 1896 was held to discuss problems of housing in slum areas of Washington. In the spring of 1896, a committee of Washington citizens concerned with problems of housing had employed a special agent to conduct a house-to-house survey of an area comprising some 35 alleys and 191 dwellings. The Women's Anthropological Society was asked to co-operate in the undertaking and voted to support the agent for an additional month in order to complete the work and tabulate the results. Part of the tabulation and analysis was done by Miss Clara de Gaffenried, a special agent of the Department of Labor, and her findings were presented in a paper read before the Women's Anthropological Society on November 14, 1896. This is the only record obtained to date of what must have been but one of many papers presented before the group. Largely at the instigation of the Women's Society, the Washington Sanitary Improvement Company was formed as a result of action by the Anthropological Society of Washington, which became a stockholder in the firm set up to handle the construction of 808 low-rent dwellings. The Women's Anthropological Society was among the other contributors and remained a continuing force in the enterprise.[9] That the women could take such concrete action to further their social objectives is eminently understandable when it is noted that they exacted yearly dues of $5.00 from each member, did not fritter away their money on refreshments, apparently did no publishing, and the likelihood is that they allowed their dues to accrue interest.

Since the American Anthropological Association was founded at about the same time that women were admitted to the Washington Society, it is not surprising to find women numbered among its charter members. Not only did women enter anthropology early, but they endured; the last surviving charter member of the American Anthropological Association, a woman, H. Newell Wardell of Philadelphia, died in 1964. The American Ethnological Society made no explicit exclusion of women, but did not number women among its charter members in 1848 or for many years thereafter.[10] However, by the time it was reorganized along its present lines, women had been fully accepted into various scholarly organizations and have thus been active in the American Ethnological Society as a matter of course. The same is generally true of the now many local and specialized anthropological societies. The International Congress of Americanists early admitted female members and in 1892 the membership, listed according to country, included Caecilie Seler of Germany and Zelia Nuttall of the United States, *"aide spécial pour l'archeologie mexicaine au 'Peabody Museum of American archaeology and ethnology' de Cambridge (Mass.)."* [11] The Peabody apparently accepted without question those women who were sincerely interested in its work, and published studies by both Nuttall and Fletcher in Volume I of the now famous *Archaeological and Ethnological Papers*.

Almost as soon as women had demonstrated competency in anthropology they were called upon to take an active part in many anthropological endeavors. Alice Fletcher was in charge of Indian exhibits at the New Orleans Industrial Exposition of 1884–1885, but it pained her to see her friends represented only by crude aboriginal artifacts, and she accordingly wrote a letter which was printed to be circulated among Indians. She stressed the importance of education if Indian people were to take their rightful place beside the Whites in creating technological wonders. [12] The Chicago World's Fair of 1893 included a special Congress of Anthropology in which Fletcher, Nuttall, and Stevenson participated as well as Sarah Yorke Stevenson, an Egyptologist of some note, and Mrs. M. French-Sheldon who spoke on customs of the natives of East Africa. [13] Stevenson was assigned the task of collecting special display specimens of Indian artifacts for the Louisiana Purchase Exposition of 1904–1905, held in St. Louis, [14] and Nuttall served in an official capacity at this exposition. [15]

The lack of opposition to women in the early days of American anthropology is strikingly demonstrated in the career of Erminnie Smith who holds the honor, at least by a year or two over Alice Fletcher, of being the first woman to receive professional recognition for her work. Of special interest is the fact that Smith had already found scientific acceptance in another field before she became interested in anthropology. Her scientific work began with geology, and, according to her various biographies, she amassed one of the finest private collections of mineral specimens in the United States.[16]

Born Erminnie Platt at Marcellus, New York, in 1836, she was educated at Miss Willard's Seminary at Troy, and in 1855 married Simeon Smith. Her economic circumstances were quite favorable and she traveled widely. During one stay of four years in Europe with her two young sons she studied languages and also took a degree at the School of Mines at Freiburg.[17] Her first paper before the A.A.A.S., "Monograph on Jade," reflects an interesting combination of her long-standing concern with minerology and her new found fascination in anthropology. It details the trade and work in jade throughout the world.[18] Two years later, in 1881, she again appeared on the A.A.A.S. program and gave two papers on Iroquois language and mythology,[19] subjects that occupied her attention for the few remaining years of her life. It is probably safe to surmise that residential propinquity to the Iroquois as well as the widely known studies of Lewis Henry Morgan prompted the development of Mrs. Smith's interests.

She was probably the first woman to do anthropological field work, although biographical data are equivocal on the exact date. It is implied that she began work with a remnant Tuscarora group in Canada in 1878, but it may have been 1879, the year Matilda Stevenson first visited Zuñi. However, Erminnie Smith set out purposefully and alone, whereas Mrs. Stevenson simply accompanied her husband to Zuñi and developed her anthropological interests after getting into the field. Mrs. Smith was adopted by the Tuscarora, "having won their affection," and was named Beautiful Flower, Ka-tei-tci-tsa.[20] This charming incident, if it may be taken at face value, suggests that she was an ethnographer who understood the niceties of rapport.

In 1882, when anthropology was first designated as Section

H in the A.A.A.S., the ladies were out in force. Erminnie Smith presented three papers based on her field work among Iroquois groups; Alice Fletcher gave two papers dealing with observations among Plains tribes; and a single paper was read by Virginia K. Bowers of Newport, Kentucky, who is long since forgotten. Nothing more than the title of her paper is listed, and more's the pity because it's a humdinger: "The Bleaching of the Aryans. Was It Done By The Law of Repetition; The Accumulation of Effects?"[21] At least Virginia Bowers has the distinction of being the first woman on record to concern herself deeply with physical anthropology this early in the history of the discipline!

Mrs. Smith continued to present one or more papers at the annual meetings of the A.A.A.S. until her death in 1886. At the 1885 meeting at Ann Arbor she was the secretary of Section H, the first woman to serve as an A.A.A.S. officer. When the A.A.A.S. journal, *Science*, was founded in 1883, the first paper contributed by a woman was by Emily A. Nunn; numbers 17 and 18 of Volume I carried her two-part article on the "Naples Zoological Station."

Although Mrs. Smith did not get around to submitting an article, "Artificial Wampum," until 1885, she managed to be the first woman anthropologist to write for *Science*. In addition to taking Maj. J. W. Powell's part in a theory concerning wampum, she provided a detailed and little-appreciated account of her visit about 1884 to what must have been the last wampum manufactory catering to the fur trade.[22]

Erminnie Smith enjoys yet another "first." Her Iroquois language studies are reported by Powell in his "Director's Report" for Volume I of the *Annual Reports of the Smithsonian Institution*, then simply the Bureau of Ethnology. The *Second Annual Report* carries the first contribution by a woman to this famous series, "Myths of the Iroquois," and establishes Smith as a gifted scholar. Her work with the Bureau is detailed in Powell's

"Reports" until Volume VII when melancholy note is taken of her untimely death at her home in Jersey City.[23] Nor do her achievements end here. Utilizing a technique to be followed by Alice Fletcher, Edward Sapir and other scholars, Erminnie Smith led a "native" informant into the fold of professional anthropology. John Napoleon Brinton Hewitt, an educated, part-Tuscarora Indian, became interpreter and amanuensis to Mrs. Smith early in her work. He went on to achieve recognition for his own work, taking up Mrs. Smith's unfinished tasks with the Bureau, and pursuing research among both Iroquoian and Algonkian groups.[24] Considering Mrs. Smith's work in the short space of eight years, had she been blessed with Alice Fletcher's life span she would have doubtless contributed greatly to the development of American anthropology.

Alice Fletcher, born in 1838 and only two years Erminnie Smith's junior, like Smith entered anthropology rather late in life. Little is known of her early years except that her family background possessed a certain remarkability. Fletcher was born in Cuba during her parents' temporary residence on the island. Presumably there was some wealth since she traveled widely and eventually gave public lectures in New York on the Passion Play at Oberammergau. Perhaps this endeavor was for her support as family finances waned, for she was not wealthy when she took up the serious study of anthropology at about the age of forty.

Through the offices of F. W. Putnam of the Peabody Museum at Harvard, a special fellowship was set up by Mrs. Mary Copley Thaw of Pittsburgh in 1891 to enable Alice Fletcher to pursue her Indian studies for the rest of her life. Alice Fletcher's scientific studies of the American Indian grew out of an earlier philanthropic concern with their welfare. Even before she took up field work she was appointed by the Women's Indian Association as administrator of funds whereby small loans were made to Indians to enable them to buy their own land and build homes as a step toward acceptance and assimilation into White society. Commitment to the social philosophy implied in this benevolent endeavor was to be a dominating force for the rest of Miss Fletcher's life.[25] Though she was to become a respected scholar and an exceedingly perceptive thinker in many areas of Indian culture, her unwavering adherence to her original "solution" of the Indian problem blinded her to the persistent force of social identity among American Indian peoples and the real significance of interrelationships between economics and other aspects of culture. In the final analysis, the views she shared with many well-meaning Whites and the energy with which she particularly promulgated their legal implementation account in part for continued and increasing hardships to the present day among the people she strove so selflessly to help.[26]

Alice Fletcher's ethnographic studies, each detail faithfully recorded and checked for accuracy, are among the classics of American anthropology. Furthermore, her theoretical and historic interests ranged beyond mere collection of facts or broad ascriptions of traits and complexes to overall evolutionary speculations so common in her day. Her studies of Omaha religion carried her into comparative work among other Siouan speakers of the Plains, and, suspecting even older layers of cosmology and ritual from other sources, she turned to the Caddoans as the likely carrier of the more ancient forms. She had observed the Pawnee Hako Ceremony in the 1880's and as her awareness of problems of diffusion increased, she returned to the Pawnee and in the early 1890's recorded the ceremony.[27] An experienced field worker by this time, and sensitive to the deeper nuances of Indian religion, her account of the Hako ceremony, though reflecting the immaturity of anthropology when it was published, was for its day a model of painstaking scholarship coupled with philosophical perception. Throughout her life, however, the Omaha, her "first" tribe, remained her particular interest and source of closest personal associations among Indians.

By the time Alice Fletcher died in 1923, at the age of eighty-five, she was a sort of living legend in anthropology, active to the end in promoting scholarly enterprises and benevolent works. Mild of manner, entirely lacking in petty contentiousness though she was often required to take a stand on controversial issues, her determination was unswerving and her power to sway others almost charismatic. "Some of her opponents never were quite sure what quiet, deep river had just drifted along and left them stranded far from their selfish hopes. She didn't fight—any more than the snowflake and the sunbeam fight. Like them, she Just Kept On—."[28] Her cheerful obliviousness to reality as others saw it was at times exasperating, and at least one anthropologist who knew her personally remembered her only as a "dreadfully opinionated woman."[29]

In the early years when her concern with Indians pivoted entirely on their welfare, she met Thomas Henry Tibbles—experienced frontiersman, minister, journalist, and ardent worker in the cause of Indian rights. His account of the meeting gives a fascinating glimpse of Alice Fletcher at the beginning of her anthropological career, her charitable concerns, her ideas about the special role of women in anthropology, and above all, her determination.

> While we were in Boston in 1879, a lady told me that after studying ethnology for years in books and museums she now wished to visit Indian tribes in their own lodges, living as they lived and observing their daily customs herself—especially the women's and children's ways.
> "Did you ever camp out?" I asked.
> "No, never."
> I found it hard to take her plan seriously. She, a thorough product of city life, was evidently nearing her forties. I could not imagine her leaving all her home comforts to go out to the far frontier and live among the Indians in an Indian

lodge. Still, she was so earnest that I reluctantly agreed to take her someday with our group for the trip she wished. But I gave her fair warning:

"You can't stand such a trip. You'll have to sleep on the cold ground. The food will be strange to you. You'll meet storms on the open prairie and be wet to the skin. Burning sun and wind will blister your face and hands. Long days of travelling will exhaust you. You'll have no privacy night or day. I'm sure you never can endure it."

"Yes, I can!" she insisted.[30]

On September 1, 1881, Alice Fletcher arrived at Omaha, Nebraska, and was met by Tibbles and Bright Eyes La Flesche, an educated Omaha woman who was associated in Tibbles' benevolent work and who soon became his wife. Tibbles assembled a camp outfit for the three-day trip across the prairies to the Omaha Indian Reservation. Fletcher came armed with letters from the Secretary of War, the Secretary of the Interior, the Post-Master General and many scientists, but her real arms and buckler were a surprising physical stamina for a small and seemingly delicate woman, a thorough delight in her task, and that unbreakable will. After introductions to members of the Omaha tribe, the two women, Tibbles, and an Omaha helper named Wajapa set off north the next day on a journey to the Winnebago Reservation, the Ponca settlement north of the Niobrara River comprised of removed Ponca who had returned to their old haunts, and finally to the Rosebud Sioux Reservation in South Dakota. Alice Fletcher had made an immediately favorable impression on the Omaha so that the Wajapa willingly answered her questions about his people and told her myths and stories. He also gave her a name from his own Eagle clan. Throughout his account, Tibbles does not identify Fletcher but designates her only by her Omaha name as "High Flyer."

Tibbles had not underestimated the hardships, bad weather, and inconveniences Fletcher could expect to encounter on her trip. One matter that he had not mentioned was the demands of Indian hospitality. The entire party suffered the results of having to partake of any food offered, no matter how sated they felt from a previous host's generosity. But she equally withstood all difficulties with only one instance of petulance at Wajapa's mild criticism of her skill as a camper. Wajapa went off and sulked at her sharp retort but soon they were on good terms again. However, despite his bestowal of an Indian name, and the good-natured friendliness, Alice Fletcher's final acceptance by the Omaha would hinge on more than a favorable first impression. In explaining her presence in the party to the Poncas, Tibbles overheard Wajapa saying, "She has come to see the Indians. She seems to be a very nice woman, but I haven't known her long enough to say for certain."[31]

Miss Fletcher was impressed by Tibbles, Bright Eyes, and Wajapa, and she was grateful to them. That her initiation into the rigors of field work was successful was largely due to them. Because they were knowledgeable, conversant in the several languages encountered on this first journey, and could communicate easily with her, a lady newly arrived from Boston, it apparently never occurred to her how atypical were the two Indians, or that Tibbles' philosophy of Indian administration derived not from his amazing familiarity with Indian life, but from White Christian values which he shared with her. Wajapa resolutely wore his White man's clothing as a matter of principle on the entire journey, although aware that his acceptance at Rosebud would be accompanied with far more gifts and favors had he come there in Indian dress. That the Rosebud Sioux did not think much of the stronger sentiment for White ways exhibited among the Omaha evidently did not impress Alice Fletcher as significant.[32] If any Omaha shared the views of the Sioux, they were the unacculturated folk whom Fletcher felt needed the educated leadership of such families as the White-oriented La Flesches.

Even educated Indians who remained knowledgeable bilingual informants could not see beyond solutions ready-made for them by kind-hearted Whites as is reflected in the touching obituary of Alice Fletcher written by Francis La Flesche, brother of Bright Eyes. La Flesche collaborated with Fletcher in writing the famous monograph, "The Omaha Tribe," and worked closely with her throughout her studies. He was her protege and virtually an adopted son. In time, the excellence of his work resulted in his transfer from the Department of the Interior, Bureau of Indian Affairs, to the Bureau of American Ethnology where he continued to make original contributions to the ethnographic literature on the Siouan-speaking Plains tribes.[33] La Flesche describes what happened when Alice Fletcher settled down to concentrate on work among the Omaha after her tour of reservations in Nebraska and South Dakota.

> She visited the Indians in their homes and began to make friends with them. At first, they were not disposed to talk, but after a time it occurred to one to ask: "Why are you here?" She replied: "I came to learn, if you will let me, some things about your tribal organization, social customs, tribal rites, traditions and songs. Also to see if I can help you in any way."
>
> At the suggestion of help, the faces of the Indians brightened with hope. The Indian continued: "You have come at a time when we are in distress. We have learned that the 'land paper' given us by the Great Father does not make us secure in our homes; that we could be ousted and driven to the Indian Territory as the Poncas were. We want a 'strong paper'. We are told that we can get one through an Act of Congress. Can you help us?"[34]

Alice Fletcher set about drafting the desired Act. She satisfied herself that not only was it the best thing for the Indians to be given small plots they could farm — after all, this was the view of all enlightened and sincere White friends of the Indians — but that this was what the Indians had come to recognize as their only hope. She spoke to each family head to gather proof of the Omahas' industrious devotion to their land. La Flesche states that as people came to Miss Fletcher for help, "Each one uttered the oft-repeated cry: 'I want a 'strong paper' which will make my home secure.'" Alice Fletcher worked out the details of an act whereby every adult Omaha would be allotted eighty acres to remain tax-free and held in trust by the government for a period of twenty-five years after which time adult, competent Indians would be granted fee patents and control over their holdings. Lands left over after distribution of allotments were to be sold for the benefit of the tribe to finance development of their farms. Fletcher had influential friends in Washington and through their efforts the act was pushed quickly through legislative procedures and was passed August 7, 1882. The frail-appearing ethnologist was appointed a special agent to oversee the surveying and allotment and in subsequent years performed similar work among the Winnebago and Nez Perce, who, along with many other tribes, were allotted under the Dawes Severalty Act of 1887 which was patterned after the Omaha Act.[35]

In 1910, after an absence of many years, Alice Fletcher returned to the Omaha for a brief visit. Considering her personal involvement in the Act of 1882, her assessment of results is fairly objective. She observed, ". . . the act has not been altogether evil nor has it been wholly good for the people." The Omaha were certainly far better off materially and were more cheerful than when she first knew them and it is small wonder that she viewed their future with optimism. She saw in the tendency to lease rather than to work the land nothing more than an unfortunate phase of adjustment to land ownership; it was really an indication of a major trend. Where Miss Fletcher assessed a few well-run farms as models for the general welfare, they were to prove short-lived exceptions. Finally, those items which she noted as "quaint survivals of old customs under a new guise," were really illustrative of adaptations and cultural persistence that have characterized Omaha life to the present day.[36]

In 1930, Margaret Mead spent a summer with the Omaha, the tribe disguised, but not for long, under the pseudonym, Antlers. In keeping with her desire to conceal the identity of the group, Dr. Mead does not mention Alice Fletcher by name but pays her respectful tribute by stating that the traditional life and history of White contact had been so completely recorded for the Antlers that she chose to work with this group because she would be able to devote her attentions entirely to modern conditions. Furthermore, Mead does not identify the anonymous scholar who provided so much of the excellent ethnographic data on the Omaha as also being the "well intentioned lady of missionary leanings" whose benevolent efforts resulted in the social and economic chaos Mead observed. Given "the psychology of American frontier days," Dr. Mead believed that individual ownership of land was probably the only solution philanthropic Whites could see for the Indians' economic problems attendant upon the loss of the buffalo.

> But the arrangements were none the less shortsighted and quite inadequate. . . . [The government] was giving this land to a people who had never owned land, who had no item of customary law or usage to govern their disposal of it. The Antlers had no sentiments for land beyond the vivid affection they felt for a familiar landscape and for the resting place of their dead. They witnessed with terror the eviction of the "Short Robes," [Poncas] their unhappy banishment to more barren lands and the pitiful return pilgrimage which a few of them attempted. But this was not the terror of the landowner, the man who had, for generations, regarded his own and his children's welfare as inalienably connected with certain plots of arable land; it was rather the fear of exile, of an unknown existence in an unfamiliar land.[37]

The course of events among the Omaha was paralleled on reservations throughout the country where allotment took place. First, several years of unprecedented prosperity were provided by the remaining natural resources, women's gardening and

half-hearted farming with livestock, machinery, and seed supplied by sale of unallotted land. Homes, and furnishings, also
derived from land sales, were new and any monies received
from old annuities or farm income were used for luxuries of
travel, staying in hotels, eating at restaurants, and buying expensive clothes. In time the remaining wild plant foods and
game, as well as money, all began to be exhausted, but systematic farming on a large scale had never really been developed.
Homes began to deteriorate, machinery broke down, livestock
was sold to maintain the new standard of living, and the in-
credibly complicated problems of heirship began to set in.

Allotments were divided into ever-smaller and more scattered
plots among heirs who, after 1900, began to increase with each
generation. Leasing of Indian lands to White farmers proved
the easiest solution; money, at least, could be fairly divided
among the many heirs sharing interests in a given allotment.
The occasional land-burdened individual, descendant of several
generations of only children, could also lease his land and realize
some return on his capital of acreage that exceeded his ability or
inclinations to cultivate. The unwieldy bookkeeping, delays and
squabbles about lease payments arising from the difficulties of
assembling the names of all the heirs, and the often ridiculously
small sum of lease money received by each heir created a clamor
among the Indians to sell the land. The Omaha happened to
have been allotted some of the richest farm land in Nebraska,
but on all reservations there were usually Whites who were
eager to buy Indian land and who were not above getting Indians in their debt so they would favor selling the family property. Between the time fee patents were issued and the beginning
of the administration of John Collier as Commissioner of Indian
Affairs in 1933, two-thirds of allotted Indian lands had passed
into White ownership.[38] And so it came to pass that Fletcher's
"strong paper" of individual allotments was far weaker than
the tribal treaty relating to undivided lands.

It is possible that if Alice Fletcher had studied the Omaha thoroughly, as she later did, instead of plunging first into the matter of lands, she would have sought some other solution to the Indians' economic problems than the one she brought with her into her field work. She certainly recognized the "tribal tie" as an obstacle to "progress" as she defined it, and realized that the tribal organization could be attacked effectively by breaking down the communal ownership and occupation of land. Had she reviewed the situation exhaustively before taking action, she might have discovered that devastating side-effects would accompany her plan; and time might have also shown her that the pattern of diversified subsistence farming which she tried to impose on Indians was becoming increasingly impractical even to Whites with a strong agricultural tradition. On the other hand, she might never have overcome her basic predilections, although her outlook became progressively more relativistic in matters other than economics in which she had by then such an important emotional stake.

During Miss Fletcher's first visit among Indian groups, Tibbles strongly disapproved of her encouragement of Indian dancing and singing and her desire to observe ceremonies. To him such matters were part and parcel with the "savagery" from which he sought to raise the Indian.[39] Alice Fletcher was impressed by the sophistication of Indian artistic achievements and the contrast they afforded to the Indians' material culture. She accepted and went beyond the tolerant belief in the psychic unity of mankind and recognized that while she thought the White man's house superior to the skin tipi or earth lodge, Indian music deserved to be respected and perpetuated as uniquely valuable.

> I was perhaps as free from race prejudice as most students,
> but at the outset I was not prepared to admit what I was after-
> wards forced to acknowledge, — that my eyes and ears were

unconscious slaves of my previous training, — race training, if you will. . . .

It is not many years since the notion prevailed that the speech of savages was a mere jargon with an exceedingly limited vocabulary . . . but we now know . . . there can no more be a jargon in music than in speech.

The Indian is not a primitive man, nor properly a savage, but he is untutored; and yet we hear him voicing his aspirations and his loves in accordance with the same laws that are intelligently and consciously obeyed by a Wagner. . . .[40]

Only after the mistakes of forced cultural change were apparent could anthropologists as a group analyze objectively the points on which the mistakes had turned. Although Powell used the term "acculturation" in the First Annual Report of the Bureau of Ethnology, for Powell and other early scholars the effects of changes as the result of White contact were perceived only as a hindrance to ethnological reconstruction of precontact culture, not as a proper subject of anthropological inquiry into social and cultural process. To the early investigators it was an unfortunate, but total inevitability for Indian culture to disappear and for Indians to become assimilated beyond recognition in the general society of the country. The massive acquisition of material culture early in the contact between Indians and Whites suggested that the process of change occurred with remarkable speed and completeness. Many anthropologists of Alice Fletcher's era reacted at times to this conviction with field techniques that can only be described as ruthless. Their first obligation was to science and history, and if information could not be obtained by patient good nature, then cajolery, trickery, and pressure were justified.[41] Fletcher, for all her misguided benevolence, must at least be respected for regarding the welfare of the people she studied as her primary obligation. As a result she encountered little resistance to her work, collected highly secret data with relative ease, and maintained the good will of her informants for those who might follow after her in pursuit of scientific information.[42]

Alice Cunningham Fletcher maintained generally excellent relations with both colleagues and informants by a combination of humor, patience, total unselfishness, and lack of vindictiveness when crossed. Her small stature and seeming frailness apparently disarmed people who had no inkling of her reserves of strength. During one field trip she suffered a severe siege of "inflammatory rheumatism" which was to leave her crippled for life. As she lay on her bed of pain, her Indian friends gathered daily to cheer and console her by songs. As soon as she was able, and with a display of musical aptitude and memory that was particularly amazing in view of her painful illness, she managed to transcribe a large number of the songs she had heard.[43]

The pity is that the full force of such determination should have been thrust behind programs for Indian welfare that were tragically inappropriate to the Indians' needs. Although Fletcher's decisions and actions had unforeseen repercussions, one can only wonder if the reliability and thoroughness of her ethnography would have been so great had she not approached the Indians first as a helpful friend and then as a scientist. The Omaha wanted friends among influential White people in the hope that they could thus be saved the fate suffered by the Ponca at the hands of an unfriendly government. The Omaha were in no position to analyze or question what Fletcher proposed, it was only important that she had their welfare and devotion to their "homes" at heart and was *Doing Something* about it.

By contrast, Matilda Stevenson, who was younger than Fletcher, although her contemporary in research, was far more directly scientific in her field work, and she also obtained a great deal of valuable information. However, the Zuñi with whom she first studied labored under no particular fears or anxieties for their lands. They were free to pick and choose among items of White culture which the Stevensons introduced — lamps, candles, soap, and window glass. While Stevenson never enjoyed the reverent esteem of an entire tribe, the friendships she made were intensely personal and those who called her "Washington Mother" thought of her as a real kinswoman. Furthermore, the Zuñi priests did not finally open their secret ceremonies to Matilda Stevenson out of gratitude, as the Omaha leaders welcomed Alice Fletcher, but out of respect for her intellectual ability to grasp their meaning and her sense of reverential respect which exceeded even that of some of the lay Zuñi. As time went by and the various pueblo groups began to feel the threat posed by White people, Mrs. Stevenson encountered rebuffs and resentment among peoples with whom she did not have the depth of friendship and long acquaintance that she had at Zuñi. Her own personality was such that she reacted much too aggressively and she is probably accountable for some of the hostility toward anthropologists that continues in the Southwestern pueblos.

Matilda Stevenson witnessed striking changes in the pueblos and she stressed the need for studies to be carried out before data were irrevocably lost. Doubtless this sense of urgency underlay her increasing tendency to throw rapport to the winds. Mrs. Stevenson came to conclude that Indians learned White ways all too successfully, thereby losing much that was precious and valuable which they should have cherished. She was deeply distressed by signs of crass commercialism and selfish individuality in the once generous and politely considerate people of Zuñi. Where Alice Fletcher had worked vigorously to endow the Omaha with the comfort, security, and quiet pleasures of White ruralism — gifts they were unable to appreciate — Matilda Stevenson noted with dismay that the Indians she knew best, when left to their own devices, all too readily acquired the profane values and behavior of the marketplace.

Matilda Stevenson became an anthropologist by marriage, but she outlived her husband by many years. Her work completely overshadowed James Stevenson's brief career in anthropology, a point well illustrated by the short and belated obituary of him which appears as a sort of afterthought, trailing her lengthy obituary in the *American Anthropologist*.[44]

Shortly after Matilda Evans' birth in Texas in 1850, her family moved to Washington, D.C. As was customary for people in comfortable circumstances in her day, her family sent her to a "female seminary," Miss Anable's School in Philadelphia, for the education that would prepare her for her eventual position in society. In 1872 she married James Stevenson, a geologist with the U.S. Geological Survey. With the founding of the Bureau of Ethnology, James Stevenson was added to the staff to report archeological remains and to collect specimens as he pursued geological research in the Territories. In 1879, Matilda accompanied her husband on an anthropological expedition which included Frank H. Cushing and J. K. Hillers.

The group spent six months at Zuñi; and there she discovered ethnology.[45] Her husband, an anthropologist by courtesy rather than training or primary inclination, was her teacher. Though always acknowledging her debt to him, Stevenson displayed a natural aptitude and intelligence uniquely her own. Like Mrs. Smith and Miss Fletcher, she was, in effect, self-trained. The Philadelphia-educated girl was no better prepared for the rigors of field work than the city-bred but intrepid Fletcher, as is shown in her straightforward account of her efforts to introduce soap and the washing of clothes among the Zuñi. "Never having had any experience in that work herself, she soon had most of the water from the tub on the floor and was drenched to the skin." Undaunted by invidious comparisons to the efficiency of the missionary's wife in the laundry, she persisted in her gospel of cleanliness until her work had attracted many followers.

The details of this small incident are revealing of Matilda Stevenson's ability to rise objectively and matter-of-factly above her sheltered rearing. She chose a transvestite as her first pupil in the art of washing and ironing, recognizing in Wé-wha qualifications of role and personal influence for initiating new ideas. At first, Wé-wha was considerably less than enthusiastic about the project. However, the beauty of freshly laundered clothing, enhanced by the male strength he brought to what in those days was an exhausting task, appealed to his vanity. Furthermore, he was enterprising, a trait Stevenson counted on when she selected him as her student. He soon set himself up in the laundry business for the ethnological expedition and then solicited business among other Whites in the area. His gleaming clothes served as a billboard, and before long other Zuñi were washing their clothes by Stevenson's methods. Matilda Stevenson noted with scholarly interest that they made no sex designation in the new task; men washed their own clothing, and women washed their own and their children's clothing.

Mrs. Stevenson's forthright acceptance of Wé-wha illustrates a degree of scientific and personal sophistication noteworthy for her time and her sex. She described Wé-wha as the largest of any Zuñi she knew; he was over six feet tall and muscular. Speculations by local Whites that he was a hermaphrodite seemed incorrect to her and she believed him to be physically a male, but psychologically and socially entirely female. In referring to Wé-wha, Mrs. Stevenson would employ only feminine pronouns and would not close the words in quotation marks. Her deep affection and admiration for this remarkable person were entirely those of a close and unquestioning friendship between any two women.[46]

While Erminnie Smith was being accorded rave notices by

Powell in the first volumes of the Bureau of Ethnology, Matilda Stevenson labored unheralded; and only her husband's work was mentioned in the first four "Reports" of the Director. Although she published in 1881 a thirty-five page study, *Zuñi and the Zuñians*, it was privately printed and evidently brought her little scholarly attention. Her first important recognition was bestowed by Edward Tylor in his comments about her field work, and her publication of the "Religious Life of the Zuni Child" in the *Fifth Annual Report* of the Bureau of Ethnology. She had concentrated purposefully on affairs concerning women and children in the belief that as a woman she could obtain particularly complete information, a point that figured in the philosophy of the Women's Anthropological Society founded and first presided over by Matilda Stevenson.

However, Mrs. Stevenson, being attracted to religion even in her study of children, soon concerned herself with far more than womanly matters. In 1881 she and her husband made an archeological tour of ruins in Arizona and New Mexico and visited the various Hopi villages where she made ethnological observations. James Stevenson died in 1888 at the age of forty-eight. His widow outlived him by twenty-seven years. Initially, she devoted herself to working up her husband's notes, and was accorded a staff position with the Bureau of Ethnology. In 1890 she went back alone to the field to begin work at Sia Pueblo. Although she worked at several pueblos, she returned frequently to Zuñi and by 1895 succeeded in gaining admission to heretofore forbidden rites.[47]

Perhaps childlessness and widowhood before the age of forty contributed to a self-sufficiency of attitude that came to characterize Matilda Stevenson, or perhaps she was naturally a rather humorless person. Certainly, those assessments we can make of her personality reveal a woman who insisted on being taken very seriously. W. H. Holmes, who recalled her with deep gratitude for nursing him through a critical illness while he was in the field, describes her as "able, self-reliant, and fearless, generous, helpful and self-sacrificing."[40] Admirable traits, indeed, but equally applicable to Alice Fletcher. Tibbles, however, noted Miss Fletcher's ready smile and amused laughter, and La Flesche remembered warmth and an easy friendliness.

Matilda Stevenson's sometimes overbearing disposition may have been justified in her own mind as selfless devotion to continuing her husband's work in the cause of Science. It is common knowledge that she had a low tolerance of criticism of her work, even from Major Powell with whom she argued vehemently. She herself admitted that when the "populace" — though not the priests — at Zuñi opposed her taking photographs of ceremonies and sacred paraphernalia because they feared having these things "carried away on paper," she managed to sketch everything secretly.[49] On another occasion, her insistence on obtaining data led to her being held prisoner in a kiva at the Hopi pueblo of Oraibi until she was rescued by the trader, Thomas Keams. She brought the trouble on herself; the Indians "had repeatedly warned the white people not to attend their ceremonials and to keep away as much as possible from the pueblo. . . ."[50] Actually both James and Matilda Stevenson were involved. A lurid account of the incident appeared in the *Illustrated Police News* of March 6, 1886, in which Matilda is credited with saving the day under the headline and subheading:

## COWED BY A WOMAN

A Craven Red Devil Weakens in the
Face of a Resolute White Heroine
— Exciting Adventure in an Indian
Village in Arizona.

The reporter places the capture and threats of violence on a roof-top rather than in a kiva, and attributes the hostility of the Hopi to a generalized antipathy to White people rather than to any particular grievance against the Stevensons.

> Col. Stevenson says that while the situation was highly interesting, it was probably less alarming than it would have been to people unacquainted with the natural timidity of the Pueblos. Mrs. Stevenson who has sojourned with her husband among many wild tribes and knows the Indian character well, created an opportune diversion by shaking her fist in the face of a hunchbacked savage, whose vindictive eloquence seemed to exert a most mischievous influence over his fellows, addressing to him at the same time several brief but vigorous remarks in English and Spanish, which he was, of course, quite unable to understand. Before the man had recovered his self-possession, the strangers had backed down the ladders, and then slowly made their way, with the whole howling pack — men and women, children and dogs — at their heels, to their ponies, mounted and rode down to camp.

Meanwhile, the article explains, word of the disturbance had reached Keams who rode out with a rescue party and, finding the Stevensons safe, captured the Hopi leaders and held them prisoner at his camp for four days, threatening more dire action should they repeat such behavior as their treatment of the Stevensons.

Matthew W. Stirling notes that although Matilda Stevenson had died in 1915, when he first came to Washington in 1921 she was still a "lively legend."

> *When I became Chief of the Bureau in 1928, I inherited the office secretary of my predecessor, J. W. Fewkes. This was May S. Clark, who as a young woman had worked with Tilly at Sia in the 1880's.*
>
> *During the several years that she worked for me, Miss Clark related to me a number of Stevenson anecdotes.*
>
> *Because she wanted her hands free for note taking and did not otherwise wish to be interrupted in making ethnologic observations, Tilly turned over her camera to Miss Clark, who made the photographs illustrating the Sia report (11th Ann. Report BAE). She had*

*never taken a picture before. The [photographs of] interiors of
kivas etc. were [made by] flashlight, many of which later had to be
retouched or redrawn by an artist.*

*When Miss Clark arrived at Sia, Mrs. Stevenson had preceded
her. On the day she reported, Tilly told her that an important kiva
ceremony was being held and that they would attend it and make
notes and pictures. It was here that Tilly handed over the camera
and informed May that she was the photographer. Miss Clark protested that she did not know how. Tilly said: "Never mind that,
I'll show you!" — which she proceeded to do. They went to the kiva
where there was a guard by the ladder at the entrance. He protested
that they could not go in. "Never mind him" said Tilly, "Go on
down. I will follow you." Frightened half to death, May, clutching
her camera in one hand and her skirts in the other, entered the dark
and smoky chamber; Tilly right behind her. They sat in a vacant
spot against the wall until their eyes adjusted to the darkness. The
no doubt horrified participants in the ceremony sat sullenly and
stopped completely whatever they were doing. They refused to move
and finally after a half hour wait, Tilly gave up and left.*

*After this bad start, it took a lot of tact and the intervention of
the agent before she began to get cooperation. However, Tilly was
nothing if not persistent and eventually she did get access to a
number of kivas and permission to record the ceremonies, apparently at the same time getting the respect of the Indians who
admired her obvious fearlessness.*

Leslie White has commented that Matilda Stevenson's sense
of self-importance took some curious forms. He had seen the
original photograph of a Sia altar in the Stevenson materials
at the Bureau of American Ethnology and noted that along with
clearly aboriginal objects there were two small ceramic dogs
of Chinese origin. When a hand-drawn copy was made for
reproduction of the photograph in Stevenson's Sia study, she
had simply had the dogs deleted without comment.

Nevertheless, for all her personal idiosyncracies, Matilda
Stevenson's relationships with the Zuñi were decidedly cordial
and her admiration for the people and their ways both sincere
and affectionate. It should be remembered that the Zuñi met

her as a young woman, still admittedly capable of making mistakes but eager to learn. There was also the softening influence of her husband to whom she was deeply devoted. During her married years she often signed herself as "Tilly," even in publications, and not until later did she consistently use the more dignified "Matilda." More than any other portrait of early women in anthropology, the studio photograph of Stevenson that accompanies her obituary reveals the person and her devotion to her work. She is shown full of years and dignity, a stern, matronly woman with white hair carefully coifed, pince nez glasses adding to the severity of her facial expression. But on the magnificent and elegantly garbed bosom resposes, gaudy and incongruous, a clankingly enormous squash blossom necklace.

The bibliography accompanying her obituary sets forth the varied and yet limited nature of her interests. She wrote of the need for overall, coordinated studies of the pueblo groups, but her own researches were fragmented and scattered — ranging among legends and irrigation ditches, games and ethnobotany, with a strong emphasis on the study of religious matters. She collected facts, set them forth precisely and in detail, and analyzed them largely within their own context. Her works, particularly on Zuñi, remain standard references for any student of the Southwest. It was left for later scholars to assess broader meanings and develop wider, interpueblo conceptualizations.

Like Alice Fletcher, Matilda Stevenson was able to return at intervals to her "first love," and after a period of twenty-five years she reported on changes that had occurred among the Zuñi. Where Fletcher's later observations of the Omaha pictured the people on the road to a better life in their adaptations to White ways, with perhaps a few unfortunate consequences, Stevenson was appalled to discover:

. . . great strides have been made in certain directions; but in 1904 the people were found to be in a deplorable moral condition. . . .

The general improvement in living is due principally to additional trading stations scattered through the country. The adoption of foreign ways, however, has brought with it, the evils of intoxication and trickery in dealing with the white man whom they delight to lie to and cheat, though among themselves the Zunis are still honest.

. . . but alas, the Zuni as a man and a good citizen has fallen far below what he was before he came into contact with the White man. In 1879 no amount of money would have purchased a genuine Zuni mask, and not for the world would they have manufactured a bogus specimen. . . . At present the less orthodox men will manufacture almost anything a collector may desire and spurious ancient fetishes are made by the sackful and passed off as genuine.[52]

Despite her introduction of the use of soap to the Zuñi in 1879, Mrs. Stevenson was not so impressed with the greater cleanliness of the village and houses in 1904 that she did not feel that as one thing might be gained a greater thing might be lost. Matilda Stevenson, always a little apart from people, nevertheless understood far better than did the fully accepted Alice Fletcher that it is the integrity of a people rather than their standard of living that makes for contentment and a deeply meaningful existence.

In the final paragraph of her major work on the Zuñi, Matilda Stevenson begged scholars to study all the pueblo groups so that local details and indications of overall relationships among them might be fully explored and understood before the information would be lost forever.

For this work the passing hours are golden, for not only are the villages losing their old-time landmarks but the people themselves are changing, are adapting themselves to suddenly and profoundly altered environment; and the Zuni at least, whose religion teaches them to speak with one tongue, to be gentle to all, and to subdue the passions, thereby winning the favor of their gods, are under the influences of modern conditions, losing the restraining power of this religion, and as a result, are changing for the worse.[53]

In her last years, Mrs. Stevenson made her home near San Ildefonso where she continued her researches. To one young archeologist working in the region she was a relic of other days, and her overbearing officiousness finally caused her to appear a silly old woman to Indians and anthropologists.

> *I never cottoned much to her nor did the Indians at the pueblo, I think. Anyhow, she once told me that they called her "Little Flower" and when I passed that on to the linguist, John P. Harrington, he asked one of his San Ildefonso informants about her, telling him of the name she had given me. The Indian laughed and John asked him why. He said, "That word doesn't mean 'Little Flower,' it means 'Big Bottom!' "*[54]

It is common knowledge that as she grew older, Matilda Stevenson took increasingly to drink, but as Stirling notes, "It would probably be unfair to consider the disagreeable alcoholic of these later times as being the same person as the strong willed, able person that she was during her productive years. . . ."

Matilda Stevenson's primary failing as an ethnologist was not her aggressiveness nor her tendency to deal with isolated phenomena, but her woeful lack of a saving sense of humor. Almost any other ethnologist, even before the days of modern acculturation studies, would have welcomed those Chinese dogs on a Sia altar as a chance to inject a mildly amusing comment to relieve the pedestrian pace of ethnographic reporting. Mrs. Stevenson was outraged, and firmly removed the offending objects from view.

However, Matilda Stevenson was not the only female anthropologist in the early days to enjoy a reputation for antagonizing people, trusting in the utter verity of her own ideas. Zelia Nuttall was also notable in this regard, although Zelia confined her contentiousness to colleagues. This, of course, was largely a matter of opportunity since Mrs. Nuttall concentrated on archeological and ethnohistorical research rather than on ethnography. Like Matilda Stevenson, Zelia Nuttall is remembered for her personality rather than for her works. Yet, Matilda Stevenson's official obituary tells us little about the woman except that she worked hard and diligently in the cause of anthropology; we must seek her idiosyncrasies between the lines of her writing and the less formal recollections of those who knew her, or perpetuate the legends about her. However, even Tozzer's restrained memorial cannot hide the fact that Zelia Nuttall was a controversial, sometimes wrong-headed, but delightfully colorful and brilliant woman.[55] Mrs. Nuttall never felt obliged to collect data especially pertinent to her sex as did Mrs. Stevenson, at least early in her career; her applications of anthropological knowledge had no particular relationship to social welfare according to the philosophy of the Women's Anthropological Society, but Zelia Nuttall was a *woman* anthropologist. Her work might have been done by either a man or a woman, more so than some of Matilda Stevenson's work relating to children, but the zest she brought to her studies and her squabbles with her colleagues are unmistakably feminine. One is reminded of the prima ballerina or first soprano. It is a mark of anthropology having come of age that a woman entering the field could be an esteemed scholar and remembered as attractive or exasperating as a woman. As noted, Mrs. Nuttall was among the first women to represent the United States in the International Congress of Americanists. "At meetings she was the center of interest," able to speak all the major European languages, but fascinating to those gathered about her for her "majestic presence, her wit, and her knowledge."

Zelia Nuttall's role of urbane sophisticate was provided by a most unusual family background; she simply brought to it a remarkable intellect and a surprisingly disciplined scholarliness, if not a contemplative calmness, in argument.

Zelia Nuttall was born of wealthy and socially prominent parents in San Francisco, California, in 1857. Her family moved to Europe in 1865, where they spent the next nine years, and young Zelia acquired a remarkable facility in languages. Although a number of years were to pass before she actually visited Mexico, her childhood reading about the history and antiquities of that country had already sparked her archeological inclinations. In 1880 Zelia married Alphonse Louis Pinart, a French anthropologist, whose special interests were linguistics and folklore. She bore one daughter, Nadine, in 1882. But the marriage was not happy and two years lated this early, ill-starred team of anthropologists separated. Zelia resumed her maiden name and kept custody of her child after her divorce in 1888.

She made her first trip to Mexico in 1884 in company with her daughter, mother, and younger brother, and began serious study of Mexican archeology. In 1902 she returned to Mexico, after extended travels throughout the world, and made her permanent home there. Her residence, Casa Alvarado at Coyoacan, is recalled by older members of the discipline who worked in Mexico as an impressive mansion and a haven to visiting scholars, graciously presided over by a charming hostess.

One bit of folklore is so revealing of the woman and occurs so persistently when Zelia Nuttall's name is mentioned that it should be noted here in the hope that the date and participants can be identified. On one occasion, the story goes, two young archeologists paid a visit at Casa Alvarado. As they gazed about the magnificent home, their hostess, beautifully dressed with trailing skirts, started across the room to greet them. Suddenly, her drawers slithered down around her ankles but she stepped gracefully out of them without breaking stride. A maid immediately gathered up the offending garment and hastened off, and

Zelia Nuttall with unruffled aplomb greeted her guests as if the incident had never occurred.

Her first scholarly work dealt with the Mexican calendar system on which she read and published a number of papers. Her studies evoked such favorable notice that in 1886 she was appointed an honorary assistant in Mexican Archeology at the Peabody Museum of Harvard University, a rank she held for the rest of her life. She became fascinated by problems of diffusion and her largest work, "Fundamental Principles of New and Old World Civilization," was published by the Peabody in 1901. She always considered it her major opus, although the kindest judgment accorded it is Tozzer's assessment that before her death it had already become "archaic." However, the curator of the Peabody, Professor F. W. Putnam, shared Nuttall's views and was thus delighted to publish her work.

Other, less ambitious undertakings added new and important information to the study of Mexican antiquities and her position as a scholar rests on them. Mrs. Nuttall's special talent was in finding lost or forgotten manuscript materials and making them available to the scholarly world. Tozzer implies that there was something uncanny in the ability that led her to poke about in unlikely repositories in the Old and New Worlds. It would seem that if anyone could have put feminine intuition to work, it would have been the indefatigable Zelia. The "Codex Nuttall," published by the Peabody Museum immortalizes her name, and a long list of other remarkable documentary materials found publication at Nuttall's hands. However, "Mrs. Nuttall's vivid mind, independent will, and a remarkable belief in the truth of her theories caused her life to be punctuated with controversies." Her most notable altercation was with the Duc de Loubat over publication rights of the "Codex Magliabecchiano" which she had discovered at the Biblioteca Nazionale Central at Florence. She was often on the side of right, but it appears that she certainly did not hesitate to enter controversy with a zest. Perhaps the most harmless and at the same time most amusing of her efforts to gain recognition of some pet theory was her designation of a day in May as the ancient New Year's Day of the Mexicans. She worked long and hard to have the children of Mexico engage in special festivities around markers set up in village plazas for the occasion. She even entered into negotiations with several Peruvian associations in the hope of spreading the celebration of the holiday.

Although Mrs. Nuttall could take herself very seriously in what now seem silly enterprises, one of her little-known publications reflects a certain wicked playfulness characteristic of a sophisticated person. "The Causes of The Physical Degeneracy of Mexican Indians After The Spanish Conquest as Set Forth by Mexican Informants in 1580," was published in the English *Journal of Hygiene* in 1928.[56] Taken as a whole the accounts ascribe the degeneracy to more leisure, a greatly increased intake of meat, baked bread, more frequent changes of clothing, softer living, and comfortable beds; sybaritic luxuries one hardly tends to associate with the horrors of the Conquest. Nuttall, not content with simply providing documentary evidence of the dangers of civilization to readers of a scientific journal oriented toward health, comments at the outset that while she does not care to become involved in the argument, here apparently was ammunition for the vegetarian movement!

During Zelia Nuttall's later years, the large and beautiful gardens at her home in Mexico were her special pride and pleasure. She raised unusual plants and flowers and also developed an interest in the collection and identification of ethnobotanical specimens. She died at her home, Casa Alvarado, at the age of seventy-six, the "last of the great pioneers of Mexican archeology."

Another woman who pioneered in a highly specialized branch of anthropology was born ten years after Zelia Nuttall. Though her works were to be widely read, she lived out her life in such quiet obscurity that when she died in 1957, at the age of ninety, her passing was scarcely noted. By that time, most people assumed that she was long since dead if they thought of her at all. Frances Densmore was born in Red Wing, Minnesota, of old Midwest stock. Her interest and aptitude in music led her to concentrate in that field, and in due course after completing her education in public schools she went away to college at Oberlin, Ohio, where she took a degree in music. She studied under Leopold Godowsky in 1898, and achieved some recognition as a professional musician, notably in piano and organ performances.[57] However, for unknown reasons she did not stray far nor for very long from Red Wing during her early years. About 1893 she became interested in the music of the Chippewa Indians near her home. She saw a tremendous boon to comparative musicology in the invention of the phonograph, and some time after 1901 she borrowed a machine and cut wax cylinder records of a number of Chippewa songs. She sent them with notes to the Bureau of American Ethnology. They were received with enthusiastic appreciation, with the result that Frances Densmore became officially associated with the institution for the rest of her life.[58] In the succeeding years, she recorded and made notes on over 2,400 songs which now comprise the Smithsonian-Densmore Collection. Stirling recalls Densmore as "a very methodical person."

> *Every year she made an appointment to see me in Washington to discuss her field work for the coming year. The Bureau had an annual Government appropriation "For the Study of Indian Music" to the amount of $3000. Since she had no salary, this money was essential to the conduct of her work, which she carried on in a most economical manner. She had a feeling of insecurity about the continuation of this fund, and I felt sure that the primary purpose of her visits to me was to reassure herself that the money would be available each year, since Government funds could not be committed more than a year in advance.*

*She told me that she had been advised by Dr. Walter Hough never to read any scientific reports in advance on the people she was to visit, since these might inadvertently influence her interpretations. She took this advice very seriously, and one may be sure that her ethnological interpretations are her own.*[59]

Miss Densmore's career spanned the entire development of mechanical recording equipment from cylinders to tape. Her work took her to all the major culture areas of North America on visits to dozens of different tribes where she recorded music and gathered a wealth of related ethnographic material which she incorporated into her discussions of music, including a greater amount of good photographic illustration than can be found in many standard ethnological monographs. She also collected herbs used in connection with various healing songs and ceremonies.[60]

A cousin who knew her well provides the following personal assessment of Frances Densmore:

*. . . she was very pleasant and interesting in conversation, always abreast of the times, had a keen sense of humor, and enjoyed her circle of friends — but she had no interest whatever in social life. From the time she took up this work it was her one consuming interest and nothing was allowed to interfere or detract from it. From her early days, all through the more than fifty years with the Smithsonian, until her death . . . she lived and labored solely for this great interest.*[61]

Although she gave her life over entirely to her work, Frances Densmore lived long enough to escape the sense of urgency that would lead to haste and antagonizing of informants. Her publications reveal an easy relationship with Indian people and respect for them as individuals. She took her acceptance so much for granted that in explaining how she obtained the songs she simply stated in one publication that "Care is taken in selecting the singers and in explaining to them the nature of the material desired, and effort is made to free them from constraint or embarrassment, in order that the recorded song may be free and natural." [62]

She attained linguistic competency and ethnographic skill as essentials to further her musical analyses, and she matured quickly as a scholar and a scientist. One of her early publications, written shortly after her work had begun in earnest with American Indians, concerned a visit with the Philippine peoples resident at the Louisiana Purchase Exposition of 1904. On the basis of comparisons between Philippine and North American Indian music she presented a fine-spun and naïvely evolutionary analysis of the origin and development of music in four stages. It is very obvious that the most exciting part about this work was the people rather than their music. The affable smiles of known headhunters made her "shiver," and she was delightedly terrified at the wild clashing of shields and mock fighting that accompanied Moro music. However, in her wry comments on this choreographic production we see a charming person who could be nothing but a good ethnographer: "I was told that this too was an improvised love song, and I infer that the course of true love in Mindanao is indeed strenuous." [63]

By the time her two-volume study of Chippewa music appeared, the dedicated ethnomusicologist was concerned with the detailed theoretical analysis of non-European music, its meaning in its own cultural setting, methods of making valid written transcriptions, and the historic and social significance of given songs. Throughout Frances Densmore's long life she traveled from one Indian group to another, constantly refining her techniques of recording and analysis. Her accomplishments have generally enjoyed a greater esteem in musical than in anthropological circles since few anthropologists are trained to follow the technical complexities of her highly specialized studies. She was awarded an honorary A.M. degree at her own college, Oberlin, in 1924, and the Litt. D. Degree at Macalester College in 1950. [64] Her work was used as the basis of an opera, "Winona," by Alberto Bimoni of the Juilliard School of Music; it also inspired the composer Charles W. Cadman to write compositions with Indian themes.[65] That she continued to labor in her chosen field until the end of her life is shown in the fact that the article in *Science* commemorating her ninetieth birthday reports that she had just finished reading proof on music studies of Acoma, Isleta, Cochiti, and Zuñi pueblos. Although Frances Densmore was primarily an ethnomusicologist, her ethnological acumen was great and deserves wider attention that it has generally received.

It is noteworthy that all of the women discussed thus far were self-trained in anthropological research and that none were teachers. Elsie Clews Parsons, born in 1875, is the last representative of this older group in terms of years, but her career began well after the development of formal instruction in anthropology and continued through the modern academic professionalism of the discipline. Elsie Clews, even more impressively than some of the others, was born to wealth and a high social position. But she lived in an era when such advantages no longer could be simply enjoyed by those who wished to pursue scholarly studies or who had a sense of social enlightenment. She insisted on entering the newly founded Barnard College rather than one of the older, prestigious women's schools and eventually completed graduate studies in sociology at Columbia University. She married Herbert Parsons, a prominent New York attorney and congressman, and bore six children, four of whom lived to maturity. Elsie Clews Parsons is recalled as a woman of imposing appearance, given to rather original dress; and even during her graduate career, according to Alfred Kroeber, "her statuesque figure floated through the seminar alcoves of the Low Library on Morningside Heights as a memorably astonishing sight."[66] According to several accounts of her life, she early allied herself with the cause of feminism, but fundamentally her concern was for the right to rational individual expression, unconfined by arbitrary social limitations of sex, class or race.

During the period that her children were young, she wrote extensively on social issues, particularly on the role of women and the nature of the family. Leslie Spier says these productions were "quite in the tradition of the old 'comparative ethnologist,' but saved from their curiosity-shop speciousness by her greater keenness of insight and soundness of psychology."[67] At about the age of forty Mrs. Parsons discovered anthropology as the result of a trip to the Southwest where the pueblo peoples fascinated her. Her subsequent search for guidance in the scientific study of culture brought her into contact with P. E. Goddard and Franz Boas.

By 1915 anthropology had come sufficiently of age so that empirical methods had been developed to deal with the problems Mrs. Parsons had wrestled with only philosophically in the sociology of the 1890's. In 1915 she made her first trip to Zuñi where she returned in 1917 and 1918, years during which she also made studies at Laguna. Her interest centered in the pueblo groups although she did study the Pima in Arizona, and the plains Caddo and Kiowa in Oklahoma, in seeking for pueblo relationships in a wider area. After 1929 she concentrated on Mexican groups, the Cahitans of Sonora and especially the Zapotecs of Oaxaca, the basis of her most famous study, *Mitla: Town of the Souls*, published in 1936.[68]

Mrs. Parsons managed to maintain two specializations in anthropology. In addition to her studies among Indian peoples, she also concentrated intensively on folklore of the New World Negro, collecting accounts in the vernacular and inspiring the further recording of such data by others. Interest in culture-contact problems such as her study of Mitla led her to South America. She died only a few weeks after returning from field work in the Andes.[69] Elsie Clews Parsons' work requires no special review. Still widely read, it is in the modern tradition of anthropology, concentrating on processes rather than on the simple assembling of fact.

Of particular relevance to the present study is Parsons as a historic figure. Women who preceded her in the discipline were remarkable according to type in terms of their era. Their natural intelligence coupled with relatively high social position and refinement of education allowed them to transcend the usual avocational and vocational limitations then placed on women. Elsie Clews Parsons too was a remarkable woman, but again, remarkable according to type characteristic of her era. For Parsons, it was not enough that she, as a woman, be able to achieve what she wished to do. She was concerned that no woman, really no competent person at all, be deprived of the opportunity to realize fully his intellectual potentialities.

As the other women are remembered as outstanding examples of a type of nineteenth-century personality, so too Mrs. Parsons is remembered as exceptional even in the company of many noteworthy contemporaries in the twentieth century. She came to see the cause of feminism as but part of a larger cause, the right to individual expression. Moreover, she did not confuse the pleasures of individual self-realization with meaningless symbols of achievement acquired for the sake of professional prestige. Although eager for women to be recognized for their intellectual worth, Mrs. Parsons did not feel compelled to be the standard bearer of scholarly accomplishments of her sex before the world. Her personal inclinations were such that she did not care to take on organizational offices. Since, by chance, she was independently wealthy, she was generous and recognized her obligations to other scholars. She expressed the view that official positions should be accorded to deserving and responsible people, but to people more active in academic life than she, who would find them useful in furthering their careers. Spier notes that because of her ability and in spite of her preferences, offices were "thrust upon her." Even the distinction of being the first woman president of the American Anthropological Association occurred at the end of her career and was in no way related to her earlier efforts to win equal opportunities and respect for women. She was simply elected in the due course of events as one of the most outstanding anthropologists of her time.[70]

A glance at the voluminous bibliography of Elsie Clews Parsons' writing reveals a person who must have possessed amazing reserves of energy and tremendous will. And yet, the personal recollections recorded about Parsons depict a woman characterized by great calm, relaxed sociability, and contemplative impartiality. Gladys Reichard recalled: "She used to say that her idea of complete comfort was to have *at the same time* a cigarette, a cup of coffee and an open fire."[71] One sees in Elsie Parsons something of Alice Fletcher in the affection she evoked among those who know her and in the determination and ability to follow the dictates of conscience and conviction without shrillness or loss of personal control. However, where Miss Fletcher labored largely alone and was unable to test the validity of her ideas, Mrs. Parsons, typifying a new generation of women anthropologists, had the benefit of purposeful training and wide interchange of ideas among teachers, peers, and even students. Mrs. Parsons' natural talents were shaped and refined in ways denied her predecessors.

Although Mrs. Parsons' career as a teacher was brief — a few years as a lecturer at Columbia University and a faculty position at the New School for Social Research which she helped to found — it was enriching. Parsons disliked public lecturing but she was vitally interested in the work of younger scholars. The full accounting of her financial assistance to promising students will probably never be known. While she was pleased to help further anthropology, it embarrassed her deeply to be thanked as an individual. To Elsie Clews Parsons, anthropology was a calling rather than a profession.

Where Alice Fletcher had used her anthropological influence in obtaining what she thought was best for Indians, Parsons learned to assess the dangers of trusting in expertise rather than in anthropology itself. She gave the matter a great deal of thought and it forms the basis of the presidential address which she did not live to deliver personally.[72] She viewed with horror the misuse of anthropology in the racist schemes of the Nazis, but she was also alert to the hazards attendant upon the utilization of anthropology to achieve any specific and immediate ends. When work is so directed, no matter how benevolently, "even slow and patient searches for social laws may easily smack of divination which according to our definition is concerned not with process but with particular interests and is callous to scientific control." However, continuing to reflect her fundamental concern with the individual, she saw in the data and methods of anthropology the liberation of thought whereby people may reach meaningful understandings and valid conclusions. Anthropologists, she believed, had a primary obligation to "popularize" their subject among laymen in order to enable them to evaluate properly the facile, shallow, and ready-made opinions supplied in increasing quantities through the mass media of communication. Mrs. Parsons hoped that the pronouncers themselves might "be educated away from their conceits."

Perhaps the melancholy circumstances under which Mrs. Parsons' presidential address was delivered and the recency of her death when it was published in the *American Anthropologist* deterred expressions critical of her ideas. It would seem that at the time her ideas were presented, they might well have been open to criticism as inconsistent. Parsons believed that social commentators often erred, and even when no fault could be found in their opinions, danger lurked in the fact that their views were promulgated and absorbed on the basis of authority rather than reason. At the same time she warned anthropologists that they too ran the risk of being oracular rather than scientific. Yet, she argued strongly for the popularizing of anthropology as the means of bringing about a desirable intellectual "revolution." However, now that more than twenty years have elapsed since Elsie Parsons' death, it is possible to discern the concepts she was in the process of formulating but could not then set forth in precise and explicit terms. Applied anthropology, a new field in 1941 and the object of Mrs. Parsons' pointed criticism, as well as the even more recent development known as action anthropology, have been approaching what Mrs. Parsons apparently meant by the "popularization" of anthropology.

As early as 1941, anthropologists were free of the cultural blindness that led to the predictive errors of Alice Fletcher and the sense of personal affront experienced by Matilda Stevenson in viewing Zuñi acculturation. By then there was awareness that directed change must follow the course of voluntary change. That is, anthropologists knew that change must be congruent with the existing values and patterns of the group concerned, values and patterns to be discovered and defined by anthropologists. However, Elsie Clews Parsons' analogy of this type of anthropology to soothsaying was apt: the diviner is often exceedingly sensitive in manipulating observable social phenomena but cannot really read minds. During the last twenty years, practical utilizations of anthropology have been moving toward greater involvement and comprehension of the group served in the fact-finding and decision-making processes in the work of directed change. Ideally, the anthropologist endeavors to promote "a state of dynamic equilibrium within systems of human relationships," rather than to advance a particular program conceived of by well-intentioned and even well-informed outsiders as in the best interests of a society.[73] Elsie Clews Parsons' presidential address carries us to developments of the present in the history of women in the early years of anthropology.

Looking back over the careers of women from Smith to Parsons, it is possible to draw at least some tentative generalizations. Individual women have made specific contributions to the development of anthropology. However, the contributions of women as a group cannot be specified in comparison to contributions of men as a group. Some qualifications of these flat statements are, of course, in order and will be briefly considered, but fundamentally women have not confined themselves to the "female data" the fathers of anthropology and they themselves initially designated as their peculiar province. Even by the time the pronouncements were made, women had already branched out into other areas of investigation. Furthermore, albeit somewhat later, many prominent men in anthropology became associated with pioneer work in the intensive study of patterns of child care and training, nutrition, and other "female" data. The disbanding of the Women's Anthropological Society in 1899 was in itself a recognition of the universality of work carried out by the very first women anthropologists.

These generalizations should, however, be seen in the total social setting of American anthropology in its early years. It appears that it was not the exclusiveness, even reinforced by taboos, of male and female activities of "primitives" that suggested women might obtain data not readily disclosed to men, but the strong segregation of the sexes in Victorian society that produced the early anthropologists. Men were unwittingly reluctant to deal with matters in the field that were beneath their notice at home. Women broke the bonds of sexual ascription of ethnographic tasks, although they can hardly take credit for it. Women simply followed the dictates of their culture as unconsciously as men. Upper-class and even middle-class women of the latter half of the nineteenth century were expected to involve themselves with problems of social welfare and matters of religion, as well as to acquire an intelligent knowledge of local, national and world events. Business and politics lay in the hands of men, but women heard far more about these things than men knew about the details of domesticity. Furthermore, in a Victorian dwelling the isolation of individuals' activities by age, sex, and social status — let us not forget the "hired girl" — could not possibly occur in an earth lodge, tipi, or pueblo household. Women such as Fletcher, Smith, and Stevenson were brought up to learn from men and to listen to their views; thus in their field work they experienced little constraint in continuing to learn from male informants. Where these women exhibited a truly remarkable degree of adaptability was not with regard to sex-linked data, but in status-linked matters. Tibbles found it hard to believe that Alice Fletcher, a proper Bostonian, could accustom herself to the lack of privacy and physical hardships of life among the Plains Indians, and Tilly Stevenson herself admitted that until she visited the Zuñi she had no practical knowledge of so simple a task as washing clothes.

Women who did not conform to the norms of nineteenth-century society — and the point would apply to other periods as well — were either "bad women" or so intellectually gifted that, proverbial exceptions to the rule, they were accorded respect and egalitarian treatment by men. Women who succeeded were by definition notable for their intelligence and unconventional aspirations, but in most cases these traits were not enough, a fact to which Parsons was particularly sensitive. All of the women discussed had advantages of family wealth, social status, and an interest in education that allowed them greater latitude of behavior than if their families had been poor and ignorant. Nevertheless, limitations placed upon women did serve a useful selective function to the benefit of disciplines that they entered, although the strain imposed on individuals may have taken its toll in Stevenson's case and contributed to her feistiness. Clearly, gifted women were under far more pressure to prove themselves than were men so that the work of a surprising number of early women in anthropology was memorable. Even their mistakes, like the mistakes of early men important in the field, served to explore and mark dead-end avenues of investigation for the benefit of those who followed.

Although women were actually welcomed into anthropology because of an erroneous notion that they could and would be the only ones to obtain certain necessary information, the miscalculation worked to the advantage of women as individuals. They did not have to dissipate their energies in *fighting* for their rights but could apply them toward earning the esteem of their colleagues. On the other hand, the emphasis on the value of women in ethnological studies may have limited but certainly did not preclude their active participation in other branches of anthropology. Zelia Nuttall, for example, concentrated on archeology, and Alice Fletcher was interested in archeology long before she did ethnographic field work.[74] However, aside from some efforts to describe physical types of peoples studied, women who were pioneers in anthropology evinced no great inclination toward work in physical anthropology in either somatological or evolutionary terms. Since physical anthropology gained its major impetus from anatomists and medical men and remains a branch of anthropology having relatively few full-time practitioners, absence of women in the nineteenth century may be due to no more than statistical and occupational chance.[75]

With regard to the fields of anthropology with which most of the early women concerned themselves, unquestionably in particular instances the sex of the investigator helped or hindered her in obtaining certain types of data. Nevertheless, the fact of being a woman has been and continues to be but one of many personal variables, any one of which may figure most importantly in affecting the course of field work at different times and in various places. In addition to the individual traits of sex, age, training, personality structure, experience, and physical health and stamina, there were and are external variables influencing the amount and kind of information obtained. Among these may be listed the general political climate under which research is conducted, existing attitudes toward anthropologists and other outsiders, and the quality of interpersonal relationships among several coworkers.

Women in early American anthropology possessed in common only an exceptional amount of drive and sense of adventure to step beyond the place society reserved for the average woman. Even the personal lives of the six women discussed are dissimilar. Alice Fletcher and Frances Densmore never married; Zelia Nuttall was divorced; Matilda Stevenson was widowed at thirty-eight; and Erminnie Smith and Elsie Clews Parsons combined marriage and an anthropological career throughout their lives. However, having decided to become anthropologists, they virtually were obliged by their society to become outstanding anthropologists. Nevertheless, the problems they dealt with were influenced by the going theories and interests of their day and were not distinguished for any definably feminine characteristics. Contrary to their own opinion in 1885, there was really nothing in their "nature as women" that gave them "special adaptations" for the study of anthropology. Each brought her own unique nature and special adaptations as an individual to the study of anthropology.

This sketch illustrated a newspaper article on the visit of James and Matilda Stevenson to the Hopi pueblo of Oraibi, Arizona, in 1886. *Courtesy Smithsonian Institution, Bureau of American Ethnology.*

Officers of the A.A.A.S. at Ann Arbor, 1885. J. O. Dorsey, vice president of the anthropology section, is standing third from right; and Mrs. Erminnie A. Smith is seated in the front row. *Courtesy Smithsonian Institution, Bureau of American Ethnology.*

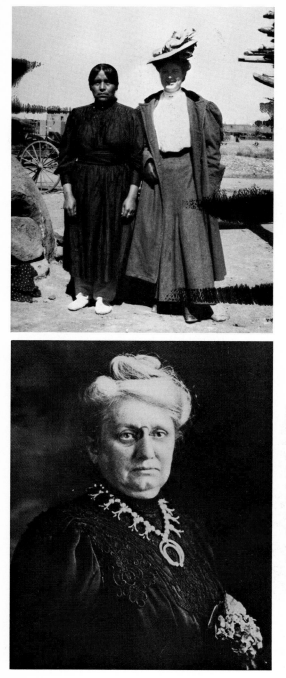

Matilda Coxe
Stevenson with
woman from Taos
pueblo. Taken
July 19, 1907.
*Courtesy Smith-
sonian Institution,
Bureau of Ameri-
can Ethnology.*

Matilda Coxe
Stevenson, "full
of years and
dignity." This
photograph ac-
companied Mrs.
Stevenson's obitu-
ary published in
the *American
Anthropologist*
in 1916.

Photograph taken by Matilda Stevenson, in 1888 or 1889, showing the Altar of the Knife Society, pueblo of Sia, New Mexico. Note the Chinese dogs in the center of the photograph. *Courtesy Smithsonian Institution, Bureau of American Ethnology.*

Painting by M. I. Wright after Stevenson's photograph. The Chinese dogs have disappeared.

Two portraits of Alice Cunningham Fletcher. *Courtesy Smithsonian Institution, Bureau of
American Ethnology.*

Alice Fletcher with Meepe and Martha. These two old Winnebago women
used to pitch and keep the tent for the allotting agents in the field. The
photograph was probably made sometime between 1887 and 1889. *Courtesy Smithsonian Institution, Bureau of American Ethnology.*

*Top, left*: Portrait of Frances Densmore "wearing dress worn when giving lecture on Indian music at the Art Institute, Chicago, on February 21, 1899." By Phillips, Red Wing, Minnesota. *Top, right*: Frances Densmore, ca. 1950's. *Below*: Main'ans or Little Wolf and Frances Densmore. Photograph by Gill, 1908. All photographs *courtesy Smithsonian Institution, Bureau of American Ethnology.*

*Top, left*: Zelia Nuttall. Photograph taken in England between 1912 and 1914. *Top, right*: Elsie Clews Parsons. *Below*: Matilda Coxe Stevenson with Taos child. Taos pueblo is in the background. The photograph was taken July 19, 1907. *Courtesy Smithsonian Institution, Bureau of American Ethnology.*

*Top, left*: Zelia Nuttall, dressed in the costume she wore to a ball at the Palazzo Vecchio in Florence in 1898. *Top, right*: Zelia Nuttall in 1927.

*Below, left*: Frederic Ward Putnam. *Below, right*: Manuel Gamio. From a photograph by Ernest Gruening printed in *Mexico and Its Heritage*.

Franz Boas.

# GLIMPSES OF A FRIENDSHIP
# ZELIA NUTTALL AND FRANZ BOAS

Based on their correspondence

in the Library of the American Philosophical

Society in Philadelphia

*by ROSS PARMENTER*

*Former music editor of the New York Times, Ross Parmenter is author of* The Plant in My Window *(Thomas Y. Crowell, 1949; paperback reprint, Apollo Editions, 1962)*; Week in Yanhuitlán *(University of New Mexico Press, 1964)*; *and a bio-bibliography of the published writings of Alphonse Louis Pinart,* Explorer, Linguist, and Ethnologist *(Southwest Museum, Hodge Anniversary Publications, Vol. IX, 1966). Pinart was married briefly to Zelia Nuttall, whose correspondence with Franz Boas is highlighted in the present article.*

# AUTHOR'S NOTE

*The footnotes exist only to cite references. Their numbering is according to the position of the references in the alphabetized bibliography at the end of the book.*

*I have many people to thank: Muriel Rukeyser, for instance, who first told me of the existence of the letters. Then there was Gertrude D. Hess, the librarian of the American Philosophical Society, who drew them from the society's beautifully kept files. She was also kind enough to read the manuscript. And I want to thank Dr. George W. Corner, the society's executive officer, for permission to publish the letters, all hitherto unpublished.*

*J. Alden Mason, Franziska Boas, Clarence L. Hay, Paula Jacobs, Nadine Laughton and A. I. Hallowell are the persons mentioned who read the manuscript. I thank them for the slips they caught, as well as for blessing the work on its way. Readers in the anthropological fields who read the script and gave me helpful suggestions were J. Eric S. Thompson, Nancy Oestreich Lurie, Ralph W. Dexter, John Paddock, Bertha Soren, George D. Spindler, June Helm, Pál Kelemen and Elizabeth Kelemen. I thank them, and also my sharp-eyed nonspecialist readers, Nona Balakian, Leonard Elliott, Charlotte Isler, and Ramona Weeks.*

*I would also like to express gratitude for personal kindness to the late Helene Boas Yampolsky, the late May Mandelbaum Edel, to Herbert Otten of the American Scandinavian Foundation, who was able to contact Nels C. Nelson, and to the ever-helpful filing clerks of the clipping library of the New York* Times. *Help in assembling photographs is gratefully acknowledged to Gillian Bulmer, Christine Bulmer, Carmelita Hamilton, Martha Hitchens, Ralph Dexter, Ernest Gruening, and Mr. and Mrs. Thomas B. Miller.*

Franz Boas and Zelia Nuttall must have met for the first time in 1886 at the Buffalo meeting of the American Association for the Advancement of Science.[5,12,63] Prior to that time, their lives had not provided the opportunity for their paths to cross. But they both attended the Buffalo meeting, and it was there that Boas came under the same wings that were already hovering helpfully over Mrs. Nuttall—[12] those of Frederic Ward Putnam, the association's long-time permanent secretary.

Dr. Putnam had met Mrs. Nuttall in Baltimore earlier that year and he had given her "kind encouragement"[62] as she studied the terra-cotta heads of Teotihuacán. He had helped her tangibly, too. Using his authority as Curator of the Peabody Museum of Harvard, he had named her the Museum's "Special Assistant in Mexican Archaeology,"[85] and he had helped her in the Archaeological Institute of America.[62] Recognition by the Peabody and the Institute and (at the Buffalo meeting) election to membership of the American Association for the Advancement of Science, had paved the twenty-nine-year-old Zelia Nuttall's way to fame and acceptance in an era when women archaeologists were almost unheard of.

At Buffalo, Boas was the one who had sought out Dr. Putnam. But the older man had promptly seen to it that the young German was extended the courtesy of being made a Foreign Associate Member of the A.A.A.S. for the rest of the meeting. Shortly thereafter, too, he helped Boas get a job as an assistant editor of *Science*, the A.A.A.S.'s journal.[12]

The Boas-Nuttall acquaintanceship, however, probably did not deepen into friendship until the 1893 World's Columbian Exposition in Chicago. That was a world's fair in which both were deeply involved: Mrs. Nuttall as an exhibitor[104] and Boas as a collector and arranger of exhibits.[35] And the section of the exposition to which they both contributed was the one that had a deep and far-ranging influence on American anthropology. Department M, it was called,[104] and it was devoted to ethnology, archaeology, physical anthropology, history and natural history.

The two were drawn into the fair[66,35] by the same man who had befriended them seven years earlier. For Dr. Putnam, who had helped originate the idea of the section was the chief of Deparement M,[42] and the year before the fair opened he had persuaded Boas to leave Clark University[95] to come to Chicago to be his chief assistant in organizing the anthropological exhibits.

At the time of the fair, Mrs. Nuttall was thirty-six[97] and Boas was thirty-five.[35] And they had a curious reversal of domiciles to help cement their friendship. The year of the Buffalo meeting, 1886, had been pivotal for each. Boas had left his native Germany for the field trip to Vancouver Island[101] that led to his permanent residence in the United States. Mrs. Nuttall, moving in the opposite direction, had left her native United States to live in Germany.[61]

Mrs. Nuttall, who had made her home in Dresden, had spent most of her girlhood in Europe. Her physician father, Dr. Robert Kennedy Nuttall, had traipsed the family back and forth across the Continent during her school years. Thus she had acquired little formal education and scarcely any scientific training. But after 1880 she gained some field experience and received practical tutelage when she married the French ethnologist and linguist, Alphonse Louis Pinart. The marriage, however, was short-lived; with legal separation in 1884 being followed by divorce in 1888.[97]

Divorce affirmed Zelia Nuttall's legal right to resume the maiden name she had already begun using in her publications. For the year of her separation she had made her first trip to Mexico, adopted ancient Mexico as her province and begun the series of studies that quickly brought her attention.

From the start she had shown a flair for discovery and controversy. An example is "Standard or Head-Dress?",[64] her first paper for the Peabody Museum. In it she took issue with German and Austrian scholars on the identifying uses they ascribed to a large pre-Columbian feather piece in Vienna. This had drawn counter-fire from Eduard Seler[92] of the Royal Ethnographical Museum (Museum für Völkerkunde) in Berlin. Because Seler later plays a role in the correspondence, a word needs to be said about him.

He is generally regarded as the initiator of Mexican studies in Germany.[43] Boas, before coming to the United States, had been a junior colleague of his at the Berlin Museum,[95] and by 1904 Seler had risen to be the Museum's director. He was already a name when he publicly criticized Mrs. Nuttall,[92] and his position was about to be strengthened by the support and patronage of Joseph Florimund Loubat. Loubat was an enormously wealthy New Yorker who had become generally known as the Duke de Loubat after his benefactions to the Roman Catholic Church led Pope Leo XIII to declare him a papal duke.[46] Not only did the Duke pay to have a number of Mexican codices reproduced, but he also sponsored publication of Seler's interpretations of them. In 1889, too, the Duke established a professorship of American linguistics, ethnology and archaeology at the University of Berlin which Seler was the first to hold.[43]

Mrs. Nuttall was also to make important contributions to the study of Mexican codices, and there are two with which her name is particularly associated.[70,71] It was in 1890 that her researches in Florence enabled her to bring the first of the two, the Codex Magliabecchiano, to light. This discovery had a particularly sweet by-product for Mrs. Nuttall. Through one of its drawings, this codex proved she was right and the Germans wrong about the purpose of the Vienna feather piece. It *was*, as she claimed, a headdress and not a standard.

Then in 1892, both as an exhibitor and speaker, she had made a splash at the Huelva meeting of the International Congress of Americanists.[36] Not only did she exhibit a facsimile of the Codex Magliabecchiano, but she gave a paper, supported by elaborate charts, that set forth her reconstruction of the Aztec calendar system. She had followed this up with further success at the ensuing Madrid Exposition,[67] where, in addition to displaying the Magliabecchi material and her calendar charts, she exhibited paintings of Mexican feather shields and a reproduction of the Alonso de la Cruz map of the Valley of Mexico, an important document which had been copied for her from the original in the Library of the University of Uppsala in Sweden. Her exhibits won her a silver medal. Her fame therefore was markedly increased by her participation in the Old World's celebration of the four hundredth anniversary of the sailing of Christopher Columbus for the New.

Thus a year later, when the New World celebrated that anniversary in Chicago, Mrs. Nuttall was a more commanding figure than was Dr. Putnam's assistant, who, despite a first-class education in Germany, had been, in the United States, only an obscure staff writer for *Science* and a docent at a small new university in Worcester, Massachusetts.[35]

The fair opened on May 1, 1893. The living specimens — the Pacific islanders, American Indians and various groups of

Oriental peoples — were encamped in "native villages" along the Midway Plaisance, but most of the inanimate exhibits were installed in the Anthropological Building.[9] Mrs. Nuttall's exhibits, which Boas must have helped arrange, were for the most part the items she had exhibited the year before at Huelva and Madrid. Here, too, she displayed facsimile pages of the Codex Magliabecchiano, her reproduction of the de la Cruz map, charts showing her restoration of the Mexican calendar system and paintings of Mexican featherwork shields.[104] They won her an American medal to set beside her Spanish one.

From August 29 to September 2 there was an International Congress of Anthropology at the fair. Boas and Mrs. Nuttall both participated and she illustrated her paper on the Mexican calendar system from the charts in her exhibit.[100]

Alas, though, the correspondence between Mrs. Nuttall and Dr. Boas in the Library of the American Philosophical Society reveals nothing of this stage of their friendship. Nor does it refer to their meeting in Berlin in 1899 when they both read papers at the seventh International Geographical Congress. In the Library the curtain does not rise until 1901. But the first letter preserved in the society's archives reveals that by that time the two were friends of sufficiently long standing for Mrs. Nuttall to write Boas with considerable indiscretion on a decidedly ticklish matter.

Before going further, though, a few words need to be said about the correspondence itself. Also there must be some bridging of the eight years separating our glimpses of them at the World's Columbian Exposition, which we can only imagine, and the first direct revelations of the letters.

Actually, the correspondence is not large. On Mrs. Nuttall's part it consists only of eight letters to Dr. Boas and a copy of a telegram to Mrs. Boas. On his part, there are ten letters addressed directly to Mrs. Nuttall and a letter for someone else which she refused to deliver. The correspondence spans twenty-seven years and gives us glimpses of the friends at five different periods when their paths crossed. We owe its preservation to Boas' well-known habit of never throwing anything away. Not only did he keep Mrs. Nuttall's letters, which were all written in longhand, but fortunately he also kept carbon copies of his typed communications to her. And one says "fortunately" because, although Mrs. Nuttall was a great letter hoarder herself, the latter-day owners who came into possession of her papers were not so concerned with their historical value. A few years after her death, trunks and trunks of letters she had saved were burned.[20,51]

But let us return to Chicago. When the fair ended in November something that Dr. Putnam had planned and hoped for came about. Thanks to a gift from Marshall Field, the exhibits in the Anthropological Building were not dispersed. Instead, they were moved to the Fine Arts Building at the opposite end of the fair grounds and became the first exhibits of the Field Columbian Museum.[28] In 1894, Dr. Putnam, in addition to returning to the Peabody Museum, became director of the Department of Anthropology of the American Museum of Natural History.[42] Boas was also to move to the American Museum of Natural History, but not until 1896.[35]

By then Boas had been working sporadically with the United States' government's Bureau of American Ethnology for seven years.[101] But this did not prevent him from accepting two jobs when he moved permanently to New York. For he agreed to teach a general course in physical anthropology at Columbia University[52] while he served as Curator of Ethnology and Somatology at the American Musuem.

At this time Morris K. Jesup, "the Father of Rapid Transit" in New York, and a retired banker and philanthropist, was the president of the Museum. Boas plunged into his museum work

with characteristic energy and vision and the first major project
he planned was one which would include researches on both
sides of the Bering Strait.[101] The plan was to search for evidence,
both in Asia and America, that would throw light on the hypoth-
esis that the American Indians had come to the New World
from the Old by crossing the Strait. Mr. Jesup liked the idea
and, because he agreed to finance the venture, it was called the
Jesup North Pacific Expedition. It consisted of a number of
individual field trips, starting in 1897. Boas himself was one
of the men who went to the American side of the Strait, and
in ensuing years he was to edit the publications giving the
results of the project.

Mrs. Nuttall's way took her elsewhere. When the fair ended
in Chicago she visited Washington. Then she returned to Europe. A granddaughter of John Parrott,[97] one of San Francisco's
richest bankers, she was not obliged either to teach or to work
in an institution. But not being forced to work did not mean
she was inactive. She kept on with her researches and her fame
continued to spread. In 1895 America's oldest learned society,
the American Philosophical Society (which did not elect Boas
until 1935) elected her as the seventh of the twenty-two women
it has honored with membership.

She also continued to travel, and in 1896, the year Boas settled
in New York, she made one of her biggest junkets. As a young
woman in San Francisco she had become a friend of Mrs. Phoebe
Apperson Hearst, mother of William Randolph Hearst. Mrs.
Hearst put up the money for Mrs. Nuttall to go to Russia to
collect ethnological material for the University Museum of the
University of Pennsylvania.[99] Two years later, Mrs. Nuttall had
her greatest triumph as a discoverer when she tracked down,
in England, the glorious Mixtec pictorial codex that bears her
name.[81]

The ticklish matter Mrs. Nuttall wrote to Boas about was a

faculty raid — or rather, an attempted one. And here one must remark something about Mrs. Nuttall that remained true all her life. She was not merely a scientist; she was also a socialite. She moved among the wealthy and the fashionable as a peer. This means that she was often able to serve as mediator between two worlds: the world of patronage and the world of scientific projects in need of patronage. It is curious how easily she moved from one to the other. Fellow anthropologists obviously had so much respect for her work that they did not dismiss her as an interfering society woman — as they might have done. The social world, for its part, never seemed to feel she lost cachet by being a working scientist. And her belonging to both camps made her a very good person to approach if one wanted strings pulled.

Mrs. Nuttall's friendship with the rich Mrs. Hearst is an example of her social connections. And her trip to Russia was not the only collecting trip Mrs. Hearst had paid for. By the spring of 1901, the date of Mrs. Nuttall's first letter to Boas, Mrs. Hearst's friends and agents had collected so much ethnographic material that Mrs. Hearst was anxious to have it decently housed. And she did not want it merely stored safely. She wanted a department of anthropology at the University of California that would study the material, catalogue it, augment it, and use it both as the basis for further collecting and for teaching.[50] She wanted the department so keenly that she was willing to finance it. Being wise, she asked friends to help in its planning.

Mrs. Nuttall was one of the friends to whom Mrs. Hearst turned. Their consultations were easily arranged, for in 1899 Mrs. Nuttall, after thirteen years abroad, had returned to her native land. She was often in the Berkeley area because San Francisco was the city in which she had been born and the one in which, at this time, she had decided to settle.[61] The other consultants in the project were Alice Fletcher, another pioneer woman anthropologist, and the same Dr. Putnam, who had run Section M at the Chicago world's fair.[50] Dr. Putnam was in California because he was continuing his researches in the antiquity of man on the Pacific Coast.[87]

Obviously the four had put their heads together on who would be a good man to run the proposed department. At this time anthropology was still in its infancy and few qualified anthropologists were available. There was one young man, Alfred L. Kroeber, who must have been discussed as a possibility. Kroeber, then twenty-five, had just got his Ph.D. in anthropology at Columbia, and the year before had been west on a field trip for the California Academy of Sciences.[94] Another name that might also have come up was that of the twenty-six-year-old Roland B. Dixon,[57] who had already begun his long career teaching anthropology at Harvard. But some of the consultants had their eye on bigger game: on Boas himself. And Mrs. Nuttall, being an old friend of Boas, was the one who sounded him out. Her letter, though, was clearly not the first Boas had heard of the proposed department. The way it opens shows that Mrs. Nuttall had already acted as a go-between, asking Boas questions on Mrs. Hearst's behalf. Specifically, she had appealed to Boas as an official of the American Museum of Natural History for an opinion as to how much his museum would and should cooperate with the proposed department at the University of California.

Mrs. Nuttall was visiting in the East when she put the big question to Boas. It is likely that she had refreshed her world's fair friendship with him in June of 1900, for in that month Columbia was host to the American Association for the Advancement of Science. Boas was one of the organizers of the meeting and Mrs. Nuttall gave a paper at it.[7] Boas at this time was living near the Museum at 123 West Eighty-Second Street.[106] Although

Mrs. Nuttall wrote her letter from Boston, her P.S. reveals that not long before she had been in New York and that her friendship with Boas was wide enough to include friendship with Mrs. Boas, the former Marie A. E. Krackowizer, an American surgeon's daughter, whom Boas had married the year after he settled in the United States.[106]

The Boston letter was on stationery Mrs. Nuttall must have designed herself, for in the upper left corner her superimposed initials Z and N were printed diagonally so that they formed a swastika. It was a suitable touch, for Mrs. Nuttall was awaiting publication of her most massive work, her book, *The Fundamental Principles of Old and New World Civilizations.*[69] One of its chief arguments was that the swastika was a leading symbol in common of the civilizations she was comparing.

Her handwriting is firm, bold and clear and the signature is underlined with a fine, switchbacking rubric. In this letter, too, she resorted to two devices she often used for emphasis: underlining and adding a long dash to the period at the end of a paragraph. The letter was written from the Brunswick Hotel and is dated May 14, 1901.

> *Dear Dr. Boas,*
>
> *I am forwarding your letter to Mrs. Hearst and think it contains a very clear presentation of facts.*
>
> *I note that you do not define the degree of co-operation which might exist between the New York Museum and the University of California and think it was as well to leave this point to be mutually agreed upon later.—*
>
> *I earnestly hope that, sooner or later a competent person will create a centre of investigation in California and employ a trained body of assistants.*
>
> *As an old friend and colleague, upon whose discretion you can rely absolutely, I venture to ask you whether you would consider the possibility of your going to California and undertaking the great task yourself? This would not exclude Mr. Kroeber, whose assistance would be needed, I should think.—*
>
> *When I go to California I can ascertain how matters stand. I should*

*like to know, however, whether there might be a chance for the
University to obtain your valuable aid in establishing and carrying
on the work. Simply write me: I cannot or I might consider the
possibility and I shall act accordingly.*

*Hoping that you will not think me indiscreet in asking you this
question and assuring you that you can rely absolutely on my secrecy
and on my high appreciation of your scientific worth, believe me,*
*very sincerely yours,*
*Zelia Nuttall.*

P.S. *Many cordial greetings to Mrs. Boas and thanks to you both for
the pleasant evening spent at your house.*

Dr. Boas did not take Mrs. Nuttall at her word. He did not
scribble off a hasty, "I cannot consider the possibility." Instead,
he composed the finest and longest of his letters in the Nuttall-
Boas correspondence. Indeed, one wonders if he wrote many
letters of such calmness, nobility, and breadth of view. Its tone
showed he respected Mrs. Nuttall, that he knew she was a serious
emissary (and not just a busybody) and that he was genuinely
concerned about California. Perhaps her letter hit him at a
time when he was particularly anxious to set down just what
course he wanted his life — and the study of anthropology — to
take. Perhaps, too, it was a time when he wanted to take stock.
He was then forty-three, and he may have wanted to size up
what he had achieved up to that point, when he had been working simultaneously for five years at both the Museum of Natural
History and at Columbia.

At all events, he lost no time in answering, and his reply remains of extraordinary interest, especially on the prophetic level.
Professionally, there was to be no veering from the lines he laid
down; but on the personal level there was never to be the
leisure for uninterrupted research that he was dreaming of.[106]
The carbon copy that has been preserved bears no address, but
the frequent references to "this Museum" suggest the original
must have been on the letterhead of the American Museum
of Natural History.

May 16, 1901

Mrs. Zelia Nuttall,
    Hotel Brunswick,
        Boston, Mass.

Dear Mrs. Nuttall, —

I received your very kindly note of Tuesday yesterday morning. You know how deeply I am interested in the question of California ethnology, and I feel that your question requires a somewhat full answer in regard to my general plans and the scope of the work which I have laid out for myself.

Since I took hold of the work in New York, I have tried to develop the same in such a way that it will ultimately result in the establishment of a well-organized school of anthropology, including all the different branches of the subject. I consider this one of the fundamental needs of our science, because without it we can never hope to thoroughly investigate and explore all the numerous problems of American anthropology. For this reason I am trying to develop the collections of this Museum in such a way that they will ultimately form the basis of university instruction in all lines of anthropological research. This aim of course must be combined with the general educational aims of the Museum, but I find that both are very easily harmonized. I am endeavoring to develop each department to such a point that within a very short time it will demand the care of a specialist, and this will be the opportune moment for introducing instruction in each particular line in Columbia University. My plan in taking up East Asiatic problems at the present time is on a line with this more general plan, and I am hoping to follow this undertaking with others which will lead us also into new lines. I want to see represented anthropology as well in its physical side as its psychological, comparative side, and also specialists capable of carrying on work in archaeology, in American ethnology, and in the problems found in China, the Malay Archipelago, East Indies, Africa, etc. I am fully aware of the difficulties of really carrying out this undertaking, but I am fairly confident of ultimate success.

You may notice that I have worked somewhat systematically on those lines during the last five years. The Jesup Expedition gave me the first foothold outside of our continent. This is now being followed out by our Chinese enterprises, and plans have been laid for the successive steps also, although they have not matured yet.

*I am confident that in this manner we shall be able inside of a very few years to give a young man a thorough all-round schooling, which cannot be had at the present time anywhere. Neither Berlin with its five anthropological professorships, nor Paris with its anthropological school, nor Holland with its colonial school, could give a proper training to the observers whom we need. I believe that the plans which I have in mind, based largely on the co-operation of this Museum and of Columbia University, will ultimately result in obtaining what we want.*

*Of course this end is still a long ways off, and our work in North America must be carried on now. For this reason we have taken up at Columbia a number of special lines which seem to be most important for carrying on fieldwork, and here I lay particular stress upon a training in linguistics, a general ethnological training, and knowledge of certain field methods of physical anthropology. By pursuing this method, I have been able to train a small number of young men who are able to do pretty good work.*

*You might say that to a certain extent the emphasis which I lay upon the necessity of having trained observers is a criticism of our present generations of ethnologists. This is true. I believe you will agree with me that almost every one of us is deficient in certain lines with which he ought to be familiar, and that lack of systematic knowledge may be observed in the writings of even our best men. But besides this, the number of young men is exceedingly limited, and I am very anxious that those who do take up the work should not be as unprepared as most of our generation have been.*

*I have the conviction that in certain lines at least I know exactly what is needed for furthering our knowledge of American ethnology, and I believe that the method which I am pursuing is more systematic than that followed by many others. It is only for this reason that I have ventured to concentrate in my hands a considerable part of the ethnological work that is being done on our continent. I have laid out the lines of all the ethnological work that has been done by this Museum. This embraces particularly work all along the Pacific coast of North America and work among the Indians of the Plains. It also embraces the archaeological work done on the Pacific coast of our continent.*

*I have, furthermore, always retained a certain connection with the Bureau of Ethnology, through which I have been able to expand our work over lines which do not properly fall in the scope of work in the Museum. I refer particularly to work in linguistics. One of the most important steps that I have taken in this direction is to suggest to the Bureau the publication of a handbook of American languages, which I am to edit.[13] I have been working up this point for several years, and I believe that the plan will now be carried out. Through this undertaking I hope to be put in a position to push the necessary linguistic and ethnological work very considerably. It is self-evident that the Government alone cannot spend enough money on field-work to collect all these data; but, being in charge of this work, I anticipate that I can much more forcibly suggest to other institutions the expenditure of means in this direction.*

*I think you will understand the drift of this rather lengthy statement of my activity and of my plans. I am committed here in many directions, which centre in my activity in the Museum and in Columbia; and if I were to sever my connection with these institutions, it would practically mean beginning all over again.*

*At the same time I believe that it will be of advantage to American anthropology if I can retain a certain amount of control in the direction of the various activities which I outlined before for a few years.*

*I do not believe at all in the policy of a single man retaining longer than is absolutely necessary the direction of such a multitude of plans as I have in my charge at the present time, and it is my strong endeavor to find as soon as possible men upon whose shoulders the carrying out of certain parts of these plans may be transferred. Thus I hope that three years hence, after the return of our exploring party from China, the whole division of our work will be taken entirely off my hands. I am looking forward to a time when I do not need to trouble myself about the work in comparative ethnology, and when all the various important divisions will be carried on independently; but, owing to the lack of men, that time has not yet come.*

*If you were to ask me at this moment whom to put in charge of the whole field of Californian ethnology, I should be unable to name any man in this country whom I should consider capable of doing so, while I am very confident that five years hence either Mr. Dixon or Mr. Kroeber will have gained sufficient experience to do so. I do not think that I need to enlarge on this point, because you know personally all the American anthropologists and the scope of their work.*

*As I stated in my former letter, it is a matter of the greatest importance that the work in California should be taken up with the greatest energy. If the question were asked, how greater funds could be extended advantageously, I would suggest that the following method would give the most satisfactory results: Establish for a period of five years four fellowships in ethnology and two fellowships in archaeology. Let these fellowships be made for the first few years in Columbia for ethnology and in Harvard for archaeology. As soon as one of these fellows is trained far enough to do independent work, let the fellowship be transferred to the University of California, and give the fellow an opportunity to do field-work in that State. I stated in my last letter how much it would cost to carry on field-work and to pay for publication. For the next five years, and not longer, give me the opportunity to direct the operations, in order to establish them on a definite systematic basis, and I am certain that at the close of this time a strong department in the University of California could be formed entirely independently of any further co-operation on our part.*

*I should like to add, that I consider the large amount of administrative work which I am doing at the present time a necessity, under the present conditions of American anthropology, but that I decidedly look forward with pleasure to a time, which I hope may come about ten years hence, when I can again devote myself entirely to scientific pursuits.*

*I hardly need to say how much I appreciate your very kindly expressions of confidence in my work, and how sincerely I thank you for your kindly letter.*

*Yours very truly,*

(*Signed*)                                 *Franz Boas.*

Boas, then, not only said No, but he counseled postponing the department until more trained men were available. But the enthusiasts in California were in no mood to delay. Still less were they willing to let Mrs. Hearst's money drain off to Columbia and Harvard while they waited five years for a Boas-trained staff. Benjamin Ide Wheeler, who had become president of the University of California two years before, in 1899, was one of those keen on the project. On September 10, four months after Boas' letter, President Wheeler recommended that the University's board of regents establish a department of anthropology.[50] Because it was to be the gift of Mrs. Hearst, acquiescence was prompt. President Wheeler recommended an advisory committee of himself, Mrs. Hearst, Mrs. Nuttall, Miss Fletcher, Dr. Putnam, Boas, and J. C. Merriam, a University of California assistant professor of paleontology and historical geology, who later was to become a power as president of the Carnegie Institution of Washington.[50]

Kroeber, the young man mentioned by both Mrs. Nuttall and Boas, was made the instructor of the new department. No one was named to the post Mrs. Nuttall had asked Boas to consider. That is, not for the first two years. But in 1903 it went to the man who had brought the two friends together, the sixty-four-year-old Dr. Putnam.[42] In order to accept, Dr. Putnam gave up his work at the American Museum of Natural History; but since holding two positions at a time was customary for him, he kept his older job as curator of the Peabody Museum in Cambridge.

Meanwhile, a major event had occurred in Mrs. Nuttall's life. In 1902 she had made what was to have been a brief visit to Mexico, and there, in the suburb of Coyoacán, she had fallen in love with a house.[61] Called Casa Alvarado, it was an old colonial palace reputed to have been the home of Pedro Alvarado, the chief lieutenant of Cortés. The red house, built in a hollow square with its inner courtyard open to the sky, caught Mrs. Nuttall's imagination so strongly that then and there she decided to abandon her plans of living in San Francisco and to settle in Mexico instead. She bought the house and, late in November, moved in.[61]

Altogether, 1902 was a meridian for Mrs. Nuttall, for the year also brought publication of *Codex Nuttall*,[70,81] which consisted of her commentary and her reproduction of the pictorial manu-script she had traced in England. Her reputation, therefore, continued to expand, and the acquisition of Casa Alvarado enabled her to develop a new aspect of her career, one which increased in importance with the years — that of hostess. Living in Mexico, too, enabled her to meet all the Mexican scholars. She won quick acceptance as a scientist with them, as she had earlier with her American colleagues. The two leading Mexican scientific organizations were the National Academy of Sciences (then the Sociedad Científico "Antonio Alzate") and the Socie-dad Mexicana de Geografía y Estadística. Mrs. Nuttall was elected to both, and in 1907 she was made an honorary professor of the National Museum.[61]

She did not, however, give up her American ties. At the same time as she took up residence in Casa Alvarado, she became associated with the University of California as a research assist-ant of the new department of anthropology she had helped bring into being. In 1903 it published Part I of *The Book of the Life of the Ancient Mexicans*,[71] which was the name she gave her facsimile of the Codex Magliabecchiano. This first part consisted of her introduction, as well as of the codex itself. Part II, which was to be her commentary, was also to contain a translation of the text accompanying the pictures. She kept tell-ing the university that her manuscript was almost ready. An-other work she agreed to do for the department was to prepare a commentary for the de la Cruz map, which it planned to publish, based on her reproduction of it made in time for the Huelva meeting of the Americanists.

Boas, being in the thick of American activities, forged ahead even more rapidly than Mrs. Nuttall. And in 1905 he showed he meant what he said about believing that one man should not retain too many charges, for he relinquished his work at the American Museum of Natural History.[35] He, too, acquired a house. But his was not a Spanish colonial palace. Instead, it was "like something out of a German Christmas card," a house of his own design which he built in a New Jersey suburb almost directly across the Hudson from Columbia.[41] The suburb was Grantwood, now part of Cliffside Park, and it could be reached by taking the 125th Street ferry to Edgewater, then boarding a trolley which wound up the Palisades to near the house at 230 Franklin Avenue.[41]

The changes in the friends' lives, however, were not reflected at the time of their happening in the correspondence. And for good reason. There are no letters between 1901 and 1908. But we know from other sources that they had contacts during this period.

1904, for instance, was the year of another world's fair, the Louisiana Purchase Exposition in St. Louis. In September an International Congress of Arts and Sciences was held in connection with the Exposition and Mrs. Nuttall and Boas were present. Mrs. Nuttall heard Boas urge an open mind and an inconclusive attitude on whether there had been contacts between the Old and New Worlds before Columbus, and she used his words in the opening paragraphs of her article, "Some Unsolved Problems in Mexican Archaeology," which appeared in the January–March, 1906 issue of the *American Anthropologist*.[72] The same year she published "The Astronomical Methods of the Ancient Mexicans."[73] It was her contribution to the *Boas Anniversary Volume*,[12] compiled by Boas admirers to celebrate the twenty-fifth anniversary of his receiving the doctorate from Kiel University in Germany. She went out of her way to pay tribute to her friend by closing with the words: "The actual purpose of the present communication will, however, be fulfilled only when, by its presence in this festive volume, it shall yield testimony of my high esteem for my honored colleague Dr. Franz Boas, and of my sincere appreciation of the great and permanent value of his scientific contributions."

Publication of the volume to honor the forty-eight-year-old

Boas was really a remarkable tribute for so young a man. And as 1909 approached it was clear that there was an older man whose achievements cried out for similar recognition on the part of his colleagues. In 1909 Dr. Putnam would reach his seventieth birthday. The University of California's retirement rules were forcing him out of the anthropology department at Berkeley,[42] and even the Peabody Museum was shifting his role of curator to that of honorary curator. A festive volume would soften the blows and provide the memorial that was his due.[84] And who was more suited for serving as chairman of its editorial board than the younger man whom Putnam had taken to Chicago and who had later worked under Putnam at the American Museum of Natural History? Boas himself must have been glad of the opportunity to honor a mentor. And it is in connection with this volume, which Boas was assembling in 1908, that the Boas-Nuttall correspondence reopens.

First, though, it must be pointed out that 1908 was the year the International Congress of Americanists met in Vienna, between September 9 to 14.[37] Both friends were planning to attend. Boas actually got there, and with him were Mrs. Boas and their twenty-year-old daughter Helene (who later became Mrs. Cecil Yampolsky). But Mrs. Nuttall did not attend. She had gone to Europe early in the year, but on June 4, her older brother, Robert Nuttall, a broker, had died in San Francisco.[61] She went into mourning, cancelling her plans for going to Vienna, and her letters of this year and the next are heavily edged in black.

Actually, her letter, addressed from Godesberg, Germany, was written the day after the Boas letter with which it crossed in the mail. The Boas letter is printed first, however, because it recapitulates the contents of an earlier lost Boas letter to which Mrs. Nuttall was replying. Boas, by this time, had returned to the United States. Not realizing that Mrs. Nuttall was not in Mexico, he had sent his first letter to her at Casa Alvarado. His second letter was addressed in care of Konrad Theodor Preuss, whose news that Mrs. Nuttall was in Germany made Boas realize his error. Preuss, then thirty-nine, was on the staff of Berlin's Ethnographical Museum[43] where Boas had been an assistant under Seler for three years before coming to the United States.

*Nov. 20, 1908*

*My dear Mrs. Nuttall. —*

*I learned from Dr. Preuss yesterday that you are in Europe; and in order to make sure that you know about our plans, I am sending you a copy of a letter which I addressed to you some time ago. I do hope that you will be willing to contribute a paper to the volume which we are preparing for Professor Putnam. The printing of course will continue for some time, and if I can get your contribution by the middle of January, there will be time enough, provided there are no difficult illustrations.*

*Yours very sincerely,*

Being a carbon copy, the letter bore no signature, and neither this letter, nor the next six, had Boas' name typed in.

Godesberg was the town Mrs. Nuttall's youngest sister, Roberta, had moved to eight years earlier when she had married Baron Franz Von Rigal Grunland. Undoubtedly Mrs. Nuttall was there on a family visit. Her reply to Boas was dated November 19, 1908, on the eve of her departure from Europe. There is no reference in the letter either to her sister or to the death of her brother, and therefore no explanation for the mourning stationery.

*Dear Dr. Boas,*

*I have only just received from Coyoacán your letter dated Oct. 11th, telling me of the preparation of a Festschrift for dear Prof. Putnam's 70th anniversary of birth. —*

*Of course it will give me utmost pleasure to contribute to it and I shall do my best and in as short a time as possible.*

*Unfortunately the present moment is most inopportune.*

*At all events I hope to have the pleasure of seeing you in New York. I will then be able to tell you what I can do about my con-*

*tribution, which I am most anxious to make as worthy as possible of the Festschrift. Today's mail also brought me (how tardily!) the postal card so kindly sent me from Vienna by the assembled Americanists. It has touched me deeply and I was much pleased to see, amongst other familiar signatures, yours, your wife's and daughter's.*

*With many cordial greetings to each of you and a hearty "auf baldiges Wiedersehen."*

*Very sincerely*
*Zelia Nuttall*

After this, there must have been another note from Mrs. Nuttall explaining that she was sailing on the Kaiserin Augusta Victoria, for Boas, not having the time to reach her in Germany before her departure, addressed his reply to the New York office of the Hamburg-American Line at 37 Broadway. His note was dated November 30, 1908.

*My dear Mrs. Nuttall, —*

*I am very glad that we shall have the pleasure of seeing you here. I trust it will be possible for you to come out and spend an evening with us, when we can talk over matters quietly. Mrs. Boas will be very glad to see you. Will you kindly call up Mrs. Boas by telephone, 60 Cliffside. My movements are so uncertain that this will be the safer way than if you call me up at the University. I expect to be at the University, however, on Monday from nine to eleven.*

*Yours very sincerely,*

Mrs. Nuttall took the ferry and spent that evening with the Boases. Boas' daughter, Helene Yampolsky, provided the evidence in a letter written on June 17, 1963.[105] But by this time Mrs. Yampolsky was seventy-five years old and within six months of her death, and her memories of fifty-five years earlier were understandably dim. "I have no vary vivid recollection of Mrs. Nuttall," she wrote. "I am sure that I met her and that she came to our home in Grantwood, N.J. I think my parents visited her in Mexico. I know her name was mentioned quite frequently. But I am afraid that is about all."[105]

Franziska Boas, the youngest child was only six at the time

of Mrs. Nuttall's visit, and at such an age she was afforded little opportunity to mingle with the guests. Thus her direct memories of Mrs. Nuttall are even vaguer than those of her older sister.[16] Nevertheless, owing to Miss Boas' memory of an old picture book, we know that Mrs. Nuttall played a role in the lives of the Boas children — a role that Miss Boas did not recognize until years later.

It came about through the *Codex Nuttall*. The Peabody Museum, in reproducing the pictorial manuscript, tried to make the publication resemble the deer-hide original as closely as possible. The sheets were fastened side to side and folded like the panels of a screen. As a consequence, the Codex has to be perused in the manner of the catalogue of Don Giovanni's conquests that Leporello whips out in Mozart's opera. Boas had one of the copies at Grantwood. As a little girl, Miss Boas did not associate the fascinating picture book with any friend of her father's, but, as an adult, she made the connection sometime after the work came into her possession. On May 12, 1964,[16] she wrote with continuing affection of the facsimile "which we as children were allowed to stretch out on the floor and examine."

The older Boas daughter correctly remembered about the Boases visiting Mrs. Nuttall in Mexico — as subsequent letters show. And in this connection it can be noted that Mrs. Nuttall also had a daughter, Nadine, now Mrs. Arthur Laughton. The impression made by the visitor on this daughter was more vivid; though it also shows how young people live in different worlds, not really knowing much about their parents' lives. Almost a half century later, Mrs. Laughton, in talking to her granddaughter, described Dr. Boas (who was about 5 feet, 7")[16] as "an odd, short little man, whose hair always stood on end."[17]

To finish the story of the Putnam tribute; despite the difficulties, Mrs. Nuttall did complete her paper. Titled "A Curious

Survival in Mexico of the Use of the Purpura Shellfish for Dye-ing,"[74] it is one of her most attractive essays. Nearly always she liked to start with something concrete, bringing to bear on it her imagination, her curiosity, and her learning. In this case it was a purple skirt she had seen in Tehuantepec before she left for Europe for the Congress she never attended. And although her paper required no "difficult illustrations" in the conventional sense, it did call for unusual supporting evidence — the tipping in of samples of material, dyed purple like the skirt.

From the way she referred to him later, we can be fairly cer-tain that during that evening at Grantwood Mrs. Nuttall met the Boases' seventeen-year-old son Ernst, then a student at Co-lumbia, who was to grow up to be a well-known physician.[59] The letters also provide further clues about that evening. In fact, when we combine our knowledge of the interests of the two correspondents with the comments they later exchanged we can conjecture what they talked about. The news of mutual friends undoubtedly provided a topic. If she did not know it already, Boas probably told her that the Duke de Loubat, who had earlier endowed Seler's chair in American anthropology in Berlin, had subsequently endowed a similar professorship at Columbia; that the endowment had come through in 1903 and that Marshall H. Saville was the first incumbent.[52] Perhaps, too, Boas told her that in 1906 Adolph Bandelier had come over from the American Museum of Natural History, where he had been doing research, to teach Columbia students what early Spanish sources could reveal about American ethnography.[52] Perhaps they discussed how Edgar F. Hewett's job as director of Ameri-can research for the Archaeological Institute of America had led him to become the head of the Institute's newest offshoot, the American School of Archaeology (later to be known as the School of American Research).[103] Because the scheme had been brewing in Boas' mind for several years, it is likely that he mentioned some of the ideas he had for the establishment of a new school of archaeology of his own.

Since his plans involved Mexico, he must have queried Mrs. Nuttall on conditions in that country. Didn't Mexico, for instance, have something the United States did not have, a Federal Department of Education whose head had cabinet rank? Perhaps, if he did not possess all the details, Mrs. Nuttall had filled him in on how the department, known as the Secretaría de Instrucción Pública, had been created in 1901 when education was removed from the jurisdiction of the Department of Justice, and how the historian, Justo Sierra, was its secretary or minister.[32] From her later views we can guess that Mrs. Nuttall may have denigrated Sierra a bit, saying that the man she really liked in the ministry was the subsecretary, the forty-year-old Ezequiel A. Chávez.

Boas must have been especially interested in the qualifications of Mexico's anthropologists, what training, if any, the up-and-coming students received, and how much cooperation in training and research there was between the teaching faculties and the National Museum. We can be fairly sure, too, that this led Mrs. Nuttall to open up about a man she could not abide — Leopold Batres.

Batres was an ex-militiaman who had particular pull with Porfirio Díaz, Mexico's dictator-president.[8] Some say he was even related to Díaz. Batres had long been a power in Mexican archaeology, and in 1885,[10] with the creation of the Inspección de Monumentos Arqueológicos, he had received the title Inspector y Conservador de Monumentos Arqueológicos. He had worked in the Oaxaca region at the turn of the century and three things he had done there[53] had already earned him Mrs. Nuttall's scorn and enmity. He had blocked her friend Alfred P. Maudslay from excavating in Monte Albán. He had taken credit for work at Mitla that actually had been accomplished by Mr. Saville with the financing of the Duke de Loubat. And at Mitla, Batres had ordered his own name carved in letters of gold on a lintel of the finest palace, the Hall of Columns.

In recent years his chief responsibility had been the massive pyramids at Teotihuacán. In addition to his influence with Díaz — or perhaps because of it — he had influence with Sierra, who, as Mexico's minister of public instruction, was in charge of both Batres' domain (archaeological monuments) and the forty-three-year-old national museum. The director of the museum at that time was Genaro García, and, as we shall see presently, Batres was about to acquire power in García's domain too.

The Museo Nacional, which had been inaugurated by the Emperor Maximilian in December, 1865,[60] occupied the building on Calle Moneda that had been the national mint. Besides housing the archaeological objects with which it was associated for so long, it was also an historical museum and a museum of natural history. However, the decision had been reached to remove both the historical objects and the natural history exhibits and to set them up elsewhere. Along with the decision to devote the Calle Moneda museum wholly to archaeology, came a decision to have the archaeological objects that had been accumulating classified. Seler, Boas' former boss and Mrs. Nuttall's opponent in the feather piece controversy, had been borrowed from Berlin's ethnographical museum to do the classifying.

Probably as Mrs. Nuttall and Boas were saying "auf Wiedersehen" they discussed when they would meet again. If nothing intervened, it would be in the second week of September, 1910. Since 1900, the International Congress of Americanists had met alternately in the Old and the New World. For the next Congress it was the New World's turn to host, and Mexico had already been chosen as the site for the second part of the seventeenth session.[38] Boas was planning to attend.

Owing to this and to other reasons there was no seven-year gap between the letters this time. In fact, the correspondence reopens nine months later. When it does, it points up something the correspondence has already shown. Namely, that although Boas did save a great deal, it was not literally true that he saved *everything*. Clearly some communications from Boas preceded Mrs. Nuttall's letter of September 27, 1908, but they have been lost. Thus it is necessary to sketch in a little more of the Mexican background.

By 1909 Boas had been at Columbia for thirteen years, the last ten of them as professor of anthropology. During all that time he had been concentrating on the work which, in 1901, he had told Mrs. Nuttall was so important: the production of "trained observers." Because of his efforts, more trained men than ever before were in the field. But there were still not enough. Mexico had not been a particular interest of Boas', but he was naturally alert enough to be aware of its archeological and ethnographical richness. Since such an area needed scientific study, it needed scientific observers. This had led Boas to the generous and far-sighted idea of training young Mexicans so they could not only observe their own country but transmit the principles of scientific observation to other Mexicans as well.

His friend, Zelia Nuttall, having lived in Mexico for seven years, clearly would know the most promising of the young Mexicans interested in archaeology. Why not turn to her for a nominee, since available funds dictated that the program would have to begin with a single individual. Besides, she was a woman of influence who could pull strings. Reading between the lines of the extant letters, we can see that Boas acted on these thoughts.

Mrs. Nuttall also wanted training made available to young Mexicans. Indeed, she may have discussed it with Boas at Grantwood. She fell in with the scheme with a will, and the young man of her choice was Manuel Gamio. Obviously she had already submitted his name in a letter that has been lost, for by the time of the next letter preserved in the file, arrangements for Gamio to go to Columbia as a scholarship student in anthropology had been almost completed.

Gamio, who was to become one of Mexico's most famous archaeologists and the first to use modern scientific methods, was a young man of twenty-six.[83] He was tall, dark, and handsome. After a short period of study at the school of mines, he had abandoned engineering to work on his father's ranch. In 1906, in turn, he had abandoned ranching to take archaeological courses at the Museo Nacional under Nicolás León and Jesús Galindo y Villa. He had then gone to Chalchihuites in Zacatecas to do his first excavating. It was his report on the Chalchihuites work[29] that won Mrs. Nuttall's respect and made her feel he was promising.

After the digging in Zacatecas, Gamio returned to work at the museum and he was placed in charge of the historical items that were slated to be removed to a new museum (eventually opened in Chapultepec Castle). As her first letter about Gamio shows, Mrs. Nuttall had even higher things in mind for him than training under Boas at Columbia. And the letter reveals that she was enjoying working as a power behind the scenes, as she had in 1901 when she tried to draw Boas away from Columbia and out to California.

> *Sept. 27th, 1909*
>
> *Dear Prof. Boas,*
>
> *Your welcome letter of the 22nd has just arrived, confirming your telegram of the same date.*
>
> *You will have since received a telegram and letter from Mr. Gamio who is rushing his work so as to leave as soon as possible. On receipt of your last telegram offering the fellowship and $450 to Mr. Gamio, I went to see the Sub-Secretary of Public Instruction, Mr. Ezequiel Chavez who had, as you remember, approved of my choice and promised to help in the matter.*
>
> *He kindly referred the matter to Mr. Justo Sierra, the Minister and the result is that the Government is going to behave very hand-*

*somely towards Mr. Gamio. He is given an indefinite leave of absence with the same salary that he received here as 'assistant in history' at the National Museum and a scholarship he receives from same institution. His trip to New York will also be paid for him.*

*This co-operation can but give you satisfaction, as it proves the good will of the Government towards your plan of giving young Mexican men of promise the advantages of higher training. —*

*Mr. Gamio has to hand over the department in his charge at the Museum, including some thousand historical objects. This & other formalities keep him from leaving as soon as he would wish. But I expect to get him off on the next Ward liner so that he will reach New York about the 15th.*

*Can your son meet him on the steamer? His English is not very fluent — but I am sure that he will soon acquire what he lacks. What I hope most is that you should give him a thorough knowledge of Museum work so that some day soon he can be made the Director of the Archaeological Section of the National Museum here and Inspector of Monuments in the place of Batres. This is, of course, strictly entre-nous — but I know that the places will be open to him some day & it will be in the interest of science to have him here fully equipped. He should become acquainted with the modern methods of field work also, later on. May I suggest that you hand him over to Hewett then? Of course you & he will decide what his studies are to be — but I want only to tell you what is needed most here — a thoroughly trained Museum director & Archaeologist, acquainted with modern methods. —*

*I do hope that he will become both — but perhaps that is asking too much? I will, of course, notify you, in due time, as to steamer & date of Mr. Gamio's sailing. — Things at the Museum here are in a lamentable condition.*

*Can you imagine that the present director has handled the whole archaeological Department to* Batres? *He is in charge at present — has published his opinion that Seler's classification of objects there was "all wrong" & is at present destroying all Seler's work and re-arranging everything. The result is confusion and chaos imminent.*

*We have formed the local Committee for the preparations for the Americanist Congress next September & the invitations will soon be sent out. I am on the sub-Committee of invitations also & shall do*

*all I can to help to make the Congress a success. — If you can make*
*any suggestion on the subject I shall be very glad to present it to the*
*Committee & act on it. When you come next year I hope that you*
*and any member of your family whom you may bring will be my*
*guests for at least a part of your stay here. If you can suggest the*
*names of any new workers who should be invited & who have not*
*attended previous Congresses, do send them to me.*

*I hope and believe that Mr. Gamio will prove himself worthy of*
*your kindness to him, in every way — at all events Mr. Chavez & I*
*agree that he is the best we can offer you!*

*With many cordial regards to you & yours & heartfelt fond wishes*
*to you and congratulations that we are now making the first formal*
*step towards the realization of our hopes & plans for the advance-*
*ment of science here,*

*Yours very sincerely*
*Zelia Nuttall*

In contrast to Mrs. Nuttall's warmth and enthusiasm, Boas'
reply is almost chilling in its businesslike formality.

*Oct. 7, 1909*

*Mrs. Zelia Nuttall,*
    *Casa Alvarado,*
        *Coyoacan, City of Mexico, D.F., Mex.*

*My dear Mrs. Nuttall, —*

*I received your letter and also the communications from Mr.*
*Gamio. I wish to thank you most cordially for all that you have done*
*in this matter. I appreciate your assistance very much indeed, without*
*which, I am sure, the desired result could not have been attained.*
*I feel fairly sure that we can give to Mr. Gamio some idea of method*
*which should be serviceable in his later work. I trust that the meeting*
*of the Congress in Mexico next year will be a great success.*

*Yours very sincerely,*

Boas could be more communicative, however, when he had
something he wanted to bring about, and he was beginning
to be anxious over a lag in the timetable for the establishment
of the new school he had in mind. In telling of the school it
is instructive to glance backward at Boas' first noble letter to

Mrs. Nuttall. Writing in 1901, he said "I decidedly look forward with pleasure to a time, which I hope may come about ten years hence, when I can again devote myself entirely to scientific pursuits." Eight of those years had passed. Boas, far from letting up on administrative duties, was plunging into a brand new project which was certain to increase them. But this was characteristic. He never did win entire freedom for the pursuit of science,[106] not even in the six years that remained to him when, in 1936,[56] at the age of seventy-eight, he finally gave up teaching at Columbia.

The new project was an outgrowth of his old passion: the fostering of anthropology by creating more, and ever more trained observers. Having done a great deal for the training of young Americans, he was now planning to expand beyond the borders of the United States. He was planning, too, to enroll students from other countries. But he was not thinking of undergraduates. He was thinking of "productive investigators" — advanced fellowship student who would soon be able to teach undergraduates themselves. The archaeology and ethnology of the Americas, he knew, were vital themes for exploration — and for simultaneous training in the widest sense — and his scheme was nothing more nor less than the establishment of an International School of American Archaeology and Ethnology.

Though the forthcoming revolution was to make it a poor choice, Mexico, with its marvelous wealth of both archaeology and ethnology, was to be the locale of the new school. And Boas and the others who had come to share his enthusiasm for the new project could scarcely be blamed for not forseeing the enormous upheaval that was around the Mexican corner. Mexico had never seemed so stable and so secure as she did at the time of their planning.

Apparently Boas saw little chance of getting the United States government to participate in the proposed school, but he had offset this by obtaining assurances of participation from four private American institutions:[15] his own Columbian University Harvard, the University of Pennsylvania, and the Hispanic Society of America. Using his German background and his German contacts, he had also secured the participation of the government of Prussia. The Mexican government, when it learned of the scheme, not only agreed to furnish the school with house room in its national museum, but to make a sizable grant providing the other participants paid their share. Paying their share meant that the non-Mexican sponsors must supply fellowships for the advanced students they sent and pay the salaries of professors they contributed to the school faculty.[24]

Nicholas Murray Butler, who, seven years earlier, in 1902, had become president of Columbia, was one of the enthusiasts for the school. Indeed, he has even been credited with its conception.[24] With such a powerful ally to aid in setting wheels in motion, Boas had been too canny to do all the negotiating under his own name. President Butler had easily seen Boas' logic when the anthropologist had pointed out that, for external reasons at least, establishment of the multinational school would have to be preceded by the creation of an international organizing committee. He had agreed, too, about the wisdom of the proposed timing. It was planned that the organizing committee should vote the school into existence during the period of the International Congress of Americanists.

Obviously, Mexico, the host country, had to be represented on the organizing committee; therefore someone of high responsibility in Mexico should be approached to name the Mexican member of the committee. Who was high enough in Mexican government circles to do the naming? Apparently, President Butler, who had already been in correspondence with Sierra, the secretary of public instruction, agreed that Sierra was the man. Acting on this belief, he wrote Sierra, requesting him to furnish the nomination.

Sierra had not replied. Not a peep, in fact, had been heard on the matter from anyone in the government.

This was puzzling because Mexico was anything but indifferent about obtaining the aid of foreign scholars to improve the educational facilities of the capital. Its university, the oldest on the North American continent, had been moribund for more than fifty years. The Mexican government was about to reopen it formally as a national institution.[88] And the government, in addition to agreeing to support this international school of archaeology by giving it facilities at the Museo Nacional and classroom space at the reopened university, had engaged a distinguished list of professors from abroad to offer three-month courses at the school of high studies which had been created as part of the nationalization and rejuvenation of the university.[88]

The first of these courses, "The Individual and Society,"[89] was already being conducted by James Mark Baldwin,[102] the American psychologist who a few years earlier had edited the *Dictionary of Philosophy and Psychology* that was to have so long a life. Boas knew Baldwin and asked him to investigate. But aware of the position of influence Mrs. Nuttall had won in Mexico, and knowing her capacity to pull wires, Boas turned even more hopefully to her with the problem. Gamio was due to arrive in two days and there had been no definite word about him, but the incoming student was far from uppermost in Boas' mind when he applied to his old friend for help.

My dear Mrs. Nuttall, [he wrote on October 13, 1909]

Excuse me if I trouble you again with our affairs; but your interest in American archaeology is such, that I know I can always rely upon your help when matters pertaining to the advancement of science are concerned.

You know that our negotiations with the Mexican Government in regard to the establishment of a School of American Archaeology in the City of Mexico have advanced so far that the Government has agreed to appropriate the sum of six thousand dollars annually

*toward the maintenance of a school, provided that the foreign govern-*
*ments and universities will continue the salaries of such professors*
*as may be delegated to the school; and that, furthermore, a number*
*of fellowships are guaranteed. All this has now been arranged for.*
*The Prussian Government has even gone so far as to vote an addi-*
*tional amount of salary for their representative when he goes to*
*Mexico. The next step in our procedure is now the appointment of*
*members of an organizing Committee. President Butler has written*
*to Mexico, I believe to Mr. Sierra, asking for the appointment of a*
*member of this Committee; but we have not heard anything from*
*Mexico. You know so well the condition of affairs in Mexico, that*
*you are certainly able to suggest the right man, and you may perhaps*
*be able to induce the Minister to act in this matter. I think I told*
*you that it is our present idea to bring the Committee together at*
*the time of the meeting of the Americanists' Congress; so that there*
*would be no special hurry if it were not for the fact that our affairs*
*ought to have been quite fully discussed before we meet next summer.*
*I am writing also to Prof. J. Mark Baldwin,[102] who, as you probably*
*know, is to reorganize secondary teaching in Mexico. I do not know*
*whether this matter would come under his department, but I thought*
*it might be well to enlist his interest. I should be very much indebted*
*to you if you could help us to make headway with this matter.*

*I am looking forward with much interest to seeing Mr. Gamio*
*here, and I shall do my best to make his stay here profitable.*

*Yours very sincerely,*

If Gamio had been a minor consideration in Boas' mind, he
had certainly not held so lowly a place in Mrs. Nuttall's. What
a time she had had! She had even been obliged to throw some
weight in the direction of the great dictator, Don Porfirio. But
she had triumphed and what she had obtained was published
in Spanish in a Mexico City newspaper. Translated, it read:

### COMMISSIONED BY THE MUSEUM
### OF ARCHAEOLOGY

The Secretary of Public Instruction and Fine Arts, by agreement of the President of the Republic, has commissioned Mr.
Manuel Gamio, assistant to the Professor of History of the National Museum of Archaeology, History and Ethnology, to go

to study archaeology in Columbia University, New York. Mr. Gamio will leave within a few days from this capital for the United States.

Because Mrs. Nuttall was proud of what she had achieved, she enclosed a clipping of the story in her letter to Boas. As will be seen, she had also looked into what was causing the hitch in the nomination.

*Coyoacan,*
*Nov. 3rd, 1909*

*Dear Prof. Boas,*

*I am happy to be able to inform you that Mr. Gamio left Mexico City this evening for Vera-Cruz & is to sail on the Ward line steamer "Mexico" tomorrow, for New York.*

*If I have not written for some time it is because I have almost despaired of being able to get him off. Red tape & financial difficulties seemed too much to cope with. The enclosed will show you that President Diaz had to be resorted to & that now Gamio is commissioned by the Ministry of Public Instruction — & will thus get the necessary salary. —*

*He told me, before leaving that he has two young Mexican friends in New York who will meet him on his arrival. He will go to their dwelling to change clothes etc. & will then immediately communicate with you at the University. So you need not trouble to go or send to meet him.*

*I think that you will find him a nice young fellow socially as well as an earnest student. Let us hope that this, our joint experiment will give us the satisfaction we anticipate.*

*Now about the other matter you wrote to me about.*

*I spoke to Mr. Chavez, the sub-secretary about it the other day. He had not heard of it. I asked whether President Butler's letter to Minister Sierra had been received. Two secretarys brought all their files down & made a thorough search for the letter before me & Mr. Chavez. It was not there. Mr. Chavez said that possibly it had gone to the Minister of Foreign Affairs & had got "stuck" somewhere. —*

*I suggest that you send me fresh letters on the subject to transmit personally to Minister Sierra & to Minister Mariscal.*

*You ask me whether I can designate a suitable person & I am at a*

*loss to do so. Will you write & tell me what he is expected to do &*
*exactly what duties the position entails — that would help me &*
*those concerned.*

*I hope that Sierra will not propose Batres! As matters stand he*
*might do so.*

*You can count on me for doing all I can to further the cause of*
*our beloved science.*

*With many cordial regards to you & yours, & congratulations*
*that young Gamio is off at last!*

> *Yours much relieved*
> *Zelia Nuttall.*

Boas, it seems, saw nothing humorous in this glimpse of how
business in conducted in a Latin American government office.
Nor, apparently, did he take Mrs. Nuttall up on letting her
deliver a second letter personally, even though she was on
friendly terms with Ignacio Mariscal, the minister of foreign
Affairs,[32] as well as with Sierra. Instead, he let two months go
by and then dictated the following rather peremptory letter
on January 17, 1910:

*My dear Mrs. Nuttall. —*

*I wrote to you quite a while ago in regard to the appointment of*
*a Mexican member of the Committee on the proposed Archaeological*
*School. Since I wrote to you we have heard from Germany that the*
*German Government is going not only to accept the plan, but will*
*also establish a fellowship in Mexico. It is imperative now that the*
*Mexican Government should appoint a member of this Committee.*
*I wish you would kindly let me know about the status of the matter.*

> *Yours very sincerely,*

While Boas had been procrastinating on the committee problem, Mrs. Nuttall had, through a little digging, uncovered
what proved to be her major subsurface discovery as an archaeologist. Although she did not spell out that she had put spade
to ground (perhaps because this was not authorized), she reports her discovery in her reply to Boas. Since by now she was
fifty-three, her zestful anticipation at the thought of going back

to rough it for several weeks on a windswept island is an index of how much she enjoyed making discoveries.

*Jan. 28, 1910*

*Dear Dr. Boas,*

*Your note of inquiry reached me yesterday & this morning I went to see Mr. Chavez who tells me that the Mexican Government has offered the appointment to a person of its choice, whose answer is expected in a day or so. He assured me that the appointment will be made in a few days.*

*If I am here when it is made public I will inform you at once. I expect, however, to leave next week for the little island of Sacrificios off Vera-Cruz where I am to spend some weeks making a thorough exploration of the island. A few weeks ago I visited the island & discerned thereon a wall of one of the temples described by Grijalva in 1518. The wall is covered with a mural painting of fine execution. I also found wide steps. When I reported this discovery to the Government it offered to send me on a scientific mission to the island and I have been delighted to accept the task. I shall live on the island in the rooms formerly occupied by the doctor of the old quarantine station which has not been in use for over nine years. A light house & 2 cocoanut palms are the sole land-marks on the islet which is but half a mile long. I hope to find much of interest to present to the Congress.*

*How is Mr. Gamio getting on?*

*My cordial regards to you & all members of your family.*

*Yours sincerely,*

*Zelia Nuttall.*

The man the Mexican government appointed to Boas' organizing committee was Cecilio A. Robelo,[24] a lawyer so well acquainted with archaeology that he was soon to become director of the national museum. The news must have relieved Boas. Mrs. Nuttall, too, must have been pleased, for Robelo was not on the side of Batres. Later, they both had even greater luck, for Robelo, because of illness, had to give up the appointment and it went to Chávez.[24] Chávez, who was to survive the revolution and become one of Mexico's most respected educators, was a more powerful figure than Robelo because of his position as subsecretary in the Díaz administration. Better still, his interest in the school was so genuine that he remained its president through the four years of its effective existence.

Meanwhile, perhaps Boas had come to realize that his January 17 note may have been rude. In his next letter, written on the same day that Mrs. Nuttall reported the appointment had been made, he atones for curtness by spontaneously telling her about Gamio. The letter also provides a vivid instance of one of his best teaching devices.

*Jan. 28, 1910*

*My dear Mrs. Nuttall, —*

*You have taken such a kindly interest in Mr. Gamio, that I wish to write to you regarding his progress. He is personally a very nice young man, and I am as much interested in seeing the development of his anthropological interests. He has not profited as much from his stay here as he would if his command of English were better, but he is improving rapidly in this direction. The greatest trouble that he experiences is a certain vagueness in his approach to subjects, which is undoubtedly due to a general method of training. It seems, he has rather learned the contents of books and lectures than gained experience in independent judgment.*

*I am very well satisfied with the way he is taking up the new points of view that come up, and the way in which he gradually develops critical insight. I make it a point rather to give him books which from my point of view do not seem to me to be up to the mark. I let him report on them, and then criticise the author's view and have him defend it if he can. I have given him a good many books on art to read, with a veiw of clarifying his view of symbolism and development of Mexican ornament, and I believe he has profited from this.*

*I believe he also profits very much from his work with Mr. Bandelier, who gives him a very good knowledge of the sources both of the region of Northern Mexico and the Southwest and of northeastern South America. He has been working with Saville on his South American material.*

*I am convinced that if you want to get the best results from Mr.*

*Gamio's stay here, it is quite indispensable that he should come back for another year. I do not believe that we can get more this year than to give him a rather vague and hazy idea of rigid methods of research. He needs such a thorough change of his method of approach, that I am sure we cannot get it inside of less than one year. He ought to have the time to do under our direction some special piece of research work, where his methods should be broad and constantly checked. I have not spoken to him at all about the question, but I wish it were possible to get for him another year's leave of absence. Perhaps he would not care to have it, but I should like to know whether it could be possible to get the opportunity for him. I rather think I might be able to get the required money here in New York, provided the Mexican Government should see fit to give him permission. I should be very glad if you would kindly let me know at your early convenience what you think of this matter.*

*With kindest regards,*

*Yours very sincerely,*

Gamio, incidently, did go back for a second year at Columbia. And Mrs. Nuttall refers to the proposal in her reply. But this time it was she who relegated the student to a minor position in the correspondence. Something upsetting had happened. She speaks of it in her letter, but in an understating way.

What Mrs. Nuttall had discovered on the Island of Sacrificios in December — the frescoed wall and the wide steps — had led her to plan the scientific mission she had been so excited about in her last letter.[75] She had told Boas that the government had "offered to send" her on it. In reality, officials had merely agreed to let her undertake the expedition, but had provided blessings in the form of a promise of $250 toward expenses. With the pleasure and excitement revealed in her letter, Mrs. Nuttall headed for Vera Cruz. The island was only three miles from the city, but before she could start digging she had to wait for further government papers. Three weeks passed before they came. And then what a blow! They said that the government would let her have only $100, that she must confine her explorations to a certain part of the island, and, crowning indignity, her work was to be supervised by Salvador Batres, the young son of her arch foe, Don Leopoldo.

She considered such conditions so outrageous that she abandoned her plans, turned around, and came home. Actually, the worst was yet to come. But what had happened made her feel sadly discouraged, not only for herself, but for Boas' school. What she writes here concerning the Congress is touching when one remembers how buoyantly she had written about it earlier — and how much she had been looking forward to it.

*April 6th. 1910*

*Dear Prof. Boas,*

*I am glad to tell you that Mr. Chavez quite realizes the desirability of Mr. Gamio's return to Columbia for another year's course & says that he will do all he can to arrange for it.*

*If I have not written to you for a long time it is because I have had a trying experience with Mr. Batres & the Ministry of Public Instruction. I made a test-case of it, so as to ascertain* exactly *what can be expected from the aforesaid & the result has been that I have handed in my resignation as member of the Organizer's Committee of the Congress & I renounced the title of Hon. Prof. of the National Museum* as a protest *against the treatment I received in connection with my discovery & proposed exploration of the ruins on the island of Sacrificios. —*

*I cannot give you details by letter, but will merely state that instead of being helped I was hindered in every way & that the conditions offered me were* impossible *to be accepted by any self respecting archaeologist. —*

*A radical reform will have to be made before any kind of International School of Archaeology can be installed here. The trouble is that, as the authorities went back on their given word, I do not feel any kind of security in future dealings unless the situation changes. My experience is a sample of what may be expected and, mind you!, I am assured of the highest esteem & regard on the part of the Ministry & it was, after all,* in its interest *for me to do the work so as to present it to the Congress & also to help them on the organizing Committee.*

*There is* general indignation *which may lead to an ultimate reform*

*of conditions. Meanwhile I have retired into "private life" & am working at researches which require no authorization of the Ministry. It is possible that I may not be here in September. —*
*With many cordial regards to you and yours,*
*always sincerely*
*Zelia Nuttall.*

The galvanizing outrage, however, was committed a month later. On May 8, the government newspaper, *El Imparcial*,[75] printed a story, issued by the Ministry of Public Instruction, telling of the ruins its inspector, Leopoldo Batres, had discovered — guess where — on the Island of Sacrificios. During Holy Week, Batres had done an unholy thing. He had gone to the island, seen what was to be seen, and, on returning, claimed Mrs. Nuttall's discoveries as his own.

Mrs. Nuttall had been planning to report her discoveries to the Congress in September, but after this act of piracy she decided not to wait that long. In what must have been a fine fit of sustained anger she ripped off "The Island of Sacrificios," a marvelously detailed paper, which ran to thirty-nine pages when it appeared in the April-June, 1910, *American Anthropologist*.[75] Because of the article's wealth of information about the island, it is one of the finest of her essays. And besides nailing Batres for his treatment of her, she did two other things to undercut him. She put into print something that was common knowledge among insiders: that Batres smuggled antiquities from sites he was supposed to be guarding and sold them for export. And she exposed with devastating particularity the arbitrary and misleading nature of Batres' reclassification of archaeological objects.

Seler, whose classification work at the museum was destroyed by Batres, was the president of the Congress.[38] Boas was the first vice president. Batres and Chávez were the honorary vice presidents. The seventy-one-year-old Dr. Putnam, who had retired from Berkeley the year before, was present. And Mrs.

Nuttall, having unburdened herself of her blast at Batres, had rallied the spirit to attend. In addition to giving a paper and spearheading a move to locate the bones of Cortés, she provided one of the Congress's leading social functions, a reception at Casa Alvarado.[45] With her various collections, her house was beginning to take on the aspects of a museum. The delegates naturally were interested in her pre-Columbian things. She took especial pride in displaying those which she believed antedated the known cultures of the Valley of Mexico.[76]

Most of the sessions were in the Museo Nacional, along the street from the Cathedral. But one day was taken up by an excursion to the Pyramids of Teotihuacán. The Mexican government, which was at the time celebrating the centenary of Mexican independence, treated the Congress lavishly. Clarence L. Hay, then a susceptible young Harvard man, was amazed at the "splurge" Díaz accorded the delegates. "I never saw anything before or since to equal it," he remembered fifty years later.[33] But, alas, the letters mirror none of this. Boas and Mrs. Nuttall, being where they could meet and talk, did not need to write. And the correspondence contains only one document from the period.

It gives an amusing insight into Boas' saving. Also, from the historical point of view, into his wisdom. The item was not in Mrs. Nuttall's hand and it was not addressed to him. Because Casa Alvarado was a short distance out of the city, Mrs. Nuttall sometimes resorted to telegrams to reach people for social reasons. This was a telegram addressed to Mrs. Boas.

"Expect you Wednesday. Hope you can stay for luncheon early."

Since the date of the telegram, January 31, was a Tuesday, the expected engagement was on February 1, 1911. The date is an interesting one. The Congress had been over more than four months, but the Boases had remained in Mexico because Boas had been one of the foreign professors engaged to give a three-month course at the University's new school of high studies.[89] His course, which was on general anthropology,[14] was near its end, for it began in November. But Boas was not going home yet. He was the secretary of the new school, and he wanted to keep his eye on it.

The school, even though it had only two fellows in the first year and possessed no quarters of its own, had been officially opened by no less a personage than President Díaz.[90] The inaugural ceremonies[93] had taken place only eleven days before the telegram. The school plays a major role in the final period of the Boas-Nuttall correspondence, and its development will be described in a moment. Meanwhile, let us see why February 1, 1911, was an interesting date for both Mexico and for Mrs. Nuttall.

Though hardly anyone realized it, the Mexican revolution had already begun. And the reason Francisco I. Madero's 1910 presidential campaign against the eighty-year-old Díaz did not at first seem like a revolution was because it was run — at least by the dissidents — along constitutional lines.[23] Besides, Díaz, having jailed his opponent, had won easily. Díaz, in fact, had felt so secure by October that he has released Madero. Madero, who had fled across the border, was living in exile in the United States. But two weeks after Mrs. Nuttall sent her telegram, Madero took a major step. He returned to his native land to lead the forces that were ready, if necessary, to fight on his behalf.

There may have been a farewell reason why Mrs. Nuttall was entertaining. Early in March she was scheduled to leave for a visit to the United States.[61] She left when she planned. And on May 10 the revolutionists began their triumphal progress to the capital by capturing their first city, Ciudad Juárez.

Because the revolution had taken its first violent turn, what Zelia Nuttall had planned as a short stay extended into a six-year exile. The lawlessness worried her, not only because of her property, but for the sake of her daughter, Nadine Laughton, the young married woman who had been struck by the way Boas' hair stood on end. Mrs. Laughton, her husband, a mining engineer, and their two children were still in Mexico.

The fall of Don Porfirio, whom Mrs. Nuttall had consulted about Gamio, must have seemed to her like the crashing of a great oak; and his hurried exit from Mexico, via Vera Cruz, must have saddened her. But we can be sure one attendant downfall must have lifted her spirits. Deprived of the protection of his patron, Batres, too, found it expedient to leave Mexico.[10] And on June 30 the new Minister of Public Instruction officially divested the Inspector y Conservador de Monumentos Arqueólogicos of his high-sounding title. García, the museum director who had assigned Batres to reclassify the collection, was supplanted at the same time. His successor was Robelo, the lawyer who had been the government's first appointee to Boas' organizing committee.[2]

Madero, the new president, did not prove what some feared he might be—a revolutionist with no qualms about spilling blood. On the contrary, he forgave people. Being a man of culture, too, he continued the government's support of Boas' infant school.

The school, as Boas had planned, was established during the Congress of Americanists.[24] And, again as Boas planned, it was called the International School of American Archaeology and Ethnology, or, to give the Spanish name, the Escuela Internacional de Arqueología y Etnología Americanas. Seler, the president of the Congress, was elected as the first of what were to be rotating annual directors. Thus Seler, too, stayed on in Mexico. But much of his year as director was consumed in preliminary organization. Boas, who never ceased being the secretary of the *Junta Directiva*, became the second director in 1911.[27] His year was the most productive of the four active years the school was slated to have. Gamio, Mrs. Nuttall's protegé, was again under

Boas' wing, for, back in Mexico, he was one of the two fellows nominated and financed by the Mexican government.

Another student of the second year was J. Alden Mason, who had his fellowship from the University of Pennsylvania. Thirty-two years later Mason was to evaluate Boas as an archeologist.[47] He noted that archaeology had never been a leading concern for Boas, but he pointed out that one achievement gave Boas "major claim to foremost rank and lasting reputation as an archaeologist." The achievement was "his work in establishing the fundamental elements of the sequence of cultures in the Valley of Mexico."

As a fillip, Mason added, "He and Manuel Gamio determined the three major periods in their proper sequence." Gamio himself has described how this was done.[31] First, Boas, Mason, Gamio, and other assistants gathered thousands of potsherds and figurines, most of them pieces that had come to light on the surface or by casual excavators.[25,30] Study showed the workers that they represented three different cultures. Then, and not till then, did Boas set Gamio the task of finding the proper sequence of the three.[26] And he did this by obliging Gamio to use a method that until then had been unknown in Mexico: stratigraphical excavation. The types found consistently at the deepest level automatically would be classified as the oldest.

Gamio did most of his digging at Azcapotzalco, which he knew to be a promising site. Thus both Mrs. Nuttall and Boas got their wishes. Although Gamio was not handed over to Hewett, as Mrs. Nuttall had suggested, he did receive training in modern methods of field work. And by having him under his tutelage for this third year, Boas was able to set Gamio a special research project which he could keep checking, always insisting that broad methods be employed.

The joint work of mentor and student confirmed a chief fact that Mrs. Nuttall is commonly acknowledged to have been among the first to discern.[21,82,98] The property she bought in

Coyoacán was so close to the vast lava bed in the southern part of the Valley of Mexico that the bed extended into her orchard, which was in front of her house. Shortly after she moved in, she noticed some children playing in a quarry that had been made nearby as workmen cut into the lava for building material.[76] The children were playing with small clay heads. Because they were so different from the familiar Aztec clay figurines, the heads caught Mrs. Nuttall's interest. She bought them from the children and hoped that others would appear. In 1906 she found several more such heads and a seated figure that was complete. These led her to believe that an archaic culture had existed in the valley, one older than any of the cultures generally recognized. Boas may well have been among the Americanists to whom she showed her figurines in 1910. Gamio certainly must have known about them. His digging through 1911–1912 established that what she had deduced from comparatively little evidence was indeed correct.[26]

Jorge Engerrand, a French geologist who had been working for the Mexican government since 1907, was the third director of the school.[18] It was during his year that military leaders revolted against Madero. "The Ten Tragic Days" that led to the overthrow, capture, and murder of Madero caused one of the American fellows of this year, Dr. Paul Radin, to decide it would be safer to get home than to stay to finish his work. But the others remained, and Mason has written vividly about the ten days of murderous gunfire.[49] Victoriano Huerta, who succeeded Madero, was a less-cultivated man, but he, too, favored the school. And a fourth year, directed by Alfred M. Tozzer, began.[96]

As it turned out, what really killed the school was not Mexican violence, but American. Some interests in the United States were convinced that Huerta must go, and, if necessary, through intervention. They found their pretext when some American Marines were arrested briefly at Tampico and President Huerta refused to order what was considered a proper apology — a twenty-one-gun salute to the American flag.[80] United States forces were dispatched toward Vera Cruz. Understandably, anti-American feeling, already high because of earlier threats of intervention, had flared higher when the humiliating salute was demanded. The anger became dangerous when it was known that President Wilson had ordered the invasion. Dr. Tozzer and Mr. Hay, one of the American fellows that year, had an adventurous time getting away from the capital. Indeed, they were among the last of the Americans evacuated and they arrived in Vera Cruz just in time to see the invasion begin.[54] This was on April 21, 1914.

With the outbreak of World War I a little more than three months later, it is doubtful that the International School would have survived much longer anyway. At least, certainly not with the government of Prussia as one of the friendly participants. But an attempt was made to keep the school alive in name and on p. 150 of Volume 18 of the *American Anthropologist* (1916)[3] one reads, not without a smile in remembering Mrs. Nuttall's efforts, "At a meeting of the Managing Committee of the International School of Archaeology and Ethnology held in New York Jan. 24, Luis Castillo Ledon was elected President of the Managing Committee and Señor Manuel Gamio 'encargado de los trabajos.' The work of the school for the present year will be under Señor Gamio's direction."

Mrs. Nuttall was a founding member of the American Anthropological Association,[1] and this issue of its quarterly probably reached her in San Francisco, where she was visiting. She must have read of her protegé with pleasure. She and Boas had indeed made a wise investment. It must have given her satisfaction, too, to know that the man she had helped groom to succeed Batres had actually done so, for Gamio had risen to be Inspector General de Monumentos Arqueológicos.

Mrs. Nuttall and Boas met in 1912 when the International

Congress of Americanists was held in London.[39] But the absence of letters suggests that they did not correspond again for many years; not, in fact, until 1928 when the Congress assembled in New York. By this time she was seventy-one and he was seventy. His fame had far outstripped hers. He was president of the Congress and to the generation of anthropologists which was taking over he was a vital and respected figure. Mrs. Nuttall, on the other hand, had been out of the country for a long time, and her reputation as hostess at Casa Alvarado had begun to obscure the fact that she had done serious scientific work. Moreover, she had grown somewhat stout, and no doubt, with her floor-length skirts and her slightly old-fashioned clothes, she struck some of the younger delegates as a relic. To two of those delegates to whom she had been particularly kind and helpful, George Vaillant and Frans Blom, she was known as "Aunt Zelia."[11]

If Vaillant and Blom could be regarded as members of the junior generation and Boas and Mrs. Nuttall as members of the senior, anthropology had been established long enough by this time to also have a middle generation. This was well represented at the Congress too. One of its members was Alfred Kroeber, the man whom both Mrs. Nuttall and Boas had felt unready for the leadership of California's department of anthropology in 1901. Kroeber had subsequently amply vindicated Boas' prophetic judgment as to his ultimate capability, but he had been obliged to wait more than five years to take full charge in California. His opportunity did not come until Putnam's retirement in 1909. Since then he had built California's department of anthropology and its museum into outstanding institutions.[94]

Mrs. Nuttall had remained associated with California, but with ties that frayed after the retirement of Dr. Putnam. By the time of the Congress in New York, Putnam, her chief link to many United States organizations, had been dead for thirteen years, and her affiliation was not with any institution in this country, but with the Mexican Sociedad "Alzate." She was still very much of a social power, however. One of her strengths, for instance, was that she was a long-time friend of the eighty-year-old Robert Weeks de Forest and his wife, the former Emily Johnston. This cut considerable social ice because Mr. de Forest, an immensely rich philanthropist, was president of the Metropolitan Museum of Art. Another social strength for Mrs. Nuttall was that she was a friend of Mr. and Mrs. Dwight W. Morrow. This had important implications south of the border, for the year before Mr. Morrow had become the United States Ambassador to Mexico.

Most of the sessions of the Congress were held at the American Museum of Natural History, and when Mrs. Nuttall came she stayed across the street from the Museum at the Manhattan Square Hotel, 50 West Seventy-Seventh Street. "At the Gateway to Central Park," as the hotel's stationery put it. The Congress met from September 17 to 22 and, because Mrs. Nuttall must have seen Boas every day, no correspondence stems from the week of the session. We do not know, therefore, what Boas thought of Mrs. Nuttall's paper on "Sculptured Rebuses."[77] But we do not have to remain in the dark about the Congress because it is well written up in the *Proceedings.*[40]

Boas delivered the opening address on Monday, September 17. Following custom, he cited the members who had died since the Congress in Rome two years before. Death, he said, had reaped "a rich harvest." One who had been gathered was the Duke de Loubat, aged ninety-six. And what, one wonders, were Mrs. Nuttall's feelings when she heard Boas say, "Doctor Leopoldo Batres, honorary vice president of the meeting held in Mexico, died in December, 1926." Did she, perhaps, detect a note of irony in the faint praise mustered for the departed member: "He was a collector deeply interested in the remains of the Ancient Mexican civilization."

The other entry in the *Proceedings* that is relevant to our story is a paragraph in the report of the third and final meeting of the Congress' council. Though Mrs. Nuttall was not an officer, she was a member of the council. The meeting took place on September 22, the last day of the Congress. The paragraph read: "Mrs. Nuttall expressed her desire to establish at her residence, Casa Alvarado, Coyoacan, D. F., Mexico, a home for anthropology and anthropological studies."

The last phase of the correspondence opens nine days later. On October 1, Boas wrote the following note, which shows he had something urgent on his mind.

> My dear Mrs. Nuttall:
>
> *I was going to call on you this morning but they told me at the hotel that you were not in. I have been so exceedingly busy during the last week that I had no time to get away from the University.*
>
> *If I can arrange it I will call on you sometime tomorrow or the day after. Please let me know what your plans are. You can reach me by telephone in the evening, Cliffside 60.*
>
> *Thanks for the money which Mr. Nelson gave me at the Museum.*
> Yours very sincerely,
> Franz Boas
>
> FB:B

Because so little is made of it, the money matter was probably not important. Perhaps it was something in addition to Mrs. Nuttall's registration fee, for the man mentioned was Nels C. Nelson, the Museum's curator of anthropology, who was the Congress' secretary-general. The mystery is likely to remain unsolved because when Mr. Nelson was queried about it shortly before his death he said he could not even remember Mrs. Nuttall being at the Congress.

But what was in the wind that obviously was important? Why was the "exceedingly busy" Boas so eager to call on Mrs. Nuttall? It was because he wanted her to do some string pulling for him He was also after that house of hers. Perhaps her words at the council had given him the idea. At all events, Boas was as far as over from devoting himself "entirely to scientific pursuits," even though the ten more years of administrative work, which he had envisaged to Mrs. Nuttall as his limit in 1901, had now stretched to twenty-seven. And because he was still passionately concerned with training "productive investigators" he was initiating the project about which he wanted to see Mrs. Nuttall.

Boas' scheme is revealed in the one letter in the collection that is not addressed to Mrs. Nuttall, the one that got in the collection because he wanted Mrs. Nuttall to deliver it for him. Before that letter is reproduced, though, something is needed concerning the political situation in Mexico.[23]

From the United States' point of view, the situation seemed to have taken a decided turn for the better the year before. Morrow gave every appearance of being the most popular ambassador the United States had ever sent to Mexico. Charles A. Lindbergh's well-publicized flight to Mexico City on December 14, 1927, had generated even greater expressions of mutual good will and friendship between the two countries than had been expected. The foes of Gen. Alvaro Obregón had been crushed, and on July 1, 1928, General Obregón had won the election that would reinstate him as president, after the four intervening years of Gen. Plutarco Elías Calles. Obregón was an acknowledged friend of the United States and during his first term — and in large part because of his efforts — diplomatic relations between Mexico and the United States had been resumed. They had been broken off in 1920 when Venustiano Carranza, the Mexican president recognized by the United States government, had been murdered by insurgents.

Obregón, too, was known to be a man who had the power to keep peace. His own uprising against Carranza had not put an end to violent attempts to seize power, but it had reversed the fortunes of such attempts. And because all subsequent revolts had been quelled, Mexico had not had an overturn of regime in eight years. The Mexican revolution, it seems, had at last been brought under control. And there were hopeful signs for archaeological cooperation between Mexico and the United States. It is true that under Calles a setback had occurred when Gamio, the Boas-Nuttall protegé, had been fired from the high government post to which he has risen — that of subsecretary of public instruction.[55] But Obregón was likely to be more friendly, for it had been during his first term that the Carnegie Institution of Washington had been granted permission to embark on its notable work in excavating and restoring the ruins of Chichen Itzá.

All these factors justified considerable optimism on Boas' part. But Mrs. Nuttall, living in Mexico, knew that matters were not so rosy as they seemed. Dramatic proof that her view of things was more accurate than Boas' had been provided two months before the opening of the meeting of the Americanists. On July 17 General Obregón was shot and killed by an assassin.

This sudden drastic change in the picture may have shaken Boas slightly, but the letter he wanted Mrs. Nuttall to deliver shows that he was not considering seriously all that the assassination entailed. Nor was he taking into account that Mr. Morrow, a Republican appointee, might lose his Mexican assignment if the Democratic Al Smith won the election that was coming up the next month.

Actually, the letter was merely a draft. It involved Mrs. Nuttall's house and Boas knew he could not proceed further with his project until Mrs. Nuttall had given her approval. And although the letter contained no request for money, it is clear that Boas planned to plant the idea of a substantial contribution in the mind of the recipient to whom, ostensibly, he was appealing for moral support only. The target was Mrs. Nuttall's rich friend, Mr. de Forest, the president of the Metropolitan Museum. And there was an element of tactlessness in the letter that Boas could hardly have been expected to know about. Mrs. Nuttall's family money had dwindled sadly. She was about to turn in the de Forest direction herself with the offer of a mortgage on Casa Alvarado that would bring her some needed cash.[51]

The correspondence indicates that some time in the two weeks after Boas' note of October 1 Mrs. Nuttall and Boas did find a mutually convenient time for the "call." Clearly, too, they discussed the future of Casa Alvarado. But it is not plain whether Dr. Boas told her he was planning to write Mr. de Forest about the house. However, he was. And with a covering letter, now lost, Boas mailed to Mrs. Nuttall the draft of his letter to Mr. de Forest. His lost note of transmittal must have implied that he wanted her to deliver the letter to Mr. de Forest personally.

The handwritten changes in the typed draft of Boas' letter to Mr. de Forest show that Boas was picking his words with especial care. The undated draft is given below. In it the reader will recognize the reappearance of an old friend. He will gain proof, too, as to how close to Boas' heart was the project that had faltered fourteen years earlier.

*New York City*

*Dr. Robert W. De Forest*
*President Metropolitan*
  *Museum of Art*
*Fifth Avenue*
*New York City*

*Dear Sir:*

  *At the meeting of the International Congress of Americanists, just closed in this city, the problem of serious work on the archaeology of Mexico was discussed very fully and the strong desire found expression of reestablishing the International School of American Ethnology and Archaeology, which was founded in 1910. This school did good work for a few years until, owing to the World War and to the revolutions of Mexico, its work was suspended. The archaeological conditions of Mexico are such that a study of the chronological sequence of art styles is paritcularly easy on account of the clear stratigraphic succession of remains. Still many problems relating to art and archaeology remain to be answered.*

*I discussed the matter also with Mrs. Zelia Nuttall who has, for a considerable time, been interested in the revival of the school work. At the time when we conducted the school one of the great difficulties was the lack of a center in which a library, specimens for study, and other material could be assembled. It so happens that Mrs. Nuttall would like to give up her house, which would make an excellent home for such a school. She believes that a reestablishment of the school on the former basis would be acceptable in Mexico at the present time. I believe also that international cooperation on the earlier basis could be attained again.*

*The problems which are to be solved in Mexico are not only of an archaeological character, but also those referring to the people of Mexico and their relation to the geographical conditions of their home are undoubtedly of the very greatest importance and should be investigated.*

*I do not doubt that if the question were placed before American scientists and also before scientists of other countries that not only a unanimous support of this plan could be obtained but that also the scientists would be glad to formulate a more detailed plan of procedure.*

*As in all other cases work of this kind depends upon financial support. I am inclined to think that if the plan were definitely formulated, such support might be obtained, either from one of the great Foundations or from interested individuals. Just at present the most important question would be whether such a plan, in which all nations should participate, would be welcome to Mexico. In this matter I am asking your advice and venturing the suggestion that perhaps you might be willing to transmit this note to Ambassador Morrow in order to learn whether a movement like the one described would meet with his approval and support.*

*Yours very sincerely,*

*Franz Boas*

*President of the Congress*

FB:B

Mrs. Nuttall's reply, on the same hotel stationery "At the Gateway of Central Park," is dated October 14.

*Dear Prof. Boas*

*Your letter was a surprise to me & showed me that you have misunderstood my plan about my house. I now understand why you think that my owning it is a drawback to my project. Some years ago a wealthy banker asked me to let him know whenever I wanted to sell it & since then has repeated his desire to buy it. As you know it is a fine specimen of Colonial architecture & its garden that I have worked over for 26 years makes it a show place that I need not consider unsaleable — on the contrary. But I love the old place & wish to have it a public building after my death so that my library and collections can remain in it & it can be enjoyed by my colleagues & countrymen. Therefore I am going to establish in it an institution for the promotion of science in Mexico, in which many of my friends are now interested. If I had known that you had been planning* "to re-establish the International School of American Archaeology & Ethnology on its former basis" *I would have told you that, under the changed conditions in Mexico & the decided anti-foreign animus, this project is absolutely out of the question. Contrary to what you write I do* not *believe that a* re-establishment *of the school on the former basis will ever again be acceptable in Mexico. Nor do I share your optimism that international co-operation could be obtained.*

*Nor do I* "want to give up my house" *— for I intend to live in it until I pass away. I have spoken to many influential persons about the plan I have in mind, including Mr. Morrow whom I shall again see in a short time. He thinks that I know more about the attitude of Mexicans towards foreigners than he does & knows that as a Member of the leading Mexican scientific societies I am in close touch with the Mexican intellectuals. While they are sympathetic with my project I know they would oppose yours.*

*Mrs. de Forest is doing all she can to prevent Mr. de Forest from being intruded upon, for he is seriously ill.*

*As to Mr. Morrow — it is useless to ask him at this critical time to divert his attention to affairs non-political. Moreover should there be a change of administration he will have to resign his post.*

*For these reasons, dear Dr. Boas, I cannot deliver your letter or endorse your views which seem based on a misunderstanding not only of my project but also of Mexicans at the present day.*

*Shall I return your letter to you or may I keep it as the expression of your views?*

*I trust that the institution I expect to found will be on so broad*
*a basis that it will not only include all scientific branches & also be*
*cosmopolitan, extending aid to foreign students, though not based*
*on "international organization."*
*   I much appreciate your kindness & send you & Mrs. Boas my best*
*regards.*

*Yours sincerely,*
*Zelia Nuttall.*

Perhaps Mrs. Nuttall's letter was as great a blow to Boas as
his must have been a shock to her. But he betrayed no emotion
in the terse but not unkind reply which he dictated to his secretary, Ruth Bryan,[106] three days later.

*Oct. 17, 1928*

*My dear Mrs. Nuttall:*

*   I am sorry that I have misunderstood your plans. So far as I can*
*see I merely repeated in my letter what we agreed upon the other*
*day. I do not quite know what other type of organization you wanted*
*and I do not recall that you expressed yourself in regard to that point.*
*I am perfectly willing to do all I can to further a matter of this sort.*

*Yours very truly,*
*Franz Boas*

*FB:B*

After this there was an eight-week silence. Mexico was still
in a state of ferment.[23] Emilio Portes Gil had been named to
take over the presidential reins which would have gone to the
murdered Obregón. But because he was provisional president
only and November 20, 1929, had been set for the election of
a constitutional president, Mexico was in for a political campaign that gave every promise of being stormy and perhaps
bloody. Meanwhile there was immediate tension and the possibility of violence very close to Mrs. Nuttall's house. For on
November 2 the sensational trial of the assassin of Obregón
began in the courthouse of the adjoining suburb of San Angel.
   Mrs. Nuttall had not planned to return home directly after
the meeting of the Americanists, for there were friends she

wanted to visit in Baltimore, Philadelphia and Washington. She had, however, set her departure for December, which would give her time enough to consult a number of experts on her proposed institute. One person she discussed it with was Ralph Van Deman Magoffin,[103] head of the classics department of New York University, who for the last seven years had been president of the Archaeological Institute of America. Mrs. Nuttall had a particular feeling for the Institute because, in 1886, its Journal had accepted and published her first paper, "The Terracotta Heads of Teotihuacán." [62]

As Mrs. Nuttall's departure date neared so did the date for the eighty-fifth meeting of the American Association for the Advancement of Science. She had been a member of the association for forty-two years and she was strongly tempted. The seven-day meeting was scheduled to open in New York two days before Christmas, and the upcoming meeting led her to write Boas again. Her letter, dated December 11, was written on the stationery of the Hotel Grafton in Washington.

Now it was her turn to be tactless. Without stopping to think how much Boas must have suffered from her frustration of his plans for revising the International School, she bubbled blithely about plans for her own competing project. The hotel's note paper had a coat of arms at the top, and across the bottom: " 'Summer Season', Saranac Inn in Upper Saranac Lake, Adirondacks, N.Y. Modern Appointments, superb cuisine. A clientele socially desirable."

> *Dear Prof. Boas,*
>
> *I received letters advising me not to return to Mexico for a while & so have arranged to attend the Meeting of the A.A.A.S. provided you can give me ten minutes for a communication with slides on "The ancient sub-gravel type of clay figurines & others found in the Valley of Mexico."*
>
> *I hope to have favorable opportunities to submit my project for the foundation of an institute to promote scientific research in Mexico to a group of advisers including you.*

*I have decided* not *to place my property in the market for two or three years to come as I wish to live therein & finish certain investigations — so it need not be taken into immediate consideration in discussing the project which can be given the time in which to be formulated.*

*Pres. Magoffin of the Arch. Institute of America has expressed a keen interest in the plan & desire that the foundation be a branch of the Arch. Institute on a broad basis however — to extend not only to Archaeology, but also to linguistics, geology, botany, etc.*

*I do hope that you will not be so "rushed" as at the Am. Congress & that I may have the pleasure of seeing you & Mrs. Boas at greater leisure. Since I left New York I have been visiting in Baltimore & Philadelphia & here, consulting colleagues in each place. I have provisionally engaged a room at the Manhattan Square Hotel for the 27th & am looking forward to a great treat.*

*With cordial regards to you both*
*most sincerely*
*Zelia Nuttall*

Boas' reply — and it is the note that ends the correspondence — may have struck Mrs. Nuttall as being devastatingly brief.

*Dec. 12, 1928*

*Mrs. Zelia Nuttall*
*Hotel Grafton*
*Washington, D.C.*

*My dear Mrs. Nuttall:*

*Many thanks for your letter. The program matter is in charge of Dr. Mason in Philadelphia to whom I am sending your abstract.*

*I am very glad to learn that we shall have the pleasure of seeing you.*

*Yours very sincerely,*
*Franz Boas*

*FB:B*

For a busy man, who had been frustrated in one of his dearest aims, that businesslike note is really not so curt. But when this investigator first read it, he felt sad. Because the note so completely ignored Mrs. Nuttall's "institute," and because it brought the correspondence to an abrupt halt, it suggested that a friendship that had spanned so many years had ended in a fight. But the name, Dr. Mason, presented another reference to be tracked down. He turned out to be the J. Alden Mason, who, seventeen years before, had been one of the five fellows of the International School during the year Boas was its director.[27] In his friendly way, Dr. Mason softened the blow by writing (February 11, 1963), "Don't get the impression that Boas was peeved at Zelia just because he sent her a one-sentence letter. That was a typical Boas letter; that's the reason he got so much work done."[48]

Dr. Mason was the man to whom Boas referred Mrs. Nuttall because Boas knew her proposed paper belonged more to one of the concurrent meetings of the American Anthropological Association than to a session of the A.A.A.S. Dr. Mason had been appointed to take over such duties for the Anthropological Association because A. I. Hallowell, its secretary, was ill. Dr. Mason himself said he could not remember the incident, so he did not know whether or not Mrs. Nuttall was granted the opportunity to make her communication.

However, the summary of the Proceedings, published in *Science*,[91] shows that she was. Her paper, "Clay Figurines of the Sub-Gravel Type and Others from the Valley of Mexico," was delivered on Friday morning, December 28, and the summary says: "Zelia Nuttall, as a result of her studies on old Mexican documents, suggested that many of the clay figurines from the Valley of Mexico represented ancestors rather than deities."

The report in the *American Anthropologist*[4] is less explicit about the paper, but, by citing exactly when Boas led the "Symposium on Art Styles," reveals that the two old friends appeared on the same program. The symposium was held immediately after Mrs. Nuttall's paper. Thus, even if they never wrote to each other again, the flare-up over the house did not prevent them from coming together as colleagues. Perhaps they had several sociable encounters. Columbia was one of the places where sessions were held and tea was served at the university every afternoon. Altogether, it must have been an enjoyable time. Jimmy Walker was the mayor of New York. He greeted the delegates personally, and the New York Philharmonic, led by Wilhelm Mengelberg, gave the scientists a complimentary concert.

The meeting was probably the last occasion the two old correspondents met, though Mrs. Nuttall must have passed back and forth through New York in the autumn of 1929 when she went to England on what was to be her last excursion away from Mexico.[61] In Mexico, however, she did not concentrate perhaps as much as she should have on her unfinished investigations. She did work from time to time on the mass of archival material she had gathered on Hawkins, the Elizabethan seaman who had been obliged to flee in defeat from Vera Cruz, but apparently she never took up the two uncompleted projects that Kroeber had waited patiently for at the University of California: her commentaries on Codex Magliabecchiano[71] and Alonso de la Cruz's map of Mexico City.[69] Nor did she complete her monograph on the Mexican calendar system which she had already begun at the time of the 1893 world's fair in Chicago.[100] Part of the trouble was her persisting tendency to become diverted into new lines by the force of new enthusiasms.

At the time of the 1928 New York Americanist Congress she was already deep in her campaign to establish the first of the two annual days when the sun cast no shadow in Mexico as a Mexican national holiday.[78] The day, generally May 17, was, she claimed, the Aztec New Year's Day. The phenomenon of the "shadowless moment" was caused by the sun being in the zenith, and Mrs. Nuttall used to demonstrate the shadowlessness to interested parties who would gather at Casa Alvarado to watch while the shadow of an upright stick diminished to nothing as the zenith was reached. The reappearance of the shadow after the zenith was passed would heighten the effect of the demonstration.

Then early in 1932 Alfonso Caso discovered the jewels of Monte Alban and Mrs. Nuttall became caught up in the ensuing controversy and excitement. She sided with Caso in holding that the jewels were genuine, but she sided against his claim (subsequently vindicated) that the jewels were Mixtec. Her contention was that they were Aztec and that they were the jewels of Cuauhtemoc, the last Aztec emperor.[79]

Thus she did not finish as much as she hoped and she was too busy to do much about establishing her foundation. But in one respect, she got her wish. She did live in Casa Alvarado until she died. In another, she and Boas were both frustrated. By the time of her death — April 12, 1933[97] — arrangements had still not been made to turn the house into "an institution for the promotion of science." Casa Alvarado fell into private hands.[51] Some of her colonial paintings and furniture and her pre-Columbian objects are still there, treasured by the present owners. But many were dispersed. Her splendid library was broken up and sold.[51] And hundreds of letters she had saved, including, probably, the originals of those from Boas, were consigned to flames.[51]

Boas lived until December 21, 1942,[58] but there is no evidence that, after Mrs. Nuttall's death, he made any further effort to secure Casa Alvarado. By this time Hitler had risen to power. Boas in his last years was too busy attacking the racial theories that were sweeping his once-beloved Germany to be concerned with rallying the nations to cooperate in investigating Mexican archaeology.[22]

Looking back on their long careers, one sees that the remarkable thing about the Boas-Nuttall friendship is how many friends in both camps never knew the two were acquainted. It was partly because their lives so often diverged, partly because both were human beings of prodigiously wide circles, many of which never overlapped. They never became Franz and Zelia to each other, and clearly neither friend was central to the other's life. But because each cared deeply for the same science, their paths had a number of significant crossings. Because each, too, was a vivid and strong-willed personality, those crossings remain quick and lively in their human interest. At the same time they reveal a good deal about the progress of anthropology in Europe and Mexico, as well as in the United States. And both friends, besides being international figures, were richly endowed individuals who, fortunately for us, still come alive in their own words.

# FRANZ BOAS

## Ethnographer on the Northwest Coast

 *by RONALD P. ROHNER*

*Ronald P. Rohner is assistant professor of anthropology at the University of Connecticut. His ethnographic field work with the Gilford Island band of Kwakiutl led him to the interest in Boas' field work among the Indians of the Northwest Coast.*

Franz Boas has influenced every aspect of American anthropology from content, methodology, and perspective to graduate training programs. One of his fundamental contributions was the establishment of field research as the foundation on which all of American anthropology rests. In this regard Robert Lowie (1937:137) has written that "Boas must be understood first of all as a field worker." Later Meyer Fortes (1953:338) cited Boas as having "Established the method of systematic field work by professional anthropologists as the basis of American anthropology." These two scholars, among many others, stress the importance of Franz Boas as a field worker. In fact, however, we know very little about Boas as an ethnographer. Leslie White (1963:48) points out some of the inadequacies of this record when he says:

> We do not know very much about how Boas conducted himself in the field, what his relationships with the Indians were like and so on. Was he ever accompanied by his wife and children? This invariably affects profoundly the relationship of the ethnographer to the people he is studying. Did he reside in a household as a "member" of a family? Did he take part in the daily life of the people? For one who "must be understood first of all as a field worker" (Lowie, 1937, p. 131), we know precious little about his life and work in the field.

This study adds to the precious little of which White speaks.[1] It focuses on Boas' activities in the field, his attitudes toward field work and his relations with the Indians of the Northwest

Coast. Information is needed on all of these points before a complete assessment can be made of Boas' contributions to anthropology. The problem is approached primarily from the point of view of Boas' observations about himself as revealed in his letters and diaries written from the field. Except in the concluding section few attempts are made to evaluate his field work or to cast the material into a broader set of theoretical questions. For the most part Boas speaks for himself about his field work.

Five specific questions guide the presentation of this paper, along with the three general points of focus mentioned above. These include: (1) how often did Boas go to the North Pacific Coast and where did he work when he was there, (2) what was the purpose of each trip and what did he do, (3) what types of problems did he encounter in the field and how did he respond to them, (4) where did he get the funds for field research, and (5) do any special incidents place Boas in particularly clear perspective as an ethnographer among the Indians of the Northwest Coast? Incidental attention is also given to what the Kwakiutl — that is, those Indians who knew or worked with him — say about Boas.

A complete evaluation of Boas as a field worker cannot be made, however, until the correspondence covering a period of forty years between Boas and George Hunt has been worked through. A large part of Boas' field research on the coast was influenced by Hunt's data, but the nature of this influence remains ambiguous.[2]

Franz Boas worked with Northwest Coast materials for almost sixty years. During this time he made thirteen field trips to the coast from 1886 to 1931, and he spent approximately twenty-nine months working among the Indians there. For purposes of examination his field work on the Northwest Coast may be conveniently divided into four periods. The first of these is his initial field trip to the coast in 1886. The second includes the five trips he made between 1888 and 1894 under the auspices of the British Association for the Advancement of Science (BAAS). The following two trips during the summers of 1897 and 1900 were guided by the aims of the Jesup North Pacific Expedition. He conducted his last five field trips from 1914 to 1931 independently of any sponsoring organization. Table 1 summarizes the total time Boas spent conducting research during each of his trips to the Northwest Coast. Figures 1 and 2 show the locations Boas visited during his field trips, and Table 2 presents a chronology of locations visited during each trip.

TABLE 1

DURATION OF BOAS' FIELD TRIPS TO THE NORTHWEST COAST

| Dates | | No. Days in Field |
|---|---|---|
| 1886 | Sept. 18 — Dec. 16 | 89 |
| 1888 | May 31 — July 24 | 55 |
| 1889 | July 18 — Sept 14 (?) | 59 |
| 1890 | June 9 — mid-Sept. | c. 98 |
| 1891 | July 5 — early Sept. | c. 64 |
| 1894 | Sept. 10 — Dec. 15 | 96 |
| 1897 | June 3 — Sept. 14 | 104 |
| 1900 | June 21 — Sept. 9 | 81 |
| 1914 | Aug. 4 — Aug. 25 | 22 |
| 1922 | Aug. 15 — Aug. 30 | 16 |
| 1923 | Nov. 13 — Dec. 18 | 38 |
| 1927 | ca. June 29 — ca. Sept. 2 | c. 66 |
| 1930–31 | Oct. 21 — Jan. 12 | 83 |
| | | c. 871* |

*This means that Boas spent approximately two years and five months on the Northwest Coast.

# TABLE 2
## LOCATIONS VISITED DURING EACH OF BOAS' FIELD TRIPS

| *Dates* | | *Location* |
|---|---|---|
| 1886 | Sept. 18 — Oct. 3 (?) | Victoria |
| | Oct. 4–5 (?) | Transit to Nawiti |
| | Oct. 6–17 | Nawiti |
| | Oct. 18–23 | Alert Bay |
| | Oct. 24–25 | Transit to Victoria |
| | Oct. 26 — Nov. 2 | Victoria |
| | Nov. 4–10 | Cowichan |
| | Nov. 11 (?) | Nanaimo (Transit to Comox) |
| | Nov. 12 — Dec. 2 | Comox |
| | Dec. 3 | Transit to Nanaimo |
| | Dec. 4–9 | Nanaimo |
| | Dec. 10–13 | Victoria |
| | Dec. 14–15 | Vancouver |
| | Dec. 16 | Victoria |
| 1888 | May 31 — June 2 | Vancouver |
| | June 3–7 | Victoria |
| | June 8 | Cowichan |
| | June 9–14 | Victoria |
| | June 15 | Transit to Port Essington |
| | June 17 | Arrived Alert Bay going North |
| | June 18 | Arrived Rivers Inlet and Bella Bella going North |
| | June 19–26 | Port Essington |
| | June 29 | Arrived Comox going to Victoria |
| | June 30 — July 11 | In and around Victoria (e.g., Cowichan) |
| | July 12 | Vancouver to Lytton |
| | July 13–14 | Lytton |
| | July 15 | Left Lytton; arrived Golden |
| | July 16 | Golden |

*Table 2 Continued*

| Dates | Location |
|---|---|
| July 17–19 | Windemere |
| July 20–24 (?) | Golden (?) |
| **1889** July 18–30 | Victoria |
| Aug. 2–12 | Alberni |
| Aug. 20–21 | Victoria |
| Aug. 25 — Sept. 3 (?) | Albert Bay |
| Sept. 6 | Harrison Hot Springs |
| Sept. 8–14 (?) | Kamloops |
| **1890** June 9 | Portland |
| June 12–29 | Siletz |
| June 30 — July 12 | Grande Ronde |
| July 4 | Portland |
| July 6–8 (?) | Seaside |
| July 9 | Ilwako |
| July 10–23 (?) | Bay Center |
| July 24–26 (?) | Portland (?) |
| July 27 | Tacoma |
| July 28–29 (?) | Port Townsend |
| July 30 | Victoria |
| July 31 — Aug. 10 | New Westminster |
| Aug.11–21 | Ladners Landing |
| Aug. 23 | Victoria |
| Aug. 25–27 (?) | Port Townsend |
| Aug. 28 — (?) | Tacoma |
| end Aug. — mid-Sept. | in Washington (?) |
| **1891** July 5 | Portland |
| July 9–21 | Bay Center |
| July 25 | Portland |
| July 29 — mid-Aug. | Bay Center |
| Aug. 19 — early Sept. | Victoria |

*Table 2 Continued*

| *Dates* | *Location* |
|---|---|
| 1894 Sept. 10–12 | Glacier |
| Sept. 13–14 | Enderby |
| Sept. 15 | Sicamous |
| Sept. 16–18 | Kamloops |
| Sept. 19–20 | Spences Bridge |
| Sept. 21–24 | North Bend |
| Sept. 25 | Vancouver |
| Sept. 26 — Oct. 2 | Victoria |
| Oct. 3–9 | Transit to Nass River |
| Oct. 10 — Nov. 9 | Kincolith (Nass River) |
| Nov. 10–14 | Transit to Fort Rupert |
| Nov. 15 — Dec. 5 (?) | Fort Rupert |
| Dec. 6 | Transit to Victoria |
| Dec. 7–9 | Victoria |
| Dec. 11 | Vancouver |
| Dec. 14–15 | Lytton |
| | |
| 1897 June 3 | Vancouver |
| June 4–6 | Spences Bridge |
| June 14–15 | 16 mi. below Lillooet |
| June 18 | Fountain |
| June 21 | Kelly Lake |
| June 22 | Big Bar |
| June 27 | Williams Lake |
| July 6 | Hanceville (?) |
| July 12 | Puntzi Lake |
| July 19 (?) | Soda Creek |
| July 20 — Aug. 2 | Bella Coola |
| Aug. 7–9 | Namu |
| Aug. 11–21 (?) | Port Essington |
| Aug. 26 | Transit to Rivers Inlet |
| Aug. 28 — Sept. 7 | Rivers Inlet |

*Table 2 Continued*

| Dates | Location |
|---|---|
| Sept. 13 | Transit to Victoria |
| Sept. 14 | Victoria |
| 1900 June 21 | Spences Bridge |
| June 25 | Coultee, Nicola Valley |
| June 29 — July 2 | Vancouver |
| July 3 — Sept. 9 | Alert Bay |
| 1914 Aug. 4 | Vancouver |
| Aug. 6 | Transit to Cranbrook |
| Aug. 7–25 | Cranbrook (St. Eugene) |
| 1922 Aug. 15 | Victoria |
| Aug. 30 | Spences Bridge |
| 1923 Nov. 11–12 | Spences Bridge (to Vancouver) |
| Nov. 13–14 | Vancouver |
| Nov. 15 | In transit to Bella Bella |
| Nov. 16 — Dec. 16 (?) | Bella Bella |
| Dec. 18 | Vancouver |
| 1927 June 29 (30?) | Portland, Oregon |
| July 7 (?) | Berkeley, Calif. (probably for one week) |
| July 21–25 (?) | Oakville, Washington |
| Aug. 3 | Portland |
| Aug. 17–26 (?) | Oakville, Washington |
| Aug. 30 — Sept. 2 (?) | Victoria |
| 1930–31 Oct. 21 | Vancouver |
| Oct. 24 — Dec. 25 | Fort Rupert |
| Jan. 5–10 | Alert Bay |
| Jan. 11 | On board boat |
| Jan. 12 (?) | Victoria |

INITIAL FIELD WORK ON THE NORTHWEST COAST (1886)

Boas began working on Northwest Coast materials in Berlin in 1885 while several Bella Coola Indians were being exhibited in the Museum of Ethnology there. Active field research on the Northwest Coast itself, however, did not begin until September 18, 1886, when he arrived for the first time in Victoria, British Columbia, at the age of twenty-eight. Prior to leaving for the field he had unsuccessfully tried to solicit money for his trip from several organizations. He did receive letters of recommendation and other forms of support, however, from such organizations as the American Association for the Advancement of Science and the Smithsonian Institution. His uncle offered him $500 but Boas decided to accept no more than $400 for the trip. Apparently he was also given some financial aid by personal friends (Boas 1909:307), and he was able to solicit a free pass for train transportation to and from British Columbia.

Boas remained in Victoria for two weeks before moving up the coast of Vancouver Island. During this time he attempted to familiarize himself with the area and people. He spent a great deal of time searching for suitable informants and often complained about the time lost in doing this. On his fourth day there, for example, he wrote to his parents, "I regret every lost hour, but unfortunately in this kind of work, it is necessary to lose many in order to find suitable people with whom to work" (Boas: 9/21/86). A few days later he again wrote, "I am unhappy for every moment lost but one cannot put one's head through a stone wall and I must bear these fruitless hours patiently" (Boas: 9/26/86).

He was able to get the cooperation of a number of informants — especially Tsimshian, Bella Coola, Tlingit, and Bella Bella — from whom he collected primarily language materials and mythological tales. Despite his annoyance at lost time, he was generally satisfied with his productiveness in Victoria, and on

September 30 he wrote, "It is strange how 'luck's scale moves up and down.' In the last few days I have been overwhelmed with material so much so that I can scarcely handle it all" (Boas: 9/30/86).

Even when he found a good informant, however, Boas could not be confident of collecting the material he wanted when he wanted it. He became angry, for example, when a Tsimshian with whom he had been intensively working suddenly disappeared:

> *I am cross because my Tsimshian has deserted me and so far he has been the best one I have had. From experience I should know that such things happen, but it is easier said than done not to be angry about it. I told the good man, who by the way is one of the most religious, that he was the greatest liar I had ever known, since he did not keep his word. I told him I would tell his pastor about it. I immediately went in search of another and hope I shall be successful tomorrow* (Boas: 9/24/86).

Later in the same day he wrote: "I hope I shall find another good Tsimshian tomorrow to replace Mathew, whom I cannot curse enough. He was able to dictate so very well. It reminds me so vividly of the Eskimo — they also ran away in the middle of a tale" (Boas: 9/24/86).

One of the important tasks which he undertook during this field trip was to begin identifying the language and tribal groups along the coast. He found this exceedingly difficult: "Such a confusion of dialects and languages exists here that it is very difficult to accomplish anything in a short time. The material overwhelms me" (Boas: 9/23/86). But a week later, after an especially productive afternoon, he wrote in his diary, "This mass of stories is gradually beginning to bear fruit because I can now discover certain traits characteristic of the different groups of people. I think I am on the right track in considering mythology a useful tool for differentiating and judging the relationship of tribes" (Boas: 9/30/86).

## FIGURE 1

### LOCATIONS VISITED BY BOAS IN BRITISH COLUMBIA: 1886–1931

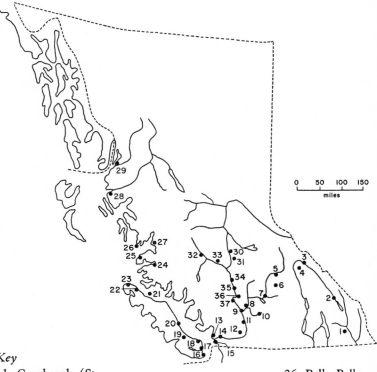

*Key*

1. Cranbrook (St. Eugene)
2. Windemere
3. Golden
4. Glacier
5. Sicamous
6. Enderby
7. Kamloops
8. Spences Bridge
9. Lytton
10. Coultee, Nicola Valley
11. North Bend
12. Harrison Hot Springs
13. Vancouver
14. New Westminster
15. Ladners Landing
16. Victoria
17. Cowichan
18. Nanaimo
19. Alberni
20. Comox
21. Alert Bay
22. Fort Rupert
23. Nawiti
24. Rivers Inlet
25. Namu
26. Bella Bella
27. Bella Coola
28. Port Essington
29. Kincolith
30. Soda Creek
31. Williams Lake
32. Puntzi Lake
33. Hanceville
34. Kelley Lake (?) (Alkali Lake [?)
35. Big Bar (?)
36. Fountain
37. (18 mi. below Lillooet)

After several more days of work in Victoria, Boas boarded
a steamer for the Kwakiutl village at Nawiti which was the first
isolated Indian community that he visited. The villagers viewed
his presence with curiosity and an element of suspicion. Shortly
after his arrival a potlatch was given and Boas made a speech
explaining who he was and what he wanted in the village:

> Finally I noticed that I had become the subject of their
> speeches, but naturally I had no idea what they wanted. At
> last they sent a young man who had been in Victoria for
> some time to interpret for me. I must add that the natives
> were not too clear about why I was there and what I wanted
> and that they were making all kinds of conjectures. At first
> they thought I was a priest, and now because I had bought
> nothing, they thought I might be a government agent come
> to put a stop to the festival. The missionaries and the Indian
> agent have done this. They would refuse to take orders and
> continue to celebrate. The agent had said he would send a
> gun boat if they did not obey, but they did not believe him
> and were not going to pay attention to the warning. Whether
> I wanted to or not I had to make a speech. So I arose and
> said: "My country is far from yours; much further even than
> that of the Queen. The commands of the Queen do not
> affect me. I am a chief and no one may command me. I alone
> determine what I am to do." (I was introduced as a chief as
> soon as I arrived here and am so introduced wherever I go.)
> "I am in no way concerned with what Dr. Powell (the In-
> dian agent whom all the natives dislike) says. I do not wish
> to interfere with your celebration. My people live far away
> and would like to know what people in distant lands do.
> And so I set out. I was in warm lands and cold lands. I saw
> many different people and told them at home how they live.
> And they said to me 'Go and see what the people in this land
> do.' And so I went and I came here and I saw you eat and
> drink, sing and dance. And I shall go back and say; "See
> that is how the people there live. They were good to me and
> asked me to live with them." This beautiful speech, which
> fits in with their style of story-telling, was translated and
> caused great joy. A chief answered something or other, but

unfortunately they mistook me for a very important personage and demanded a written statement from me that no gun boat would be sent. So I had to explain to them that the Queen was somewhat more powerful than I, and promised to say that I liked to see them sing and dance. They were satisfied with this and promised to make a big celebration for me tomorrow. I think I managed the affair quite well. Until a few minutes ago all the chiefs have been coming to see me to tell me that the 'hearts' of all people were glad when they heard my speech (Boas: 10/7/86).

At another potlatch the following day Boas announced that he would distribute food if the people would end the celebration with a dance. He recorded in his diary: "Naturally they were more than willing. The chief came to me and said: 'When a chief comes to visit we do not celebrate with a dance, but because the big chief from a distant land came to us, we shall hold a dance. Go to your house and await us.' In the meantime the house was cleaned and all the . . . [?] for the family were taken out. A very large fire was made" (Boas: 10/8/86). The dance lasted about half an hour and the following afternoon he gave his feast:

I had a large fire built in the middle of the house over which two big bowls of rice were cooked and then roasted [?]. The house had been cleaned for the festival and soon all the men assembled. The first to come were three greybeards who are always together and always to be found on the platform [?] in front of the houses. Gradually everyone came and sat down on the platform which extends around the house. A drum was brought, and while the boy whom I had engaged as cook stirred the concoction, the entire company sang their songs. So far I have transcribed only one melody. The melody is so foreign to me that I find it difficult to record and I am very much out of practice. After four or five songs had been sung, I have hardly described this, the dishes were passed and everyone ate busily. When they were almost finished the chief arose and held a long speech, which was interpreted for me. "This chief," he said, pointing to me, "has come to us from a distant land, and all our hearts are glad. He is not like the other whites who have come to us. His heart is pure [?reinlich] and kind towards us Indians. None of the King George men (English) or the Boston men (Americans) gave us [?] festival. But his people must be good and he shows that he has the heart of a chief. Whoever of us shall meet him, will be glad and recognize him as a great chief. We are glad he came and hope he will return. My heart is friendly towards him and if he wants anything from us we shall do our best to do what he asks." I accepted the speech with proper composure and gave some tobacco to every man. There were thirty men, one woman and a few children. It seems women take part only if no male member of the family is alive. When all was over they got up and carried what was left of the food to their wives (Boas: 10/9/86).

Boas devoted most of his time among the Nawiti to sketching the settlement, individual houses within the settlement, house posts, masks and other representations of material culture. He purchased sixty-five masks and other articles for a museum collection, and he attempted to record the associated tale for each. The day before he left Nawiti he wrote in his letter-diary to his parents, "I certainly would not sell what I have now for less than $200. It is the only collection from this place that is reasonably well labeled. I, too, have not been here long enough to understand everything completely, but I have accomplished a good deal" (Boas: 10/15/86).

He arrived in Alert Bay on October 18 where he stayed for a week acquiring five pieces for his museum collection and recording tales in Kwakwala, the native language of the Kwakiutl. The day he left Alert Bay he wrote:

I haven't much to tell about my life here. It is pretty monotonous. I go about visiting, listen to stories and write until my fingers are lame. It has become difficult to get much that is new because I am pretty well acquainted with the mythology. I shall have to work hard in Victoria, reread everything and if possible copy it. Otherwise I shall lose control of my material (Boas: 10/23/86).

A few days after his return to Victoria he took stock of his work. He had recorded 119 tales — "among them a whole book full that have not been copied" (Boas: 10/31/86). He estimated the value of his museum collection at $200 according to prices in Victoria; he paid $70 for it. He hoped to increase the value of the collection to exceed $500 in order to pay for his expenses which at that time amounted to $280.

Boas collected Bella Coola and Tlingit tales and attempted to understand the grammar of the languages during most of the week that he spent in Victoria. Regarding the former Boas complained:

> I am not very well satisfied with my results, although during these last three days the grammar of the language has become much clearer to me. But progress is very slow. I want very much to collect folk tales but I have no opportunity to do so as there is no sensible person here. So I shall have to give it up. The Bella Coolas tell me the most beautiful stories in their own language. The stories themselves were not worth much but on the other hand the language is very much worth while (Boas: 10/28/86).

As part of this plan to survey significant locations along the east coast of Vancouver Island, Boas proceeded next to Cowichan where he encountered suspicion and resistance from the Coast Salish Indians living there:

> I was cross last night and did not want to write. I could accomplish nothing. This morning I had gone to Somenos, the village two miles from my house and got a few things, hoping to continue this afternoon. But for some inexplicable reason I could not get the people to talk. They evidently think I come with some evil intent. As a result I wasted three hours without accomplishing a thing. This morning I had quite a scene in the upper village. I had my camera

with me [which he picked up in Victoria] and photographed a handsome totem pole in front of a house. Shortly afterwards, the owner appeared, a young man, and demanded that I pay him, which naturally I refused to do in order not to deprive myself of the possibility of photographing whatever I might wish. He declared that he was master of his land and would not permit me to leave until I paid. I replied just as quietly that I would leave when I felt like it. They always try to bluff strangers, and I know by this time how to counter them. I quietly proceeded to another house and continued with my work and lo and behold it was not long before friend Indian followed and asked whether he might not interpret for me. So I accepted if he would make himself useful, and to-day he sought out all the people who have the information I am seeking and helps me as much as he can. I was here in the afternoon and wanted to photograph a painted house. Earlier I had held conversation with the owner but he did not want to tell me anything. While I was putting up the camera he merely said it was his house and he wanted a picture of it. The whites look upon the Indians not as humans but as dogs and he did not wish any one to laugh at things that were their laws, as painted houses and articles used for celebrating their festivals. In spite of anything I could say, I could get no where with him and as I want something from this man, I did not insist and said I cared nothing about the picture and spoke of other things. In this way I learned a great deal by subterfuge. A young man came with a stag and wanted me to take a picture of it. I placed him in front of the house I wished to photograph and so attained my end. But I got nothing from the Indians out here. My host promised to accompany me to the village tomorrow and since the people trust him I hope the ice will be broken. Last night I was completely out of sorts (Boas: 11/6/86).

Two days later he encountered similar problems:

I find that my notes are very scant these days due to the slow progress I am making. I must admit that this week has been the most unpleasant one I have spent in this region. I have to run about all day, twice a day two miles to the settlement and there is very little to be gotten there. At least I know that the people here have an entirely different cycle of myths from those in the north and this strengthens me in my belief that the myths here originate from two different sources. I was up there again yesterday and almost became impatient because of the long drawn out manner in which they told the stories. It really was a test of patience. In the afternoon I tried my luck in the other settlement but was unable to accomplish a thing. I persuaded my host to talk to them, as he knows them well, and I hope that will make things easier. This afternoon I was in Somenos again and could do nothing for the strangest reason. An old man who usually tells me stories was in best form when an equally old woman interfered. He said a man had laid dead for nine days and she said ten, whereupon he became so angry that I could not get another word out of him. These sessions are most amusing, however, not the one I just passed through. Yesterday two young men appeared and laughed when they heard the old man tell stories. He was ashamed because of it and said he would refuse to talk if others were present. Every five minutes he assured me his is the best among all the men here and knows everything. In the meantime screaming, dirty children run about; sometimes a meal is eaten. Dogs and chickens force their way between the people, the fire smokes so badly one can scarcely see [?]. The old man watches that I write down every word that he says and if I fail to do so he takes it as a personal insult and holds a long speech of which I do not understand a word. This evening I went to the settlement of Cowichan which is in front of my house. My landlady's talk really helped and the old rascal who had forbidden everyone to tell me anything, gave me a long speech saying that he feared the chief, but now he would tell me some things because he knew I was a good man, but I should repeat nothing. I already know these big lies. I also had trouble in Somenos this morning because I wanted to make a drawing. The Indians always try to bluff strangers with their impudence. Nowhere have I had such trouble as here. This morning I went down to the village, as had been arranged, only to find that my new friend, who goes under the name of Bill, was not at home. His wife held a long speech of which I did not understand a word, so I left and asked for him outside. I did not have to ask long for I heard his stentorian voice issuing from one of the large houses standing on the steep bank of the river. He was holding a long speech. I climbed the stairs (a euphemism) which led to the house and found a large number of men assembled, crouching around two fires. Well, I found them all assembled in front of the fire discussing the case "Boas" or just about to begin. I understood an occasional word and gathered that they were discussing my wishes. The end of the matter was that Big Bill, who up to now had forbidden them all to tell me stories, said in the best Chinook that he would help me and he has really kept his word. But there was nothing to be done then, as the big, warm dinner had first to be eaten (Boas: 11/8–9/86).

Boas also began collecting skeletal materials in Cowichan — especially skulls, which he took from the Indian burial grounds. He continued collecting skulls at Comox, his next stop.

Boas' unpleasant experiences were sharply reversed when he reached Comox on November 12. Here the Indians were pleasant and cooperative, and his problem became one of keeping up with his material. A few days before he left Comox he recorded in his diary: "So far this has been the best place I have visited. From the beginning the Indians were friendly and willing to talk. I have not found them so any where else" (Boas: 11/29/86). Ten days earlier he had written, "The Indians were in good humor and so I got a good deal. As a matter of fact I get so much material that I cannot possibly work it over every day as I would want to" (Boas: 11/19/86).

In Comox he concentrated on language studies — vocabularies and texts in Pentlatch, Comox, Sechelt and Lekwiltok — and on the further development of his ethnographic map of Vancouver Island. He spent long hours each day recording new data and reworking them in the evening. Even though he was very busy, his life was monotonous because each day was like the preceding:

> I am always very tired evenings because I really have to work very hard. I get up at 6:45, have my breakfast and work in my room until 8:30. I then go to the settlement [a twenty-five minute walk from the hotel where he was staying] and start work there at about nine. I return at 11:45 and am out again by 1:30. By 5:00 I am back here and work over my material as well as I can and prepare myself for the following day. By that time it is 10:30 or 11:00 and I am really tired (Boas: 11/20/86).

One of Boas' last stops in his 1886 field trip was Nanaimo on December 3. He planned to spend a week or so there working on Salish, and he hoped to find a native speaker of Squamish (Coast Salish) so he would not have to go to Vancouver. Six days after he arrived, however, he read in a newspaper that William F. Tolmie, a scholar who had been working with Northwest Coast materials for many years, had died, so Boas left Nanaimo to attend the funeral in Victoria. He tried to acquire Tolmie's manuscript on the Indians which the latter had been preparing for publication.

While he was in Nanaimo, Boas contacted people from whom he hoped to get sketches of several languages such as Tsimshian, Haida, and Kwakwala. "I consider it the duty of a field worker," he wrote, "to obtain as much additional material as possible in this way" (Boas: 12/5/86). By this time his own manuscript had grown to 326 pages.

For several weeks Boas had become increasingly impatient to leave British Columbia, and when he received a letter from Adolf Bastian[3] offering him $250 for the purchase of museum specimens Boas wrote to his parents:

> *Unfortunately it is too late. Three months ago I would have accepted with thanks. He writes: "In order to facilitate the purchase of objects for a collection you may count on us for a preliminary sum of*

*1000 Marks. It will not be difficult for us to come to an agreement as to what should definitely be included in the collection. I shall of course be very glad if, while carrying out the aims of the museum, support can be found for scientific researches such as yours." That is fine, my dear sir, only unfortunately a little too late. Ten horses will not keep me here longer than I need to finish up* (Boas: 12/8?/86).

Boas pulled the loose ends of his project together during his last week in British Columbia. He spent two days in Vancouver working with a Squamish informant. In the remaining time he copied many of his notes, worked on his ethnographic map, and completed several chores in the office of the Indian Superintendent. A week before he left he discovered that the same language is spoken on the mainland as on the corresponding part of Vancouver Island. This was important to Boas because the ethnogeographic part of his field trip had given him the greatest trouble. He recorded in his diary: "The names of the tribes were unknown and after I had found seventy tribes with the greatest difficulty, they had to be arranged according to language and dialect and their location determined. In spite of the short time, I have succeeded pretty well" (Boas: 12/12/86).

The day he left the Northwest Coast he reminisced to his parents in Germany: "It is a strange feeling to have again completed this type of work and now for a year or longer I shall have to live on the memory of this quarter of a year" (Boas: 12/16/86).

### RESEARCH PRIMARILY FOR THE BAAS (1888-1894)

The Committee of the British Association for the Advancement of Science for the Study of the Northwestern Tribes of Canada was appointed in 1884.[4] Boas began conducting research under their direction in 1888 and continued until 1894. During this time he completed five field trips in 1888, 1889, 1890, 1891, and 1894.

An explicit set of instructions from Horatio Hale, editor of the committee, guided Boas' field trips. Linguistic work was to be confined to limited vocabularies and brief grammatical sketches. "The point is," wrote Hale, "to ascertain the total number and the grammatical characteristics of the distinct stocks in the whole Province. The question whether the linguistic groups are, or are not distinct stocks is not of great importance" (Hale: 5/21/88). An ethnographic map was to be prepared and Boas was instructed to make anthropometric measurements "of the various stocks and tribes" (Hale: 4/30/88). Later Hale wrote, "It would be well to describe the complexion, features, and general appearance of the natives of the various tribes in ordinary language, noting their differences, if any" (Hale: 5/21/88).

Furthermore, Boas was requested to make a brief description of the country insofar as it helped to understand "the condition and mode of life of the different tribes" (Hale: 4/30/88). Hale summarized his initial instructions by saying: "My idea is that what is expected from you on this occasion is not so much a minute and special study of any one or two stocks or tribes . . . as a general outline or 'synopsis' of the ethnology of the whole Province, which may hereafter be completed by such special studies, in the way of monographs, by yourself or others" (Hale: 4/30/88). Boas was not expected to visit every part of British Columbia, but he was expected to "give an ethnological description of the whole region from north or south, without omitting any stock" (Hale: 5/21/88). Hale also gave Boas permission to buy skeletal specimens for the American Museum of Natural History if this did not hinder his ethnological work (Hale: 5/17/88). Finally, E. B. Tylor, chairman of the committee, requested him to purchase a limited number of Northwest Coast artifacts, but Boas was not able to do much collecting during his 1888 field trip.

Boas arrived on the Northwest Coast for the second time on

FIGURE 2

LOCATIONS VISITED BY BOAS IN WASHINGTON AND OREGON: 1886–1931

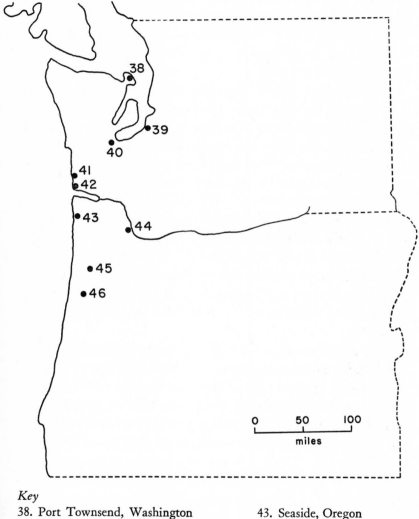

Key

38. Port Townsend, Washington
39. Tacoma, Washington
40. Oakville, Washington
41. Bay Center, Washington
42. Ilwako, Washington

43. Seaside, Oregon
44. Portland, Oregon
45. Grande Ronde, Oregon
46. Siletz, Oregon

May 31, 1888. He remained in Vancouver for three days and then went immediately to Victoria. Prior to arriving in British Columbia he had written to his parents: "I am really looking forward to getting into the 'field' again for a short time" (Boas: 3/6/88). And once he reached Victoria he recorded in his diary: "It gave me great pleasure to see all the places I had known again" (Boas: 6/5/88).

Boas worked with a Tsimshian informant during his first few days in Victoria. He received permission to make anthropometric measurements of Indians in prison and he also accompanied a photographer to a burial site where the two men stole an Indian skeleton. "It is unpleasant work to steal bones from a grave," he reported in his diary, "but what is the use, someone has to do it" (Boas: 6/5/88). On June 8, he made a quick trip to Cowichan where he passed the day measuring a collection of 75 skulls. During the remainder of his time in Victoria he worked with Haida, Tlingit and Kwakiutl informants, as well as photographed and measured prisoners, and he measured his expanding skeleton collection. He had collected 85 crania and 14 complete skeletons by the end of this field trip (Boas: 8/8/88).

His second week in Victoria was frustrating because he had to spend a considerable amount of time searching for suitable informants. He met George Hunt for the first time and made arrangements for Hunt to work with him on linguistic materials. But when Hunt did not appear for two days Boas wrote in exasperation: "The only way I can get people is to drag them in by the hair. This week was the most unsatisfactory one I have spent on the coast excepting for the time at Quamatcin [Quamicham, a Cowichan village] when I was here before" (Boas: 6/13/88).

Two days later he left for Port Essington, near the Alaska border, and wrote to his wife: "Now I am finally ready to leave and I am very glad to get away from here [Victoria] because I cannot work here at all. The Indians are so difficult here" (Boas: 6/15/88). While in transit to Port Essington he recorded in a letter on the back of his diary, "I am surprised how becoming to me this trip on the boat is. I should be surprised if I am not fat and looking well when I come home. I eat and drink well and have a good time thinking of my Indians" (Boas: 6/17/88). Two weeks later, after leaving Port Essington, he reaffirmed his good feelings about the field trip. "I think, however," he wrote, "that this trip does me a lot of good, at least I am feeling refreshed and all right" (Boas: 6/28/88).

His research at Port Essington consisted of working with a Tsimshian informant on language and to a limited degree on customs. He photographed five beautifully tattooed Haida but he took few anthropometric measurements, "as people did not like to be subjected to it" (Boas: 6/25/88). He did, however, take a skull and the lower portion of a skeleton from a small island near Port Essington.

On his voyage back to Victoria he worked with a Bella Bella informant. "Through him," Boas reported, "I have been able to complete the list of tribes and am acquiring quite a good vocabulary" (Boas: 6/29/88). He devoted most of his time to recording Haida, Tsimshian, and Tlingit, and to making anthropometric measurements in Victoria and the surrounding region. Despite the continual frustrations of field research he found pleasure in his work. A few days before venturing into the interior of British Columbia for the first time he wrote:

> I don't think I can help coming back fat and healthy. I am outdoors a lot, eat and drink well and do not overwork myself. In addition I am sleeping about 10 hours every night. I go to bed at 9 and get up at 6:30 since I prefer working by daylight rather than by the light of the bad lamps [in the hotel where he stayed whenever in Victoria] (Boas: 7/5/88).

Boas' first major stop following Victoria was Lytton in the Fraser River valley. Here he collected a few more skeletal specimens and a small Interior Salish vocabulary. He was impatient to return to his wife in New York so he moved quickly to Golden and Windemere to collect data from the Kootenay. The interior tribes did not interest Boas because they bore little relation to his former work (Boas: 7/19/88).[5] "All in all," Boas recorded during his return trip to New York, "I am satisfied with the results of my trip, although I have accomplished only about 1/4 of what I did last time. This is due to the fact that I had to travel back and forth so much and had to deal with so many different tribes" (Boas: 7/24/88).

Boas returned to British Columbia the following year. Again he worked under the direction of the BAAS as explicitly formulated by Hale. He was offered $1,100 by the Bureau of American Ethnology for two months' work on the Chinook language, but he probably did not accept it because Hale offered him $1,000 to continue with the BAAS program. Before returning to the field Boas wrote to Hale proposing the type of work he wanted to continue:

> My suggestion for this summer's work would be the following: I should go as soon as possible to Alert Bay on the northern part of Vancouver Island in order to settle a number of doubtful points on the sociology of the tribes of that region, but principally to obtain translations of a number of songs of members of the secret societies which, as I think now, will shed a new light on this important problem. Then I shall proceed to Bella Bella and devote my attention to the little known tribes of that district. I choose them because I feel convinced that we shall find here important information on the history and development of the social organization of these people and particularly regarding certain religious ideas and the original concept of totemism. I should visit the settlements of Chinaman Hat, Bella Bella, Talung, Rivers Inlet, and if I could possibly arrange so, of Gardner Inlet. I also hope to ascertain some facts regarding the conventionalism of art which I consider of importance (Boas: 7/6/89).

He also suggested that he and his family move to Victoria for a year or two to facilitate his research. "Such an arrangement," he wrote to Hale, "would make the work less expensive and more successful, as — while preparing my reports — I should constantly be able to fill up any lacunae or to ascertain doubtful points to continue my researches" (Boas: 7/6/89).[6]

Boas had been chafing under Hale's limiting directives for a long time. Shortly after proposing his alternative plan for research Boas received a chastising letter from Hale:

> *I must earnestly enjoin you to follow implicitly the instructions you receive from me. If you had done it last year — if you had kept the linguistic portion of your work strictly within the limits prescribed, and had made your ethnographic map to conform to my Oregon map (as I requested) — you would have saved yourself and me a great deal of trouble, and would have produced a more satisfactory report.*
>
> *I cannot understand why you should persist in causing me an immense amount of useless trouble, as well as much annoyance, by objecting to my instructions, which you are expressly engaged to carry out. Kindly go on hereafter, with your usual energy and ability, in the course which, after much experience and careful consideration I have marked out for you* (Hale: 7/13/89).

Boas was angered by this and other such letters, and he wrote to his wife from Victoria describing his feelings about Hale's instructions:

> *Yesterday I had another letter from Hale and I pondered a long time after reading it, as to what I should do. I have written him and Dawson and Tylor, but tore up the letters again because I thought it would not be the right thing to do to write them while I am here. Also, I do not like to complain about him behind his back because this would look so much like an intrigue. So I have resolved just not to answer his letters except in the case that he wants some information on something. When I come back I shall make excerpts from Hale's most saucy letters and send them to Tylor, explaining to him that I cannot go on working with Hale. If a new offer comes*

*from him, I'll write him the same and hope that Tylor will back me up. The old man is simply so forgetful that he forgets from letter to letter what he has said before and then accuses me of having not followed his instructions. I might also send my grievances to Wilson and Dawson and ask them to decide. Besides, his special instructions are very childish and show clearly that he knows nothing about general ethnology. I am not even angry any more about these things. Since I have agreed to work here I'll carry out my agreement. I'll see how this can be done despite his pestering me. It is clear that the only logical way out would be to write that I can't go on this way. This, however, would destroy the whole matter which has just started to work out. And yet I tell myself again and again that I am taking too much of a beating. Hale's vanity, pedantry and sensitivity are at the bottom of everything and, because I realize this, I do not want people to think that my difficulties are due to the same traits. I don't see any other decent way out than to let the people in question decide whether I have followed my instructions or not* (Boas: 7/23/89).

A few days later he wrote again to his wife who was visiting relatives in Germany:

*An especially unlucky star seems to hover over this trip. Yesterday the steamer on which I was to sail even went aground, but fortunately it was freed after 24 hours. But it probably won't leave here [Victoria] before Tuesday. I really have absolutely nothing to do here anymore. I have completely pumped all information out of my [Indian] lady and cannot do anything more with her. You cannot imagine how angry I am with Hale's instructions. Apparently he is not familiar with the existing literature of the coastal tribes, otherwise he would not state that the tribes of the west coast are the least known. The opposite is the fact. The outcome of this trip will be very meager, I am afraid, just because I have to follow useless instructions* (Boas: 7/28/89).

Boas remained in the Victoria region until late August of 1889. He went to Alert Bay for a week and finally traveled into the interior of the province. His first few days in Alert Bay were very profitable. He wrote to his wife:

*I am very happy now because I achieved good results in the past days, in my opinion. I made the interesting discovery that Nutka [Nootka] and Kwakiutl [Kwakwala] belong together. This is even clearer than the connection between Haida and Tlingit. Through a quite extraordinarily lucky coincidence, members of the very many tribes have come together here, and during these two days I got quite a lot of material* (Boas: ca.8/27/89).

His work in the interior of the province was not so successful as that in Alert Bay. Just before he left the Northwest Coast he wrote to his wife again: "The closer I get to the time to get home the more impatient I get and the harder the work — which is not very satisfactory here anyhow — becomes. Yet I am working ten hours a day and hope that this year's report will please old Hale. The last two weeks were not very fruitful and to my great distress a Lillooet [Interior Salish] Indian who had promised me the evenings has gone again and I wanted to learn something about their language" (Boas: 9/14/89).

After Boas returned from the field in 1889 he received a letter from E. B. Tylor expressing general approval of Boas' suggestion to work on one or two tribes thoroughly rather than on five or six superficially. His work during 1889 focused primarily on the Nootka, Coast Salish, and Kwakiutl, although he did go into the interior again for a brief period. The next two field trips during 1890 and 1891 emphasized linguistic research on Salish and Chinook in Oregon and Washington.

The Bureau of American Ethnology financed Boas' 1890 field trip. He was given $1,100 of which $450 ($150 per month) was for salary and $650 was set aside for traveling expenses and for the payment of informants. Hale's instructions for field work during this season were considerably limbered:

*As regards instructions, I need only say that the object of your present trip, so far as the work of our Committee is concerned, is to fill up, as far as practicable, some of the Lacunae which was unavoidably left in your former investigations. You of course, are the proper judge of what proceedings will be best for this purpose. I will not hamper you with any specific instructions. You will consider yourself entirely at liberty to act in your own judgment* (Hale: 5/21/90).

In 1890 Boas first went to Portland, Oregon, and then he went to Siletz on the Pacific coast where he worked with Chinook and Tillamook (Coast Salish dialect) speaking informants on linguistic and ethnological problems. He had difficulty with the Chinook spoken there. He also took bodily measurements of ninety-eight children. Even though he was able to collect a considerable amount of material he assessed his days in Siletz as being disagreeable. From there he traveled to Grande Ronde but he was disappointed because no Chinook speaker lived on the reservation. He did, however, learn of the existence of a language which had been unknown to him, and he made measurements of seventeen more Indians.

Boas returned to Portland on July 4, and then moved to Seaside where he stayed in the combination post office and boarding house which was three quarters of a mile from the Indian village. Initially he was disappointed because the only good Chinook speaker was an old woman who knew no English. But on the whole his stay in Seaside was agreeable and successful, and he collected a sizeable vocabulary. He continued his work across the Columbia River in Ilwaco, Washington, and then he went to Bay Center where he found an excellent informant and learned more about the Chinook language in one day than he had during the entire trip. He also collected tales. Before leaving Bay Center, he began work on another language — Chehalis — which he found very difficult. By this time he had completed one hundred thirty anthropometric measurements.

Boas' interest in historical reconstruction becomes clear during this trip when he recorded in his diary:

> Today I found an important legend which has its origin on
> Lake Superior or thereabouts. Here on the coast it is only

known in Bella Coola and here. It throws a peculiar light
on the way legends get around. Then I got a very interesting
version of a visit in heaven [?], a migratory legend which
is known all over America. I can find relatively little about
old customs. From everything I hear it appears that California culture has spread as far as the Columbia [River],
that east of the Columbia . . . [?] came while north of
here a group of tribes is living with whom I have had my
dealings up to now. My measurements make it clear to me
that here on the Columbia a migration from the east took
place (Boas: 7/16/90).

Boas experienced one of his least pleasant weeks on the coast
when he left Bay Center. He went from Portland to the Puyallup
Reservation near Tacoma and then to Port Townsend where
he wanted to work with some Indians, but he was not able to
find them. From there he went to Victoria where he expected
to catch a steamer going north but discovered that it had left
two days earlier. No other steamer was scheduled to go north
for two weeks. He searched for some Indians in Victoria with
whom he could work but he had little success because most of
them were out fishing. He found some inebriated Indians but
he could not get anything from them although he was able to
make five sets of measurements. He finally gave up and went
to New Westminster but most of the Indians there were working in the fish canneries. "I have never spent such a ghastly week
as the last one," he wrote to his parents. "Everything I wanted
to do went wrong and I wasted the whole time" (Boas:
7/31/90).

His problems did not end when he walked to a mission school
about thirty miles up the Fraser River. The priest was cordial
and allowed Boas to make his measurements on the boys but
he was received very differently when he and the priest went
to the girls' school. "The head nun almost scratched out my
eyes," he reported to his wife, "and [she] yelled that it was
outrageous, and that it has never happened before that a man

wants to measure girls. 'How can science dare thus to deal with the work of god' she yelled at me, and we finally had to leave sadly" (Boas: 8/2/90). Boas, however, did spend a great deal of time in New Westminster measuring Indians and he was able to find at least one good informant with whom he could work on ethnological problems.

He continued with his measurements in Ladner's Landing where he was able to work more easily than he had in New Westminster. He was not satisfied, however, because he could work with the Indians only when they were not busy in the canneries. Futhermore, he was dissatisfied because he could do little more than make measurements. By the middle of August he had measured about 280 Indians. He was relieved when he met one of the Bella Coola Indians with whom he had worked in Berlin before coming to the coast for the first time. As a result of working with this man many things which had been unclear regarding the Bella Coola and their relationship with neighboring tribal groups now became clear. He also collected some useful drawings from his Bella Coola informant and he continued to work on linguistic questions.

Boas wrote the last letter of his 1890 field trip from Victoria on August 24. He indicated that he planned to go back to Washington for another four weeks before returning to New York. He particularly wanted to revisit Port Townsend and then go to Seattle and Tacoma, but he does not say what he planned to do there.

Little specific information is available regarding Boas' field trip in 1891, except that he collected Chinook texts. The texture of his field work changed substantially, however, in 1894. Although he continued to work under the direction of the BAAS he was also given support by the American Museum of Natural History and the United States National Museum. He was apparently allotted $1,900 for his research, but after arriving in the field he wrote to George M. Dawson, one of the members of the BAAS committee, requesting an additional $200 so that he could remain there for an extra month during the winter (Boas: 9/21/94). Hale responded that only $100 could be made available. Thus Boas presumably had $2,000 at his disposal — including his salary and expenses.

Prior to leaving for British Columbia Boas received instructions from Dawson:

> We feel inclined naturally to leave the general character of the work largely to your own discretion. As a good deal of space has already been given to linguistic matter and as Mr. Hale thinks we now have a good basis in this respect for philologic comparisons, the investigations of this summer might profitably be directed chiefly to customs, etc., with perhaps such folk-tales as may appear to be important as historical traditions, and whatever you may consider to be necessary to complete the general anthropometric data for comparative purposes (Dawson: 5/28/94).

Boas arrived in Glacier, British Columbia — near the Alberta border — on September 10, 1894. He did not look forward to this field trip and he wrote about these feelings to his wife: "Oh, it is so repulsive to me that I have to start work now, or rather to have to start coaxing the Indians. I don't even want to think of it" (Boas: 9/12/94). The following day he began measuring Indians in Enderby and in Okanagan. Three days later he wrote a disgruntled letter to his wife expressing his views on anthropometric measurements:

> My Okanagan trip was a great failure. During the two days I stayed there I measured only five Indians and simply could not get any more without staying much longer. I came to the conclusion that my time is much too valuable to spend it with fruitless attempts to measure Indians. There are younger people who can do this. After this trip I shall never do it again. All this measuring, or rather the talk connected with it to get the Indians, is really repulsive (Boas: 9/16/94).

He continued his letter with documentation of his dissatisfaction:

*Friday [September 14] I went with an Indian to Lake Okanagan in the pouring rain to measure Indians. Unfortunately he took me to the chief first instead of letting me go from house to house. First we had to parley a lot and then the chief told me to wait, that he is going to talk it over in the evening. From the way he acted I saw right away that the good chief was afraid and that I wouldn't get what I wanted. When all the Indians had scattered in all directions in the evening I left and arrived in Enderby late in the evening and very angry. I was so cold that I could not move my fingers. The chief told me that he was the descendant of many great chiefs and that the Indians wanted to make him chief when his father died but that he did not want to be chief because he wanted to be humble. In all things he would have to ask the advice of the old people who helped him and this he had to do in my case too. And they all live within a radius of about ten miles. Well, there was nothing I could do about it. He then also told me as an example of his humbleness that the government once gave saddles, bridles and tools for farming to all the Indians but that he had not accepted them because he only wanted to have things which he had earned on his own property with his own hands with the help of the dear god. It is really interesting to find out how these people think but this does not help my work. Yesterday I got five people in Enderby. I met a missionary there who had come from the Lake. I greeted him politely and he asked me what I was doing and I explained everything to him as well as I could. He answered very politely (he is French), "That seems very foolish. What do you want to do such nonsense for?" And the Indians ask him for advice which he does not keep from them. And that is the reason for my lack of success in Enderby! I'll be glad when I am back on the coast again* (Boas: 9/16/94)!

After he arrived in Kamloops, however, he felt much better because he was able to measure twenty-five Indian children in the nearby mission school. Four days later he wrote, "The disagreeable feeling I had that I don't get along with the Indians is slowly wearing off now, and I am hopeful that I'll have good results" (Boas: 9/21/94).

Boas left Kamloops on September 18 and stopped in Spences

Bridge on his way to North Bend, Mission City, and Vancouver. He met James A. Teit—"A redheaded Scotsman who is married to an Indian woman" (Boas: 9/21/94)—near Spences Bridge. Teit later became one of Boas' principal informants for many years. On this occasion he simply employed Teit for two days to assist with the measurements, but Teit also agreed to write a description of the tribes along the Thompson River which Boas intended to incorporate in his own report.

Boas continued his measurements in North Bend and Mission City. He became increasingly satisfied with the results of his work. "I found some very interesting points working out here which confirmed my former observations on the populations of these parts of the country," he wrote to his wife. "I am slowly getting into the mood for 'field work' again. I don't get worried and just do what I can. If there is no work to be found I don't mind and take it easy. You'll see how fat and healthy I'll return. Yet I would rather be with you now" (Boas: 9/23/94)! Two days later he reported, "Yesterday and this morning I really worked hard. I wish I could cover as much as this every day. The results of my measurements confirm very nicely my previous findings which were somewhat doubtful at the time. However, I need some more material to be really satisfied" (Boas: 9/25/94). By this time he had made one hundred fifty-eight measurements, but he had done nothing else.

Boas changed his tactics in Victoria. He had been searching for a job during a large part of the year and he saw the possibility of being offered a position in the American Museum of Natural History. Consequently he began making plaster casts of Indian faces to send to the museum. He hoped these casts and the photographs he was taking of the Indians would lead to a position in the museum.

Boas did not have any success finding cooperative Indians the first few days in Victoria but then he hired a photographer and went to the Victoria prison where he made a cast of and photographed a Kwakiutl Indian from Alert Bay. Later he found one of the Indian women who had been in Chicago the preceding year during the World Columbia Exposition. After a great deal of talk he allayed her fears and she allowed him to measure her and make an impression of her face. Later she helped him find several other Indians who were willing to have casts made and measurements taken.

He boarded the *Barbara Boskowitz* for Kincolith (Nass River) on October 3. One Haida, two Tsimshian and several Kwakiutl, from whom he hoped to collect folktales, were also on the schooner. He was disappointed when he found that he knew the Kwakiutl songs and tales better than the Kwakiutl, although he made a few unimportant corrections and additions to his old material. Even though he had a great deal of free time during this voyage — as he had been having throughout the entire field trip — he did devote some profitable time to collecting Kwakwala texts. The Kwakiutl left the ship near the northern end of Vancouver Island so Boas worked with the Haida Indian during the remainder of the voyage.

He began work immediately after his arrival in Kincolith on October 10 — even though most of the Tsetsaut (Athapascan) Indians with whom he wanted to work were hunting about thirty miles away. He collected a small vocabulary from one of the remaining Indians and discovered that this tribe (which is now extinct) was Tinneh (Athapascan), as he had suspected. "They are really Tinneh who have reached the ocean here," Boas reported to his wife. "They are not even so isolated from the other Tinneh. Thus I could examine the question with greater ease since the most important part [of the question regarding the identification of this tribe] was settled and the tribe was really not as isolated as would have been possible" (Boas: 10/11/94).

Boas sent one of the Tsetsaut Indians to bring back an old and knowledgeable Tsetsaut informant. In the meantime he employed a fifteen year old boy to help him, but the latter did not speak Tsetsaut very well. Later Boas recorded in a letter to his wife, "My informant was very unsatisfactory for the first two days until I gave him a piece of my mind. Today he was all right. He was not punctual enough for my taste. This is, in general, the fault of the Indians. I am always very strict with them when I pay them" (Boas: 10/13/94). Boas remained dissatisfied with the youth for several days and was tempted to dismiss him but the boy quit first. Prior to this Boas collected some useful information on topics such as the territorial distribution of the Tsetsaut but was not able to acquire much of the linguistic data that he really wanted. Boas then found another man who spoke little English but who had more perseverance and energy than the boy. He collected language material from him, including texts, had some folktales interpreted and gathered limited ethnographic data.

Boas worked a great deal on the Nass (Niska) dialect of the Tsimshian while he was waiting for his elderly Tsetsaut informant to appear. He collected vocabularies, worked on the grammar and recorded texts which were later translated for him. He also made more measurements. Within four days after his arrival in Kincolith he had measured sixty-five Indians; he hoped to get the remaining fifteen men within the next few days. He was forced to curtail his measuring activities within a short time, however, because he was running out of paper.

His elderly Tsetsaut informant, Levi, disappointed Boas when the former finally appeared two weeks after Boas landed in the village. "The man talks so terribly fast that I cannot get any decent material out of him," Boas lamented to his wife. "He might learn to speak more slowly if I insist on it but I doubt it. I have to try my best though. I worked the whole afternoon to get the old habitat of the tribe and its relationship to the neighboring tribes. I am clear about it now. It is a very slow process with him, though. I also got two legends and some linguistic material — vocabulary only. It is clear to me that I have to make whole sentences to get anything out of him. I cannot ask him about grammatical forms as such. That makes the work much harder" (Boas: 10/25/94). Four days later Boas wrote again:

> My Tsetsaut is quite exasperating. I get some words, legends, as well as a few interesting notes on customs, but the language! The following example will explain my difficulties to you. I ask him through my interpreter, "How do you say in Tsetsaut: If you don't come, the bear will run away?" I could not get him to translate this. He would only say, "The Nass [Tsimshian] could be asked a thing like this; we Tsetsaut are always there when a bear is to be killed. That's why we can't say a thing like this." I also asked him, "What is the name of the cave of the porcupine?" His answer was only, "A white man could not find it anyway and therefore I don't have to tell you." Thus it is all the time, and you can imagine how slowly I progress. Tomorrow I want to try another method. I cannot let him speak Tsetsaut because he speaks much too fast. Therefore, I want to try to tell him his stories back and let him translate them for me sentence by sentence. I don't know if this will work out (Boas: 10/29/94).

Boas also had other problems in Kincolith. A few of the villagers suspected that he was a spy for the government and that he wanted to take their land away from them. Some of them thought he was making a great deal of money from the material he was collecting. Consequently they wanted more money for performing different services for him, including giving him lodging. Boas had been a guest of Mr. Collinson, the missionary at Kincolith, his first day in the village but Mrs. Collinson did not want the added burden of another member of her household. As a result Boas selected the neatest Indian house in the community in which to take up quarters. After two weeks Boas' hostess demanded more money or Boas must move.

*I flatly refused* [he told his wife] *since $1.25 is more than enough. I did not see her personally. In the afternoon she told me herself through the interpreter that I could leave the same evening and look for other quarters. I told her that I paid her more than I would pay a hotel and explained to her how much money she would lose if she would not keep me. I also told her that Mr. Collinson wanted me to stay. So she finally gave in. Events like this do not contribute, however, to my comfort. There is no other place here though where I could stay. I cannot go to Collinson who did not want me at the outset and besides his wife does not have any help now* (Boas: 10/27/94).

By October 31 — ten days before he left Kincolith — Boas had written 170 pages on Niska language and customs, fifty-five pages on Tsetsaut customs, vocabulary and grammar, and seventy pages on the Kwakiutl. At the end of a few more days he had completed an additional ninety-seven pages of Tsetsaut texts. The Tsetsaut language was unusually difficult for him, but he had translated all but about nine pages of these texts by the time he left the Nass River region. He does not give any indication from whom he collected his Kwakiutl data.

Whereas earlier the people had resisted being measured by the stranger Boas, they permitted him to do so after he became known. One old man agreed to be measured only after Boas promised to let him tell a story for twenty-five cents an hour, the wage Boas paid his informants during this trip. By the time he left Kincolith he had collected over 234 sets of measurements.

Boas also collected a few artifacts for his museum collection. He paid a Tsetsaut Indian to make him a marmot trap, he had a model of a Tsimshian house built, and he purchased a head-piece for ten dollars. The price of the latter was high, but Boas felt it was worth the money because he was able to elicit the tale which was associated with the head-piece.

Boas became increasingly concerned when the schooner did

not appear on its return voyage as scheduled. He had expected it to anchor near Kincolith around October 26, but when it had not come in by November 7 he wrote to his wife, "No boat yet! If it doesn't come by tomorrow we have reason to believe that something happened to it. Darling, I am so anxious to get some letters, and I am so sorry that you have not heard from me for such a long time. If I did not have to go to Fort Rupert because of my income for next year I would give up the trip there. It is really too bad" (Boas: 11/7/94). In the meantime his funds were running very low. The boat arrived two days later, however, and Boas boarded the *Boskowitz* for Fort Rupert.

One of the most notable features of this field trip was the time Boas spent in Fort Rupert observing and describing the winter ceremonial. He lived with George Hunt and his family in a one room house for the first two days in Fort Rupert, but then he began sleeping in another of Hunt's nearby houses. The morning after his arrival Boas and Hunt discussed Boas' plans for field work in Fort Rupert. That afternoon Boas invited all the Indians in the village to a feast which consisted of hard tack and molasses. He described the feast in a letter:

> *There were about 250 Indians in the house — men, women and children. They were painted red and black and wore jewelry. Each was dressed in his cedarbark cloak. First the lower tribal units came, and when they were all here, the members of the secret societies arrived. When they arrived everything was dead silent. Their place is behind the fire in the back of the room. Welcoming speeches were held for me and I was given the name of Heiltsakuls "the silent one" [literally, "the nonspeaking one"].[7] Then the master of ceremonies called the singers and told them what to sing. Every tribe — there were three tribes present — was served. In the meantime I made my speech. I said that I wanted to come for a long time and that I was glad to be here now. Then I spoke to the people who had been in Chicago [at the World Columbian Exposition in 1893] and gave them their pictures. Then they started to eat. While everybody was eating one society after the other called, "the whales are eating*

*now, that is good"; "the . . . [?] are eating now, ku, ku, ku."*
*These are the names of the societies. Then one of the Kwakiutl said*
*that a long time ago he had loaned some blankets to another man*
*and that if he did not get paid he would have to "put down a mat*
*[?]." That means that the mat would not be taken away until the*
*blankets were lying on it. Then the Koskimo brought blankets and*
*gave them away with appropriate speeches, telling the Kwakiutl*
*that they were nice people and open handed, etc. At the end I got*
*a silver dollar from him and also had to make a speech. Of course,*
*I have to give him two before I leave. The whole thing lasted four*
*hours and cost me $14.50. Of course, I gained the good will of these*
*people and got invitations to all feasts which are taking place here*
(Boas: 11/16/94).

Boas later published a partial account of the feast:

> Before the biscuits were distributed I had to make the formal
> speech depreciating my small feast and asking my guests to
> be happy and to eat to their hearts' desire. In return I was
> told that no feast like mine had ever been given and that I
> was a great chief. The figurative speech of the Kwakiutl
> Indians has it about like this: "You are the loaded canoe that
> has anchored in front of a mountain from which wealth is
> rolling down upon all the people of the whole world; you
> are the pillar supporting our world." And all this for a treat
> of hard tact and molasses. But the gross flattery of this speech
> must not be taken too seriously, as it is simply a stereotype
> formula used for expressing the thanks for a feast (1896:233).

He also spent a substantial amount of time taking anthropometric measurements in Fort Rupert. He hoped to measure
one hundred Indians; within the first few days he had measured fifty-two adults with the aid of George Hunt, on whom he
relied heavily for assistance. He also spent a great deal of time
observing the winter ceremonial and then asking questions
about it. Furthermore, he recorded songs, hired a photographer
to take pictures, and collected a few artifacts. His days were so
full that he found little time for writing. He explained this to
his wife:

*I can't find the time now to write to the parents in Germany and probably will simply copy this letter during my trip home. I don't have the time either to describe to you my impressions of the strange surroundings and of the feast; all my free time is used for making extensive notes, i.e., I make short notes and go over them the next day with Hunt and have him explain everything to me* (Boas: 11/17/94).

*I do not work too much here because the whole day is taken by feasts and dances. My time, however, is well spent. I get quite a different impression of these feasts because I witness so much of which I had only heard before. I also hope to get a number of photographs this week. If I really get them I can write a nice article for an illustrated magazine. I would really like to do this because the topic is really attractive* (Boas: 11/18/94).

According to Boas' record, as well as the account of several of my own Kwakiutl informants, he dressed and behaved very much like the Indians themselves while he was living in Fort Rupert. He wrote, for example, "I go to the feasts in a blanket and headring and am on very friendly terms with the people. I am much better off here than in Alert Bay because there are no white people here" (Boas: 11/18/94). One of my informants states that Boas also went barefoot on many occasions.

RESEARCH FOR THE JESUP EXPEDITION (1897–1900)

In 1897 Morris K. Jesup, President of the Board of Trustees of the American Museum of Natural History, organized an expedition at his own expense to study the tribes of the North Pacific Coast. The expedition was created at Boas' suggestion and Boas was placed in charge of the research. He described the purpose of the project as follows:

It seemed to me well to make the leading point of view of my discussion, on the one hand an investigation of the historical relations of the tribes to their neighbors, on the other hand a presentation of the culture as it appears to the Indian himself. For this reason I have spared no trouble to collect the

descriptions of customs and beliefs in the language of the
Indians, because in these the points that seem important to
him are emphasized, and the almost unavoidable distortion
contained in the description given by the casual visitor and
student is eliminated (Boas 1909:309).

Work undertaken by the expedition lasted for five years from
1897 through 1901, but Boas made only two field trips during
this time — in 1897 and 1900. George Hunt was a major con-
tributor under Boas' direction throughout the project. Boas
hired Hunt for $75 a month plus expenses during the 1897
expedition. The latter worked independently collecting museum
specimens and ethnographic material in Kwakwala throughout
most of the 1897 field season.

Boas made his first sweeping tour of the north central interior
of British Columbia in 1897. He began his investigations in
Spences Bridge and then went up the Fraser River to Lillooet;
he proceeded further north along the Chilcotin River to Tatla
Lake and then west across the mountains to Bella Coola. From
there he went along the coast to Port Essington and then back
to Bella Bella.[8] The major purpose of this trip was to measure
the physical characteristics of previously unstudied tribes of the
interior and to study their customs. He also did a substantial
amount of work in these terms along the coast. He devoted
very little time to the study of the language.

He spent most of his time among the Kwakiutl in Alert Bay
when he returned to the Northwest Coast in 1900. Here he
worked on Kwakwala grammar with an informant in the morn-
ings; he worked on ethnological problems during most afternoons, and in the evenings he labored with George Hunt
revising the 682 pages of texts which had been collected on previous trips. He commonly spent almost twelve hours a day in
these activities. He described a typical day in a letter to his wife:

*I get up at 6* AM. *Breakfast is at 6:30; at 7 my interpreter comes
with whom I work till noon. Then I eat lunch and at 1* PM *he*

*comes again. Then work is resumed till 6. Then there is dinner. Then another Indian comes who at present explains paintings to me. We work until 9 and then I am tired and do not want to write any more. Life is very uniform this way but I am so glad that I am getting good results. Up to now I can be very satisfied. I am slowly starting to understand the grammar of the language which is terribly complicated. The painter, with whom I am working evenings, is very good and his teaching helps me a great deal in the understanding of the art of these tribes. For the time being I see George Hunt only evenings and Sundays* (Boas: 7/8/00).

Boas stayed with a white man who owned the canneries in Alert Bay and who was married to one of George Hunt's sisters. "Since I've known all of them for years," he wrote to his mother, "I am very well taken care of" (Boas: 7/8/00). He was happy with his work in Alert Bay and continued in his letter, "It is a rare pleasure for me to be able to work absolutely without disturbances. In New York I have so many administrative duties that often I cannot really think of work. I often try to arrange my work differently but without success. The Museum and the students take most of my time" (Boas: 7/9/00). This theme was repeated throughout his period of research in 1900. On another occasion he wrote, "I am really feeling happy because I can look forward to working without being disturbed by all sorts of other things. All in all I haven't felt as well and strong as now for a long, long time" (Boas: 7/10/00).

The analysis of Kwakwala gave him a great deal of trouble. He wrote about this to his wife: "The language is terribly hard and complicated. The Chinook and Tsimshian are easy in comparison" (Boas: 7/10/00). A few days later he wrote: "The Kwakiutl [Kwakwala] is much harder than I thought. It is the first Indian language with which I have worked which has irregular verbs, etc., which are terribly difficult to handle" (Boas: 7/14/00). Despite these problems, however, language study progressed well for him during this season.

He spent many afternoons recording tales told by elderly

informants. He also occupied a considerable amount of time by collecting Indian paintings and having them explained. Later he began collecting food and medicinal plants used by the Kwakiutl. He interviewed women about their techniques of collecting, preparing, and using these plants, but he was unable to devote the time necessary to give the task systematic and exhaustive treatment.

Boas was disappointed during this phase of the field trip because he was not able to utilize the services of George Hunt, except on evenings and Sundays. Hunt worked in the canneries and did not have the free time that Boas wanted. Also, his language interpreter was becoming bored, and Boas wrote: "I hope that I can start with my ethnographic work on Monday. It's time now because my interpreter is losing his pleasure in his monotonous work" (Boas: 8/1/00). Boas wanted to work with Hunt on ethnographic material, but Hunt did not have the available time until the end of Boas' trip. Boas reconciled himself to the fact that Hunt would have to work independently, and he wrote to his wife:

> I hope that George Hunt will be able to do many things which still have to be done, all by himself. I revised much of what he had done and can see that he does everything properly and that he does not pull my leg. I find him quite dependable, more than I thought (Boas: 8/16/00).

Boas always had difficulty leaving his family for a long period of time, and he missed not regularly receiving mail from them because of the inconsistent delivery along the coast. By the end of August in 1900 he was impatient to return to New York and he wrote:

> My work is very monotonous, interrupted by nothing. I have been away from N.Y. now for 10 weeks and am counting the days to my return. I really miss the children. My first weeks were so interesting that I was completely absorbed by my work. But the more I learn the less daily progress I seem to make. In the evenings now

*I always have the interpreter with whom I work on the language
and who instructs me during the day on the customs and manners
of the Indians* (Boas: 8/23/00).

Boas concluded his field work in 1900 by casting Indian faces
in plaster of Paris, "And [he] was annoyed because it was so
hard to persuade the guys to let themselves be cast" (Boas:
9/7/00). In the same letter Boas wrote, "Now I can't wait for
the steamer to take me to Victoria. I am so glad to get away
from here. My work is finished; the trunk is packed so that I
can take the steamer as soon as it comes — when it finally does
come" (Boas: 9/9/00)!

INDEPENDENT RESEARCH (1914–1931)

Boas did not return to the Northwest Coast for fourteen years,
although he worked continually with Hunt by mail during the
intervening time.[9] He made five field trips from 1914 to 1931.
Little specific information is available regarding the financial
sources of support for his field research after 1900; apparently
Elsie Clews Parsons financed some of Boas' field work, as she
did for many of Boas' students. Boas became increasingly active
in fund raising as he became eminently established in anthropology. Presumably he was able to use some of this money to
support Hunt's long term research as well as his own.

Boas worked for less than one month on the Northwest Coast
in 1914.[10] He spent most of this time collecting texts among the
Kootenay in the interior. Boas had difficulty finding a suitable
interpreter there because most of the men were haying.

Another eight years lapsed before he again returned to British
Columbia in 1922 at the age of sixty-four. This was the only
time that his wife accompanied him to the field. They remained
there for less than one month while Boas worked on linguistic
problems among the Interior Salish.[11]

Boas returned to the coast alone in 1923. He employed most
of this time among the Bella Bella clearing up many doubtful

points of ethnology and linguistics. He hired George Hunt to work as his assistant for $90 a month. Hunt was invaluable to Boas during this trip because the former knew the Bella Bella and was able to convince many of them that they should give Boas most of the information he wanted. Throughout the Northwest Coast, Indians were reluctant to reveal family histories, tales of origin, songs, or other items of personal property which did not belong to them. Boas wrote about this to his wife: "Here it is the same as everywhere on the coast: everybody is afraid to tell something that does not belong to his family. That makes my work so hard" (Boas: 1/20/23).

Boas found the linguistic work relatively easy because of the close relationship between the Kwakwala spoken in Fort Rupert and the dialectic variant spoken by the Bella Bella. Because of these dialectic differences, however, Hunt was able to achieve only a partial understanding of the language. A Bella Bella man who lived for a number of years in Fort Rupert contributed substantially to the collection of Bella Bella tales.

Boas worked for more than fifteen hours a day recording tales, gathering ethnological data, working on the language and, in the evenings, correcting Kwakiutl materials with Hunt. He complained in several letters that he was working so hard that his hands were cramped but that he was making very good progress. He wrote to his wife, for example, "I feel like a spider in a web to which everything is flying. I tell Hunt what I want and he brings the people to me" (Boas: 11/23/23). Later he wrote, "My work progresses well but it is almost too much. Since I know the problems here so well, the material is in good order and can almost be used as I take it down. I only have to file it in the right place. The result is quite satisfactory" (Boas: 11/28/23).

Despite the fine progress he was making, Boas was dismayed by the Indians' loss of knowledge of indigenous customs and language. He wrote about this to his secretary, Ruth Bunzel:

"The work has been going on satisfactorily, only too much has been forgotten, and the old people who do remember begin to ramble along so incoherently that I do not get much out of them" (Boas: 12/5/23). Earlier he had written that "Everything is so thoroughly lost that it is very hard to find out anything reasonable. The young people have even lost much of their language — not as much of the grammar as of the vocabulary. I speak Chinook with all the people except my main language teacher" (Boas: 12/3/23).

Boas also collected folklore material from the Bella Bella. But after his return to New York he complained to Edward Sapir, "What is more peculiar is that the folk-lore of the Bella Bella is in a state of great decay. Everywhere informants were ready to tell me Tsimshian and Haida stories, also Rivers Inlet stories, but whatever I got of their own stories were very fragmentary" (Boas 12/31/23).

Furthermore Boas was concerned with problems of Kwakiutl social organization. He did not clearly understand many aspects of the winter ceremonial, *numimots* (Kwakiutl ambilateral descent groups),[12] and rank stratification, especially who the "Eagles" were. These were among the problems on which he and Hunt worked during this field trip. Over-all, Boas was satisfied with this trip, although he was happy when it ended, and he wrote to Edward Sapir:

*I just came back from British Columbia and arrived here* [in New York] *on Christmas Eve. I am very glad I made the trip because linguistically as well as ethnologically a great many doubtful points have been cleared up. The great confusion in the Fort Rupert winter ceremonial is due to the fact that they took in all the family ceremonials of the north into the winter ceremonial. The organization of the Bella Bella is quite complex, but on the whole consistent in its principles. The idea of rank is, if anything, more strongly developed there than farther south. The peculiar Eagle among the Fort Ruperts has also been cleared up through a study of the conditions among the Bella Bella. The Eagles evidently correspond to the head chiefs, of which there are two in each tribe* (Boas: 12/31/23).

Later however, he wrote to Hunt encouraging him to write more about the Eagles: "We ought to know who the Eagles are now and from whom they inherited their places, and also what Eagles exist among other tribes and why they claim that rank" (Boas: 1/11/24).

Boas was concerned almost exclusively with linguistic problems in 1927. "But," he wrote to his friend Waldemar Bogoras, a Russian anthropologist, "I had a number of young students there who did ethnological work at the same time" (Boas: 10/31/27). One of Boas' students in Washington at that time was Melville Jacobs, who reports:

> I was with him for many weeks at Oakville here in Western Washington in the summer of 1927. I can report that the Washington State Salish-speaking Indians who worked with him at Oakville in 1927 told me that they felt that he was a very fine gentleman — he was then 69 and in excellent health. It was my feeling that they liked very much his dedication, personal dignity, honesty, and interest in their language (Jacobs: 4/22/65).

Boas had earlier collected linguistic information from the Coast Salish but he did not want to publish his material without adding to it. Consequently he also made arrangements to work with some informants (apparently Saanich) around Victoria where he arranged to meet George Hunt for a few days.

Boas' last field trip to the Northwest Coast was in the winter of 1930–31. He was accompanied by a young Russian anthropologist, Julia Averkieva, a student at Barnard College. They spent three months in Fort Rupert and a week in Alert Bay among the Kwakiutl. Boas anticipated his field work among the Kwakiutl with pleasure. Upon his arrival in Vancouver he wrote to Ruth Benedict, "I am really looking forward to the coming week. It will be the first serious field work I have done for a long, long time" (Boas: 10/21/30).

Boas was concerned with a range of problems throughout this trip. He collected Kwakwala texts and revised some of his old texts with the assistance of George Hunt. He also recorded "forms of expression of different people" — styles of story telling and oratory. Language studies, however, gave him considerable trouble because of the changes in Kwakwala resulting from contact with English. In this regard Hunt wrote to Boas before the latter arrived in the field:

> I Dont know weather you will find any one of these People to talk the old fasheon language for the Most of them one word for every thing instade of useing the Defferent word for the Defferent way of answer. one thing I know that [they] last [lost] about two third of their language. for there lots of the Indians comes and ask me the meaning of the words. this is the Reason I say thes language is Disappearing (Hunt: 3/15/30).

After he had been in the field for about three weeks, Boas wrote to Benedict, "I talk with difficulty and understand after I write it. I follow conversation only partly. It goes too rapidly, but I am getting into it again" (Boas: 11/9/30).

Boas also recorded the different song styles and rhythms of the Kwakiutl on phonograph cylinders. He wrote to one of his sisters in Germany, "All in all I now have 145 which, as far as I can tell, include all existing styles of music and poetry — feast songs, boasting [Renommierlieder] songs, games, love songs, dance songs, religious songs, etc" (Boas: 12/25/30). Furthermore he made movies of dances and collected social organization material. He was generally concerned with many problems of acculturation.

Julia Averkieva worked on a different set of problems from Boas. She was interested in economic life and worked especially with the women, learning matting and basket-making techniques as well as blanket work and box making. She also learned several Kwakiutl dances and collected life history material from the women — especially about their marriages. She focused most heavily, however, on Kwakiutl string games (cats' cradles).

Boas enjoyed her company and wrote several times to his colleagues and relatives commenting on this. "We all like her very much," he wrote to Bogoras in Russia. "She has done very good work with me in Fort Rupert" (Boas: 4/24/31). She was a good companion for Boas who was grieving because of the accidental death of his wife the previous year. His bereavement is clearly apparent in a letter he wrote to his children in New York:

> *A year ago today I went to Chicago not knowing what fate had in store for me. The viaduct over 125 street broke down on mother and you lost a dear mother and I cannot find myself since then. When my work is done, my thoughts concentrate always on the same thing. . . . And I'll find myself eventually, and do what has to be done but the real enjoyment of life is gone* (Boas: 12/14/30).

His letters indicate that one important function of this field trip was to help him overcome some of his sorrow.

Both Boas and Julia Averkieva attended, and often actively participated in dances and feasts (potlatches). Boas received his second Indian name in one of the potlatches which he described in a letter to a grandchild:

> *The Indians gave me a nice mask with ermine skins and a carved cane. Then I gave them some presents too. They gave me a funny name. I do not believe you can say it. I'll try to write it*
> Mullmumla-eelatre
> *that means "if you put water on him the southeast wind will blow." It is a big rock near by here and the Indians believe that if you sprinkle water on its southeast side the wind will begin to blow* (Boas: 11/18/30).

Boas also gave at least one feast while he and Averkieva were in Fort Rupert. He described this in a letter to a sister in Germany:

*I've had in mind to invite the Indians once more and after some debate I was asked to do it. Well, I had 55 guests. I served salmon with fish oil, tea and hard tack with jam and apple sauce. The Indians used the opportunity to celebrate Christmas, i.e., they had entertainment in their old style at which the men and the women in groups made fun of each other. The men sang first and then the chief gave a speech challenging the women to speak in turn. The speaker always holds one of the staffs in his hand and the challenge consists of throwing the staff, on the floor, to the person who is supposed to talk. At first the women did not want to participate but after some time they also became gay. They sang and a few danced to the songs. Then the groups gave each other presents. Then women entered with tea spoons tied to long sticks and they danced with them in their hands. Then after a speech every man, me included, received a . . . [?] spoon. Then the men, after more dancing and more speeches, gave the women fish angles and fish . . . [?]. Then the women came with dead pigeons [?] with which they executed a lively dance. Thus it went on from 5:30 until one A.M. (Boas: 12/25/30).*

As he had done in many preceding years, Boas actively involved himself in the attempt to correct some of the social conditions and injustices experienced by the Kwakiutl while he and Averkieva were in Fort Rupert. Sanitary conditions and communicable diseases transmitted through prostitution disturbed him. He was most distressed, however, because of the effects of the anti-potlatch law and the confiscation of coppers. He strenuously criticized the government in many of his letters for the manner in which they administered Indian affairs. In one letter, for example, he wrote, "The interference with the Indians on the part of the government is really scandalous. The way they administer the law with respect to the Indians, everyone who has a formal knowledge [of the winter ceremonial] would have to go to jail" (Boas: 10/27/30). The following month he complained to his son:

*I had a council with the Indians who are really suffering because of the stupid persecution of their customs by the government. I can do nothing about* [it], *but promised to do my best in Ottawa. I am not at* [all] *certain what I can do because the missionaries here are behind it all. It goes so far that the children in school are not allowed to draw in the style traditional of their people but according to prescribed models* (Boas: 11/18/30).

Boas wrote to the Lieutenant-Governor of British Columbia and later went to see him on behalf of the Indians.[13] His first letter to the Lieutenant-Governor concerned sanitary conditions in Alert Bay. He reported from hearsay that a dysentery epidemic caused by the fact that the drinking water became polluted as it flowed past the outhouses had been instrumental in the death of a number of Indians. Furthermore he charged that dying patients were being turned out of the hospital in Alert Bay.

Later when Boas and Averkieva went to Alert Bay to study the influence of English on Kwakwala, he and Halliday, the Agency superintendent, had an argument about Boas' report to the Lieutenant-Governor. Boas wrote about this to his children in New York: "I went right away to see the Indian Agent — to be polite, and right away we had a controversy about the fact that I notified Victoria of the dysentery epidemic against which nothing was done. In any case, I achieved this much that the water from the latrines does not run into the drinking water any more" (Boas: 1/5/31).

Boas also wrote to a number of other people about the social conditions of the Indians. He even considered seeing the Premier of British Columbia. On their trip back to New York, Boas stopped at the University of British Columbia and talked to several people about these problems. He also had a two-hour conference with the Lieutenant-Governor in Victoria. The Indians were gratified by Boas' efforts to help them. In this regard Hunt wrote to Boas:

*We was very proud to have you as our visitor when you was here, my wife mist you very much when you left us, and I am glad to see you have mentioned the potlatch and the coppers to the Governor, and that you are still following it up, and I will be very anxious to hear from you again regarding same* (Hunt: 2/15/31).

*So I read your letter to the Kwagul* [Kwakiutl] *People. and to the lawels !es* [Tlauitsis?] *tribe and they all told me to thank you for keeping your Promise to them* (Hunt: 3/10/31).

Boas explained these issues very nicely in a letter to the Lieutenant-Governor of British Columbia. Regarding the potlatch, he wrote:

> *I consider the whole potlatch law a mistake. It should be understood as its basis that the Indians who do not write require publicity in entering contracts and paying debts. According to their customs, publicity means that the tribes are invited to what is commonly called a feast at which a transaction is made.*
>
> *The Indians have developed an exceedingly intricate economic system. They borrow and take interest. The amount of interest seems high, but it is actually not so high because the repayment may be delayed for years without an increase in interest. The general method of entering into a contract is that the person who requires another person to make a certain payment for services, or whatever else it may be, will give to his prospective debtor a certain amount to bind the contract, and double the amount has to be repaid after fulfillment of the contract.*
>
> *The actual effect of the potlatch law is that those who evade the payment of their debts will be law abiding, while those who honestly try to fill their obligations are punished with imprisonment for doing so* (Boas: 3/5/31).

Regarding Indian marriage customs and the loss of coppers, Boas continued:

> *There is a general misunderstanding in regard to marriage. The former missionaries always claimed that the Indians purchased their wives. Nothing can be more erroneous than this assumption. Marriage, as among ourselves, is a contract and, as in other cases of contracts, the person who enters into the contract makes a payment in order to bind the contract, while the other party later on pays double or three times, in this case, the amount paid. So the father*

*of the young man makes the first payment at the time of the marriage. It is customary that immediately the father of the girl returns to the young couple two or three times the first payment to the young man's father. This is accompanied by the gift of privileges which are valued very highly by the Indians. During the whole time before this payment it is customary for the young wife to "visit the father's house," which means that she goes there and is given ample presents of provisions and property.*

*There is one particular point that has caused them a great deal of trouble. In some way the Indians of Alert Bay were induced to deliver their coppers (that is pieces of copper of a definite form which play somewhat the role of banknotes of high denomination among them) to the police. These coppers were transported to Ottawa and are, so far as I know, in the Museum of Geological Survey. The Indians claim that they were promised payment for these coppers inside of five years. Seven years have elapsed and they say that nothing has been done. The values of these coppers are very high, running up to $1500 or perhaps $2000. When they are bought the person who holds them will generally be in debt for part of the purchase price and if he dies this debt must be taken over by his son or whoever inherits the copper. Owing to this fact we find that at the present time considerable amount of monies are still being paid for non-existing coppers and there is a general confusion and resentment on account of these conditions* (Boas: 3/5/31).

Boas maintained a strong personal interest in the Kwakiutl until his death in 1942. George Hunt died September 9, 1933, and Boas wrote, "If it is necessary I should be very glad to pay a moderate amount to his widow monthly" (Boas: 9/18/33). The offer was not accepted, but he was invited to contribute to the purchase of a monument for Hunt.

Boas had begun working with another Kwakiutl informant, Dan Cranmer, during his field trip in 1931. After Hunt's death Boas utilized Cranmer's services even more extensively. When Boas died, Cranmer wrote a letter of condolence to Boas' daughter, Helene Boas Yampolsky.

*The sorrowful tidings of your deep affliction reached me today, and oh my dear Helene if only sympathy were like waves of light, how*

*the rays would pour from my heart to illumine the gloomy veil of*
*grief which wraps you in its sombre folds, but, oh, how powerless*
*indeed are love and friendship in the presence of frail mortals last*
*great mystery, to shed one little drop of consolation over the frag-*
*ments of a broken heart, which only time can mend, having suffered*
*the loss of my own Father, I know how to sympathize with you in*
*your affliction, we heard the sad news of your dear Father's death,*
*one of my friends heard it over the radio, and told me about it, and*
*I am glad to hear about your Father's death, because I am giving a*
*potlach this winter, and I have been to Fort Rupert, and according to*
*our Indian custom I mourn for my master, the Fort Rupert people*
[Kwakiutl] *sang some mourning songs, as you know he* [Boas] *was*
*well known amongst the kwag-ol* [Kwakiutl] *people* (Cranmer:
1/9/43).

George Hunt's daughter, Mrs. Tom Johnson, describes him as
follows:[14]

Well, Dr. Franz Boas was a very kind man. And he really
know — know to be amongst the Indian people. He goes
around to every house and see — visit them and talk about
things what he needs to know. All about the things of the
Indians. And he works very well. We like him very much
because he was very kind to us. That time when my brother
was — when he was — know his winter dance — he [Boas]
use to go and [stay] close by him, because he really wants
to know what to be done. [She is referring to Boas' 1894 field
work.] That's why he come for — to know everything belong to the Indians because they was lot of Indians when he
first came. The Koskimo, and the Nawiti, and the Nakoaktok. They used to come and stay around here. They used to
come — come to Fort Rupert to gather heres for dancing
every winter and Dr. Franz Boas used to be amongst them.
He used to use button blanket and some bark on his head
and he was *really* likes to be amongst Indian people. He was
very good to us (Mrs. Tom Johnson: 6/7/64).

CONCLUSION

Comments may now be made regarding some of the issues
raised in the introduction to this paper. Questions concerning

the number of times Boas went to the field and where he worked when he was there are answered in Tables 1 and 2 and in Figures I and II. Table 3 summarizes his major activities during each of the thirteen field trips he made to the Northwest Coast. It also includes a synopsis of his activities during the intervening periods when he was not working there.

TABLE 3

Boas' Major Activities During Each Field Trip to the Northwest Coast (With a Summary of Other Principal Activities)

| Field Trips | Major Activities |
|---|---|
| | (1883–84.    Field work among the Eskimo of Cumberland Sound, Baffinland.) |
| | (1885.    Assistant in the Museum of Ethnology in Berlin; docent at the University of Berlin.) |
| 1886 | General reconnaissance; collected artifacts for museum; studied folklore; "ethnogeography" (ethnographic map of Vancouver Island); language study; collected skulls. |
| | (1887.    Appointed to the staff of *Science*: married Marie A. E. Krackowizer.) |
| | (1888.    Appointed docent in anthropology at Clark University at $1,500 (?) a year.) |
| 1888 | Reconnaissance; description of customs and beliefs; partial listings of N.W. Coast tribes and languages; anthropometric measurements; collected skeletons; photographed prisoners. |
| 1889 | Worked especially with the Nootka, Salish, and Kwakiutl; collected almost complete list of "tribes, septs and gentes [*numimots*]" of Kwakiutl. |
| 1890 | Filled in omissions of previous trips, including enthnographic and linguistic map; anthropometric measurements. |

*Table 3 Continued*

| Field Trips | Major Activities |
|---|---|
| 1891 | Collected Chinook texts (limited information available). |
| | (1892.   Resigned from Clark University; appointed Chief Assistant, World Columbian Exposition, Chicago.) |
| | (1893.   At Chicago Exposition; trained George Hunt in the rudiments of phonological transcription.) |
| | (1894.   Appointed Curator in Field Museum, Chicago — a temporary position; searched for a permanent position part of the year.) |
| 1894 | Anthropometric measurements among Interior Salish: made plaster casts and took photographs; studied Tsetsaut (Athapascan) and Niska (Tsimshian) language, customs, and bodily measurements; observed and recorded songs and customs of Kwakiutl winter ceremonial. |
| | (1895.   Searched for a permanent position much of the year.) |
| | (1896.   Appointed Assistant Curator in ethnology and somatology at the American Museum of Natural History; appointed lecturer in physical anthropology at Columbia University for $1,500 a year.) |
| 1897 | Investigated physical characteristics of Indians on banks of Fraser River north of Lytton; customs and physical characteristics of Chilcotin; studied Bella Coola customs and beliefs; studied graphic art of the Haida; physical appearance of Haida and Tsimshian; limited language study. |
| | (1899.   Appointed Professor of Anthropology at Columbia University for a term of two years at $2,500 a year, effective July 1 — position later became permanent.) |

*Table 3 Continued*

| *Field Trips* | *Major Activities* |
|---|---|
| 1900 | Revised texts; worked on Kwakwala grammar and Kwakiutl ethnology; studied Indian art; studied customary techniques of collecting, preparing, and using plants among Kwakiutl; recorded tales; cast Indian faces in plaster of paris. |
| | (1901.    Appointed Curator of Anthropology in the American Museum of Natural History, January 1.) |
| | (1905.    Resigned from the American Museum of Natural History.) |
| | (1910–12.    Spent more than one year in Mexico helping to establish and working with the International School of American Archaeology and Ethnology.) |
| 1914 | Collected linguistic materials, including texts from the Kootenay; anthropometric measurements. |
| | (1915.    Conducted field work in Puerto Rico during summer — five weeks after his facial operation.) |
| | (1919–21.    Conducted field work in pueblos of New Mexico part of each summer.) |
| 1922 | Worked on linguistic problems among the Interior Salish; wife went with him to the field (limited information available). |
| 1923 | Cleared up doubtful linguistic and ethnological points, including Kwakiutl winter ceremonial and social organization, social organization of Bella Bella, and "Eagle" of Fort Rupert; Bella Bella folklore. |
| 1927 | Largely linguistic work, especially in Washington; students did ethnological work (limited information available). |
| 1930–31 | Acculturation; motion-picture photography and sound |

*Table 3 Continued*

Field
Trips                    *Major Activities*

recordings; corroboration of Hunt's material; style of
story telling of different people, including songs and
oratory; revision of texts with Hunt; description of
feasts and wedding.

(1936.      Became Professor Emeritus-in-Residence,
            Columbia University, stipend of $6,000,
            effective June 30.)
(1942.      Died in New York in December.)

Boas rarely participated in the daily lives of the Indians,
although at different times he spent a considerable amount of
time observing and recording significant aspects of customary
behavior. Most of his activities in the field were oriented toward
or derivative from language studies. Typically he worked with
a single informant eliciting information about specific linguistic
problems as well as more general ethnological topics. His orientation in the field was toward collecting ethnographic material
in the language of the Indians. He felt this was the safest and
most efficient way to collect data which reflected the natives'
own points of view. Consequently, from the perspective of contemporary ethnography he spent minimal time observing significant features of Indian life and negligible time participating
in it. He summarized his position regarding anthropological
research — as he viewed it at that time — in a letter to A. L.
Kroeber in 1935:

> To sum up the whole situation it seems to me that there are three
> questions that should be answered in all anthropological investiga-
> tions. First, how does a culture come to be what it is at the present

*time? Second, how does the culture as it exists at the present time determine the life of the people, and how do individuals influence the culture? And third, how far is it possible to recognize tendencies to future development in the present status of the culture. Any investigator who confines himself to one of these questions without any regard to the others may contribute valuable material but he is not an all around anthropologist* (Boas: 8/5/35).

Boas encountered a number of problems in field research. One of the most trying was his attempt to find suitable informants with whom he could work. This was notably true during his earlier years on the coast. He often complained in his letters and diaries about the time he lost searching for informants or, very often, about waiting for them to appear. He sometimes encountered hostility, distrust, and passive resistance from Indians whom he wanted to use as informants. After he began specializing in Kwakiutl studies around 1893, and after the Kwakiutl learned that he could be trusted — that he was not an agent for the government or a missionary who intended to interfere with their potlatches and winter ceremonials — he was able to overcome most of these difficulties. Nevertheless he sometimes met similar problems when he went to other areas.

Several anthropologists have commented that Boas probably did not like field work. Spier (1943:114), for example, claims that, "It is probable that he did not wholly enjoy field work, that he disciplined himself to it." Goldenweiser (1941:115) makes a similar observation when he writes, "In field work Boas found a sort of chastening influence. It took him away from books, from theory, from speculation, from students and lectures." Jacobs (1959:127) punctuates the same theme: "The austere visitor probably mingled politely with the natives, but with some discomfort and always with a feeling of pressure to get the scientific task accomplished." On the whole, however, Boas makes it clear that despite the problems of field work he did get a great deal of satisfaction from it. Field work provided a welcome change for him as he became increasingly involved in academic and administrative responsibilities. But as Jacobs suggests, he always felt a strong internal pressure to get as much work completed as possible before leaving the field. Such inconveniences as an unexpected delay in transportation and tardy or recalcitrant informants were all the more exasperating because of his motivation to continue uninterruptedly with his work. Also he occasionally became bored from the monotony of doing the same thing day after day.

One of the least attractive features of field work for Boas was the necessity of being separated from his wife and family to whom he was devoted. His letters from the field are replete with references to his concern for his family, the fact that he missed them, his frustration when he did not receive letters from them, and his annoyance at the irregularity of mail delivery. Even though he became absorbed in his work, toward the end of each field period he wrote about his anticipation of returning home to his family.

Boas rarely lived in an Indian household or community unless circumstances required that he do so. He usually stayed in a hotel or some other public accommodation within walking distance from the village where he wanted to work. After he came to know George Hunt very well, however, he lived with or near the Hunt family and their kinsmen in Fort Rupert and Alert Bay.

Boas often referred to the Kwakiutl as "my dear friends" but he established a closer working relationship with Hunt than with any other Indian on the North Pacific Coast. Hunt often addressed Boas as "my Dear friend" and closed his letters with a phrase such as "Good Bye to you Dear Friend." Boas frequently reciprocated with phrases such as "my dear George" or "Now my dear friend. . . ." The relationship between the two men was one of friendship but, equally as important, it was one of respect. Because of this Boas was able to elicit information which, according to Hunt, no other white man could have possibly acquired.

Boas was the first person to make a systematic survey of the Northwest Coast and to identify the language and tribal groups there. He was also concerned with the historical relationships among these groups. He published more than 10,000 pages of Northwest Coast material, over half of which is in the form of texts. A significant portion of his North Pacific Coast publications are essentially organized field notes. Boas was aware of many inaccuracies in these publications but he rarely corrected them in print. Furthermore he published new material as it came from Hunt, but he never explained the inconsistencies between the new material and that which had been published earlier. Consequently some anthropologists have exaggerated the severity of these problems and have dismissed his work as being unusable or of negligible value.

One of Boas' most basic general contributions to field methodology was his insistence that the ethnographer must work in the language of his people. Boas' extensive use of a single informant to record texts in the native language was unusual in anthropology. Furthermore he was the first anthropologist to train an informant to record field data in the informant's own language. Boas was also original in stressing the collecting and interpretation of field data from the point of view of the Indians themselves.

Ethnologists in continental Europe did not consider field work a necessary activity at the time when Boas began working with the Eskimo, or later when he began studying the Indians of the Northwest Coast. The general attitude toward field research among many continental ethnologists before 1920 appears to have been analogous to the attitude of many historians toward the work of newspaper reporters: comparing, analyzing, and interpreting sources was considered scholarship; working in the field was *merely* collecting.[15]

Boas' career in the United States, however, did not suffer because of his interest in field work. In fact field research became a respectable and essential part of ethnology in the United States through his continuous efforts which were contemporaneous with the field work tradition created in England by Haddon, Pitt-Rivers, and Seligman, and elaborated by such men as Malinowski and Radcliffe-Brown. From this point of view Boas did indeed establish field work as the basis of American anthropology.

# FRANZ BOAS AMONG THE KWAKIUTL*

RPR: Mrs. Tom Johnson talking about Franz Boas.

MRS. T. J.: I've got to talk about Dr. Franz Boas when he came to Fort Rupert—when he came to see my father, long ago and he asked him to do little work for him for the—for the university. So he [Hunt] started in. He was living with my parents that time and they [Boas] always have little questions every date—or days—and my father give—give himself to work for him. And he went everywhere to get the stories of the first Indians. They—they gathering comes in Fort Rupert and Dr. Boas came—came to Fort Rupert too. And that time my brother was first got to begin to get his dance. The winter [dance]. And Dr. Boas was amongst them and they took lesson every date what will be going on that date. And he [Boas] started to give himself to be in the dancing part. And he did. The—1893. That the time he started and my father invite some different tribes to come—come in our—come in our Reserve. And they came in and they started. And Dr. Boas was working amongst the Indians. He used to use our customs. He don't want to be left behind. And they call him *HēíLak̠walə̣ts*. That was his name. It was given to him. [The correct date is November 16, 1894.]

RPR: How do you say that, once more?

MRS. T. J.: It's *HēíLak̠walə̣ts*.

RPR: Uh-huh. Who gave him that name?

MRS. T. J.: My father.

RPR: Ah.

*Transcription of the author's tape-recorded interview (June 17, 1964) with Mrs. Tom Johnson of Fort Rupert, B.C. Mrs. Johnson, who is George Hunt's daughter, was born in 1888.

MRS. T. J.: And his—and all—all our relations. So he was amongst the people at wintertime dance. And he used to give feast to those—to those Indians. And later on he got his work with my father. He [Hunt] used to go around each villages to find out—find out the stories—the stories of the first generations to our people. And my father used to come home and write day and night. He used to be tired when he writes. He wasn't well educated, but he learned—learned all how it goes through nicely. And he made lot of the stories and sent it down to the museum at New York [American Museum of Natural History where Boas was working]. I used to help him when he does work. When he gets tired he tell me to try and learn how to work with him. And we used to work—sometimes he used to go other different tribes and get all kinds of things that belongs to the Indians—some of the masks and some of those kind. Everything he can get. And he bought them from the Indians. And he used to send it down to—down to New York. And he was well working man that time.

And Dr. Boas left us and he went back to—back to New York. And the next time he come in he went about the same—keep on with my father, George Hunt. And he was called to go to the World's Fair [World Columbian Exposition, 1893]. And he went there with ten mens and with some womens—Indian womens. And they get to Chicago. And they did lot of things. First of all when he went to Chicago and they built a Indian House there—big hall. And they started on that and it didn't take him long to finish it. Then they used to use it for everything. They dance and the white man go and see what's going on. Some of the Indians he [Hunt] took with them were—were having a dance, and do all sorts of things. They working on what they got—working on the things of the Indians long ago. Do little work for them while they do all the works they go for.

And one time they — near the end — they — what they are
doing — they have a big hall there for dancing hall and the
— he was told by the manager of the — the one that been
called them to go to Chicago, to have a fair dance on a — on
outside the sea. It was a . . . . And it's nighttime when he
get all the mens to start on to dance that night. They was
every kinds of dances there. And it's time for my father to —
to tell the — tell his people to dance on the platform outside
the little inlet. So the — all the white man was ashore and
they was watching. And they start to dance on the — on the
platform. And he use one thing that's very — I think it's very
hardest thing to see if we don't see it ourselves. He got — he
got that dance of *hā<sup>e</sup>LíxwalaL*. They call it *hā<sup>e</sup>LíxwalaL*.
And he . . . .

RPR: What does that mean?

MRS. T. J.: And he get it ready. And the man who's going to
dance with that — he's ready. And he came out. He was dressed
up in white. And they sang for him. And he was dancing
with his — with his club. So he — so they . . . . The — the
song is end and he start to go backwards and forward and he
was using the club on his body and he said — and the blood
came out — came out of his body. The white sheet was nothing
but blood and the white people were shouting. Tell my father
to stop it or he bleed to death. Some of them were fainting
about to see — see the blood all streaming down his body. So
after that was finished and he tell them to jump in the water.
And he went down. And he stayed quite a while. Then he
come — come up at the other side of the — it's kind of scow
— and, they pull him up and change his clothes. It was all
blood. And he — he came out and dance again. He was very
clean. No more blood there. And he . . . . That's a, that's
a thing what is good to make — they made a present for my
father. They gave him a gold medal, that time. They were

pleased for him to get the first prize on that day — on that night.

RPR: That was the second time, then, that your father met Franz Boas, was it?

MRS. T. J.: Yes, that the second time that he came here. [This is not accurate. Boas met Hunt for the first time in 1888. Hunt went to Chicago in 1893, and in 1894 Boas went to Fort Rupert.] And he — and call him to with him to Chicago for the World's Fair. And he was there with his men. And they did lot of things there. And after that they all come home. That was the end of the World's Fair. And he got something else — he's got a big framed picture from the — that was his prize and — and they came home. My father was still working when he came home getting the stories from other tribes — the generation of the other tribes and the — and he's been working there I don't know how many years. I was quite a little girl when he started and now I think I was — I think I was sixty — sixty years old when he died. He was still working on that kind of . . . .

RPR: How did he get the other tales? How did he get Indian tales?

MRS. T. J.: Because he goes around to different places and he hired them to — to tell stories to them. See, he used to go to the Nootka. He, he got lot of stories there. And he used to go the Bella Coola and he had lot of stories. They used their own words — own language — and go to the Knights Inlet.

RPR: Did he ever make up any tales himself or are they all . . . ?

MRS. T. J.: Yes. He used to get some from our . . . There was lot of old people that time he was working. They — he used to get lot of — the old people goes in our home and go and tell him the stories of our old people. The first generation when they first — first saw the light. Then they kept it in their mind. Go to the next — to them . . . . The children when they getten grown up they know the story because they always tell the story they beginning.

RPR: Can you tell me something about Franz Boas himself while he was here in Fort Rupert? What he did, who he lived with, how he acted, what he was like?

MRS. T. J.: Oh, yes. He came the second time and he was living with the Cadwalladers [George Hunt's sister]. And, he did lot of things while he was here with — her name was Julia [Averkieva] — and he made up his mind to give them something for prize when he was here. [She is referring to Boas' 1930–31 field trip.] And — and I think he bought some — some clothes for the men and some towels for the womens.

RPR: Was this for a potlatch?

MRS. T. J.: Yes. And he invite them. He bought some of the Indian food. He does out — what we do with it. And he — and he told me to cook — cook it for him. So they all come in and they — and they have their supper here, and . . . Oh, he was talking — sometimes talk our language. He learned it very much. And — and he gave it to everyone of the people that gathered in here for supper. He gave it like as we do — us Indians. He gave it away to our people. Then — because wanted to be a real Indian. Yes that's when he — when he gave away his — what he bought and gave it to our people and when it's through and they, they call $w^h\bar{a}ni$ [Julia Averkieva] to come and dance, and she was dancing. We all get up and dance with her and give her name — gave her name — that's her name, $w^h\bar{a}ni$, Julia, and he's finish with that. He [Boas] wants to be a — he wants to be regal as Indian does, because we like to give our children a name when we does 'give away' that's why he did that for. Julia never been amongst Indian people. So she was happy while they were here and after that he did lot of things with the Indians. And — and he bought some things from the Indians what they have, because that's why he come for, because he wants to know really what should be done with what he bought and he gets someone to come and help him dance with him. And we dance with Julia, with $w^h\bar{a}ni$, that's her name now. That's her Indian name. Oh he did lot of things. He goes around and get some more stories from the old people that was living, because they never forget about their stories at they beginning when they come to a man when they are born and they start on with stories every night. They tell the — they second generation to know — know all the stories they have — they beginning. They all have crest, that Indians. That's why they want to keep they stories all right.

RPR: Can you tell me something about Franz Boas as a man? What he was like as a — just a man? Describe him?

MRS. T. J.: Well, Dr. Franz Boas was a very kind man. And he really know — know to be amongst the Indian people. He goes around to every house and see — visit them and talk about things what he needs to know. All about the things of the Indians. And he works very well. We like him very much because he was very kind to us. That time when my brother was — when he was — know his winter dance — he [Boas] used to go and [stay] close by him, because he really wants to know what to be done. That's why he came for — to know everything belong to the Indians because they was lot of Indians when he first came. The Koskimo, and the Nawiti, and the Nakoaktok. They used to come and stay around here. They used to come — come to Fort Rupert to gather heres for dancing every winter and Dr. Franz Boas used to be amongst them. He used to use button blanket and some bark on his head and he was *really* likes to be amongst Indian people. He was very good to us.

RPR: Did he get along well with people and people liked him, generally?

MRS. T. J.: Yes

RPR: Did he seem to be relaxed when he was with people? Enjoy himself?

MRS. T. J.: Yes, yes he does. You see, you see we used to invite him, everyone that—they really like him. He used to invited by our friends and he go in with Julia. And they eat all our food. ᶜ*Lìᵉnə* [oulachon oil], *hā̄ᵉmas* [dried salmon] and some berries, dried berries. He likes them all. And everything we cook for him he eated.

RPR: Did he eat grease [oulachon oil]?

MRS. T. J.: *Yes.*

RPR: Very good.

MRS. T. J.: Oh, he likes it, because he want to be a real Indian. Oh.

RPR: You said earlier this afternoon that Boas never did bring his family with him. Is that correct?

MRS. T. J.: No.

RPR: He came alone every time except for the once—the one time he came with Julia?

MRS. T. J.: Yes. He was alone. Nobody . . .

RPR: How long did he stay while he was here?

MRS. T. J.: I don't remember. Maybe—maybe two months when he goes to different tribes. He used to go around to different tribes.

RPR: How did he get around?

MRS. T. J.: Oh, he used to go in a steam boat . . .

RPR: Did he ever go fishing with the men or work with the men?

MRS. T. J.: No.

RPR: Or do anything with the men other than his own work?

MRS. T. J.: No.

RPR: He didn't actually live with the people and—sort of day to day do the things everyone else was doing?

MRS. T. J.: No.

RPR: But he did—he lived with your family for awhile?

MRS. T. J.: Yes, he was living in our home. He stayed there over month. My father at Bella Coola—he was writing to him to go and meet him at Bella Coola. He was a walking this road behind us from Vancouver and he traveled with two men beside him and they met this — I don't know what he call those people — are living close to the road. He just sit down on a horse [?] both of those three and they go to a house under the ground. Maybe it's a — they stay there all the time and they — they were invited to the house and they get in there. Get something to eat. They eat some fried fish. They wasn't much tea around that time, so they went to Bella Coola.

RPR: This was with your father?

MRS. T. J.: Yes, with my father, because he went and met him [Boas] there.

RPR: I once heard a story about Dr. Boas. I wonder if you can tell me whether or not you heard it too, or maybe it's just a joke. He walked out of a house somewhere here in the village [at Fort Rupert] and a group of men were cutting wood on the beach. And one of the men said to the other man, in Kwakwala, something like, "If I had a face that looked like his," pointing to Boas, "I wouldn't be seen out in public." And they didn't know that Boas understood Kwakwala so he walked over to the edge of the beach where the men were standing and said, spoke to them in Kwakwala, and said, "Good morning gentlemen. It's a fine day, isn't it?" The men were — the man who made the comment was very embarrassed because he didn't know that Boas could understand Indian. Have you heard that story before?

MRS. T. J.: No. [Laugh]

RPR: Do you think that might be true? Something like that?

MRS. T. J.: Well, he used to go to other people when they — when he see them and they talk to him. [Laugh]

RPR: I also heard another story about him, that he used to be around taking notes. Did he take a lot of notes, by the way? Did he write much while — with people around?

MRS. T. J.: Yes

RPR: I heard that people didn't mind — they liked him — that they didn't mind his being around. He would come for dinner — and would be there for supper, that is — and he would still be there by the time everybody went to bed. They didn't mind that — with his pencil and paper. But they did get a little mad when he was still there in the morning with his pencil and paper, watching. Have you ever heard that?

MRS. T. J.: Oh, no. [Laugh]

RPR: I think Henry Bell [a Kwakiutl] told that story once. I don't know how he found out, or who told him that.

MRS. T. J.: Well, somebody must have remembered that.

RPR: Oh, how old were you, approximately, when you were working with your father who was working with Dr. Boas?

MRS. T. J.: Dr. Boas. I think I was twelve. Well, I was quite small when he first came that time in 18 — 1893 [1894]. I was — I think I was only five or six.

RPR: Did your father talk much about Dr. Boas?

MRS. T. J.: Yes, he used to tell us story when he was in New York and Chicago. He tell us a story what he see, what he hear, and talk about Dr. Boas always being amongst the Indian at Chicago.

RPR: Uh-huh. How was Dr. Boas — did he pay your father for each thing he sent him or did he pay him in advance, or how — how did that work? Do you remember?

MRS. T. J.: I think he paid for it — all of them. Sometimes be big box full — two sometimes, because he got it from — from other tribes.

RPR: Uh-huh.

MRS. T. J.: I used to help him for the numbers to put it on.

RPR: For the page numbers you mean?

MRS. T. J.: Yes, and put it in the book.

RPR: Ah. Dr. Boas really didn't spend much time actually living in the village then did he?

MRS. T. J.: No.

RPR: How much would you say just off hand, all-together, he might have spent?

MRS. T. J.: The time he staying around here?

RPR. Yes.

MRS. T. J.: Oh, well, only once he stayed around here maybe two months and next he came he didn't stay much longer around here. Maybe three weeks. I think it was three weeks because — because he went back early. Left us.

# NOTES AND REFERENCES

# IN SEARCH OF EXPERIENCE

1. For recent treatment of biography in general and the nineteenth-century life-and-letter tradition in particular, see John A. Garraty, *The Nature of Biography* (New York: Alfred A. Knopf, 1957), and C. C. Gillespie's "Bibliographical Essay" in his *Genesis and Geology* (Cambridge, Mass.: Harvard University Press, 1951).

2. Leo Tolstoy, *War and Peace* (New York: Heritage Press, 1938), II, 525–26.

3. Isaiah Berlin, *The Hedgehog and the Fox* (New York: New American Library, Mentor Books, 1957).

4. See A. J. Pomerans (trans.), René Taton's *Reason and Chance in Scientific Discovery* (New York: Philosophical Library, 1957, for an interesting discussion of the extent to which chance, in all of its ramifications, has played a part in scientific discovery. Although recognizing the possibility of such factors, however, Taton stresses much more the preparation of the scientist himself to recognize the accidental ("chance only helps those whose minds are well prepared for it") and the cultural level of scientific attainment which makes certain scientific steps possible and certain problems acceptable. The net effect of his argument as well as the thrust of his examples is to diminish the role of the scientist qua person while extolling the individual role in scientific activity.

5. Joel H. Hildebrand, *Science in the Making* (New York: Columbia University Press, 1957), p. 7.

6. Loren C. Eiseley, *Darwin's Century* (New York: Doubleday and Co., 1959); "Charles Darwin, Edward Blyth and the Theory of Natural Selection," *Proceedings of the American Philosophical Society* (1959), 103:94–158.

7. For a more detailed discussion of Brixham Cave and the importance of its excavations, see my "Brixham Cave and the Antiquity of Man," in M. Spiro (ed.), *Context and Meaning in Cultural Anthropology* (Glen-

coe, Ill.: Free Press, 1965), pp. 373–402, an expanded revision of a paper delivered at the meetings of the Society for American Archaeology in 1960.

8. See William Stanton's very interesting *The Leopard's Spots* (Chicago, Ill.: University of Chicago Press, 1960) for a treatment of this theme in America; there is no comparable description of the European phase, the central theme of which was the maintenance of the concept of the essential unity of the human species.

9. Paul Broca, "Histoire des Progres des Etudes Anthropologiques," *Memoires d'Anthropologie*, Paris, 1874, Vol. 2, pp. 488–509 (originally read July 8, 1869). See also George Stocking, "French Anthropology in 1800," *Isis* (1964), 55:135–50.

10. *Queries Respecting the Human Race to be Addressed to Travellers and Others* (London, 1841).

11. Thomas Bendyshe, "A History of Anthropology," *Memoirs of the Anthropological Society of London* (1863–64), 1:335–458.

12. An interesting study for intellectual history would be one in which the anthropological interests, concepts, etc. of the 1950's were compared to those of a generation earlier with some attempt to assess the impact of the war on the anthropological concerns.

13. This realization is part of a more widely dispersed appreciation of the role of the observer in science. As Leach points out (E. R. Leach, "The Epistemological Background to Malinowski's Empiricism," in *Man and Culture*, ed. Raymond Firth [New York: Humanities Press, 1957], p. 120) it was just this recognition that contributes to Malinowski's greatness: For Malinowski, culture consisted "in what the field-worker himself observes; it is intelligible in terms of the field-worker's personal private intuitions. No data outside the immediate subjective-objective present need to be considered."

14. Carl Resek, *Lewis Henry Morgan: American Scholar* (Chicago, Ill.: University of Chicago Press, 1960); Bernhard J. Stern, *Lewis Henry Morgan: Social Evolutionist* (Chicago, Ill.: University of Chicago Press, 1931); Leslie A. White, *Pioneers in American Anthropology: The Bandelier-Morgan Letters, 1873–1883* (2 vols.; Albuquerque: University of New Mexico Press, 1940). See also White's editions of Morgan's field trip notes in *American Antiquity, American Anthropologist,* and *Rochester Historical Society Publications.*

15. W. C. Darrah, *Powell of the Colorado* (Princeton, N.J.: Princeton University Press, 1951).

16. R. R. Marett, *Tylor* (New York: John Wiley and Sons, 1936).

17. A. Hingston Quiggin, *Haddon the Head Hunter* (Cambridge, Eng.: Cambridge University Press, 1942).

18. Melville Herskovits, *Franz Boas* (New York: Charles Scribner's Sons, 1953).

19. Robert E. Lowie, *Robert H. Lowie, Ethnologist* (Berkeley and Los Angeles: University of California Press, 1959).

20. Margaret Mead, *An Anthropologist at Work* (Boston: Houghton Mifflin Co., 1959).

21. Walter Goldschmidt (ed.), "The Anthropology of Franz Boas", *Memoirs of the American Anthropological Association*, No. 89; Raymond Firth (ed.), *Man and Culture*. See also the earlier A. I. Kroeber, et al., "Franz Boas, 1858–1942," *Memoirs of the American Anthropological Association*, No. 61.

22. Raymond Firth, *Man and Culture*, p. vii.

23. See particularly Margaret Mead, "Apprenticeship under Boas," and Clyde Kluckhohn and Olaf Prufer, "Influences During the Formative Years," in Goldschmidt (ed.), *Memoirs of the American Anthropological Association*, No. 89; and E. R. Leach's "The Epistemological Background . . ." in *Man and Culture*.

24. C. P. Snow, *The Search* (New York: Charles Scribner's Sons, 1959), pp. 103–04.

25. See particularly, Joseph B. Casagrande's edited *In the Company of Man* (New York: Harper Bros., 1960), in which twenty anthropologists describe their informants.

26. See A. I. Hallowell, "The Beginnings of Anthropology in America," *Selected Papers from the American Anthropologist 1888–1920*, ed. Frederica de Laguna (Evanston, Ill.: Northwestern University Press, 1960), pp. 1–90; also the much less satisfactory Panchanan Mitra, *A History of American Anthropology* (Calcutta, India, 1933).

27. Margaret Mead, "Apprenticeship under Boas," *An Anthropologist at Work*, pp. 33–35.

28. Raymond Firth, "Malinowski as Scientist and as Man," in *Man and Culture*, p. 10.

# WOMEN IN EARLY AMERICAN ANTHROPOLOGY

1. This paper is exploratory rather than definitive. Collections of letters and other important manuscript materials were identified at the

Peabody Museum, Harvard University, and the Archives of the Bureau of American Ethnology; but time limitations on this paper prevented me from consulting them. I hope that each subject may some day be accorded full-scale treatment, and that interest may be sparked to bring the existence of little-known biographical source material to the attention of anthropologists. In beginning my research I turned to various people who might direct me to source materials or who might have personal recollections of some of the women. In this regard, I wish to express my sincere thanks for the kind interest taken in my project by Professors Volney Jones and Leslie White, University of Michigan; Professor Arnold Pilling, Wayne State University, Detroit; the late Dr. A. V. Kidder, Sr. and Miss Margaret Currier, Harvard University; Professor A. I. Hallowell, University of Pennsylvania; Dr. Matthew W. Stirling, retired director of the Bureau of American Ethnology, of Washington, D. C.; Dr. William Sturtevant and Mrs. Margaret Blaker of the Bureau of American Ethnology; Dr. Clifford Evans, United States National Museum and Dr. Betty Meggers, Washington, D.C.; Dr. J. Alden Mason, Philadelphia; Mr. Ross Parmenter, New York; Dr. William N. Fenton, New York State Museum, Albany; the late Dr. S. A. Barrett, Berkeley, California; and Miss Mabel Densmore, Red Wing, Minnesota.

2. George Rosen, and Beate Caspari-Rosen, *400 Years of a Doctor's Life* (New York, 1947), pp. 87–92.

3. Rossiter Johnson (ed.), *Twentieth Century Biographical Dictionary of Notable Americans*, Boston, 1904; Vol. I, "Myra Colby Bradwell," n.p. Hereinafter cited as Johnson, 1904; Vol., ". . ."

4. Edward Lurie, *Louis Agassiz, A Life in Science* (Chicago, 1960), pp. 166–67, 200–01, 380–81. Acceptance of women in the various sciences was not unique to the United States in the nineteenth century; *cf.* Alexander F. Chamberlain, "Johanna Mestorf" (obituary), *American Anthropologist*, Vol. XI, No. 3; 536–37. The career of this German archeologist, 1829–1909, included curatorial and professorial appointments.

5. Whether the American Association for the Advancement of Science ever discriminated against women or whether it was simply a good platform for arguing women's rights is difficult to determine, but in 1880 an impassioned feminist plea was entered in a paper by Ellen Hardin Walworth under Natural History — not Anthropology, entitled, "Field Work By Amateurs," A.A.A.S. *Proceedings*, XXXIX, 597–602.

6. Edward B. Tylor, "How The Problems of American Anthropology Present Themselves to the English Mind," Anthropological Society of

Washington, *Transactions*, Vol. III, 1885, 81–95 (quotation on 93). The address was first printed in *Science*, IV (1884), 545–51.

7. W. H. Holmes, "Matilda Coxe Stevenson" (obituary), *American Anthropologist*, Vol. 18, No. 3, 1916, 552–59. Hereinafter cited as Holmes, 1916. Holmes designates Stevenson the founder of the Women's Anthropological Society, 555.

8. Daniel S. Lamb, "The Story of The Anthropological Society of Washington," *American Anthropologist*, VIII (1906), 564–579. Lamb provides the sequence and details noted regarding the joint meetings between the A.S.W. and W.A.S. that led to the eventual disbanding of the women's group, but does not discuss the Sanitary Improvement Company.

9. I am indebted to Dr. Evans and to Dr. Meggers for providing information concerning the Sanitary Improvement Company and making available to me the pamphlet regarding the W.A.S. as well as drawing my attention to George M. Kober, *The History and Development of the Housing Movement in the City of Washington, D.C.*, Washington, D.C.: Washington Sanitary Housing Companies (1927), p. 10, which details the work of Miss Clara de Gaffenried.

10. *Transactions of the American Ethnological Society*, I (New York, 1845), *passim*, sets forth information regarding the constitution and organization and a list of charter members.

11. *Congrès International des Americanistes Compte-Rendu de la Huitème Session Tenue a Paris en 1890*, Paris, 1892, 11, 13.

12. Alice Fletcher, *A Letter From The World's Industrial Exposition at New Orleans, To The Various Indian Tribes Who Are Interested in Education* (Carlisle, Pa. [1883]), 4 pp.

13. W. H. Holmes, "The World's Fair Congress of Anthropology," in *Selected Papers from the American Anthropologist, 1888–1920*, ed. Frederica de Laguna (Evanston, Ill., 1960), pp. 423–34. Five of the 38 participants listed by Holmes were women.

14. Holmes, 1916, 554.

15. Alfred M. Tozzer, "Zelia Nuttall" (obituary), *American Anthropologist*, XXXV (1933), 475–82. Hereinafter cited as Tozzer, 1933.

16. Johnson, 1904, Vol. X, "Erminnie Smith." In reply to my letter, William N. Fenton reported having read at the Bureau of American Ethnology the correspondence of Erminnie Smith, "a wonderful letter writer," to Major Powell; Fenton also notes the existence of correspondence between Smith and Fletcher. He considers Smith to have been

a good linguist and a "much better scientist than Harriet Maxwell Converse" who also did early work in Iroquois folklore.

17. Johnson, 1904, Vol. X, "Erminnie Smith."

18. An abstract of Smith's paper on jade appears in A.A.A.S. *Proceedings*, XXVIII (1879), 523–25. Thus far, the location of the entire paper remains unknown.

19. A.A.A.S. *Proceedings*, XXX (1880); abstracts of "Comparative Differences in the Iroquois Group of Dialects," 315–19, and "Animal Myths," 321–23.

20. Johnson, 1904, Vol. X, "Erminnie Smith."

21. A.A.A.S. *Proceedings*, XXXII (1882); Smith, 402–03, 595; Fletcher, 580–84, 595; Bowers, 595.

22. *Science*, V (1885), 3–4.

23. See, "Report of the Director," Smithsonian Institution, Bureau of Ethnology, *Annual Reports*, I–VII (1879–1885). VII, xxxi, notes Smith's death and continuation of her work by J. N. B. Hewitt; Vol. II, 47–166 contains Smith's "Myths of the Iroquois": with illustrations of the stories apparently done by an Iroquois informant.

24. John R. Swanton, "John Napoleon Brinton Hewitt" (obituary), *American Anthropologist*, XL (1938), 286–90.

25. Walter Hough, "Alice Cunningham Fletcher" (obituary), *American Anthropologist*, XXV (1923), 254–58. Hereinafter cited as Hough, 1923. Hough notes that Fletcher was actively interested in the work of the Peabody as early as 1880 or 1881 but was not officially listed among the personnel until 1886. She was instrumental in the preservation of the Serpent Mound in Ohio and her first scientific interest in anthropology was as much archeological as ethnological.

26. Among the many benevolent groups interested in the welfare of the American Indian was the "Mohonk Conference" founded in 1882 by a philanthropist, Albert K. Smiley, who opened his estate, now a summer resort, at Lake Mohonk to visitors who gathered each year to discuss Indian problems. The group was not a society and had no regular membership but the U.S. Board of Indian Commissioners, a semiofficial investigative body under the Indian Bureau made up primarily of interested private citizens, often met with the conference and held special sessions at Mohonk. The conferences continued more than three decades, and well into the twentieth century, with cooperating organizations, clung to the ideals of individual enterprise and assimilation of the Indian. Among the cooperating groups were the Society of American Indians

and the Women's National Indian Association. See *The Quarterly Journal of the Society of American Indians*, II (1914), 172–74; and "Mohonk Platform of Principles, adopted by the Mohonk Conference, October 9, 1885," *Publications of the Women's National Indian Association*, pamphlet, 4 pp., no date, no site.

Fletcher was a primary force in these organizations and, in the present day, it seems incredible that she could have been imbued with ideas of using force to get Indian children educated, spending as quickly as possible any capital held by tribes, and reducing tribal lands. The nine points set forth in the 1885 Mohonk Platform are understandable to some extent only if it is recalled that in the 1870's and 1880's Indian reservations were, in effect, prison camps designed to keep "hostile savages" in control. Kindly whites, guilty in the realization that the Indian had been misused, sought to grant human dignity and rights of citizenship to Indians although their methods were drastic and threatened the Indians' only remaining source of security, community life. The almost religious fervor concerning the sacredness of private property is a most notable feature of these groups.

27. Alice Fletcher, "The Hako: A Pawnee Ceremony," Smithsonian Institution, Bureau of American Ethnology, *Annual Report*, XXI (1904–1905). A complete bibliography of Fletcher's scholarly works accompanies the Hough obituary.

28. Charles F. Lummis, "In Memoriam, Alice C. Fletcher," *Art and Archeology*, XV (1923). See also "Alice C. Fletcher Memorial Meeting," *El Palacio*, XVI (1923), 83–88, which discusses Fletcher's remarkable powers of gentle persuasion, work in behalf of education in American archeology, and her "practical" approach to Indian problems.

29. Paul Radin, personal conversation with N.O.L., 1958. This impatient dismissal of my casual inquiry whether he had known Alice Fletcher distressed me at the time. I simply wished to know more about the woman who did field work on the Plains before the echoes of Little Big Horn had barely ceased reverberating and the hostilities of the Ghost Dance of 1890 were yet to come. On the basis of the present research, Radin's reaction is entirely understandable. With almost anyone else Fletcher could be all sweet reasonableness as the "expert" on Indian policy, but Radin was one of the few people in the early 1900's who actually saw what was happening to her beloved Omaha and other tribes. He was probably at no pains in Fletcher's presence to conceal *his* opinions based

on a great deal more scholarly objectivity than Fletcher's emotional commitment to the allotment system.

30. Thomas Henry Tibbles, *Buckskin and Blanket Days* (New York, 1957). Hereinafter cited as Tibbles (1957). The item noted occurs on p. 236. Tibble's manuscript was actually written in 1905, but additional materials were gathered by the publishers, including a biography of Tibbles, for the 1957 publication.

31. Tibbles (1957), p. 261. Pages 268–70 recount one argument Fletcher lost although she won the day. Tibbles was terribly distressed that Fletcher's outspoken criticism of Indian policy and questioning of Indians about injustices would get the party into trouble and even land them in prison — he had had experience with the amazing power wielded by Indian agents on the frontier. What really exasperated Tibbles, however, was Fletcher's combination of foolhardy crusader's zeal and insistence on the proprieties of cultured society. "Quoth our Boston dame to me, 'The House is the proper place for the agent to receive a lady.'" She was finally prevailed upon to visit the Rosebud Reservation Agent at his office and to Tibbles' relief opened conversation politely with a pleasantry about the weather; but Tibbles' heart sank when the agent, obviously considering the party nothing but nosey busy-bodies remarked, "I regulate everything here but the weather." Fletcher chose to consider this a lighthearted witticism — she had an ace up her sleeve. She presented her official credentials and the agent wilted as she knew he would.

32. Tibbles (1957), p. 260.

33. Francis La Flesche, "Alice C. Fletcher" (obituary), *Science*, LVII (August 17, 1923), 115. Hereinafter cited as La Flesche, 1923.

34. La Flesche (1923), 115.

35. La Flesche (1923), 115–16; Tibbles (1957), 295. Tibbles takes full credit for the Dawes Severalty Act. Actually, experiments of the Indian Bureau in granting patents in fee to individual Indians and gifts of land for family homesteads by benevolent groups were the model on which Fletcher's views and the Dawes Act were based.

36. Alice Fletcher and Francis La Flesche, "The Omaha Tribe," Smithsonian Institution, Bureau of American Ethnology, *Annual Report*, XXVII (1905–1906), 640–42. Actual publication of the *Reports* lags behind the sequence of volume dates so that information collected in 1910 was included at the end of this volume. Fletcher's assessments are given on pp. 640–42; comparisons are derived from my own observations

of Nebraska Winnebago and Omaha, 1950 and 1954, and discussions with Omaha people at the American Indian Chicago Conference, June 13–20, 1961, as well as from Mead (*See* n. 37).

37. Margaret Mead, *The Changing Culture of An Indian Tribe* (New York, 1932), p. 51. It is striking that while Mead's study shows the effects of tremendous changes between 1882 and 1930, particularly from *ca.* 1910, some thirty years later her descriptions of life among the Omaha in 1930 are still generally applicable.

38. *Cf.* Harold C. Fey and D'Arcy McNickle, *Indians and Other Americans* (New York, 1959), pp. 72–79, for an historical analysis of the Dawes Severalty Act and statistics on land losses.

39. Tibbles (1957), pp. 278–79.

40. Alice Fletcher, "Music As Found in Certain North American Indian Tribes," *Music Review* (August, 1893), 534–38. Quotations from first and final pages of article.

41. In 1946 when I was a young graduate student at the University of Chicago, well indoctrinated in the importance of rapport and empathy and had even had some field experience, I attended a lecture by Paul Radin and was outraged at his matter-of-fact account of obtaining certain data by means of psychological and economic pressures. In later years, when Radin and I became friends and even worked together, I was able to understand somewhat better the sense of urgency that motivated early field workers to obtain data by almost any means that would not actually skew the information or cause the anthropologist to be ousted from the group. In truth, some data would have been irrevocably lost but for the work of Radin and others. However, the wounds still smarting as a result of Radin's methods did not simplify my first field work among the traditionalist Winnebago.

42. La Flesche (1923), 116, recounts a traditional ceremony held specially as an expression of thanks to Fletcher for her work in behalf of the Omaha. At the close, the leader "told Miss Fletcher that she was free to study this and any other tribal rites."

43. Hough (1923), 254–55.

44. Holmes (1916), 557–59.

45. Holmes (1916), 552–56.

46. Matilda C. Stevenson, "The Zuni Indians: Their Mythological, Esoteric Societies and Ceremonies," Smithsonian Institution, Bureau of American Ethnology, *Annual Report*, XXIII (1901–1902), 310, 380. Hereinafter cited as Stevenson (1901–1902).

47. Holmes (1916), 553.

48. Holmes (1916), 558–59 lists Stevenson's bibliography.

49. Stevenson (1901–1902), 17.

50. J. Walter Fewkes, "Contributions to Hopi History, 1890 — II. Oraibi in 1890." *American Anthropologist*, XXII (1922), 268–83. Kiva incident and quotation, 273.

51. I am indebted to William Sturtevant for his kindness in drawing my attention to both the article and illustration from the *Illustrated Police News* and for providing me with copies. Dr. Sturtevant brought the first draft of this paper to the attention of Dr. Stirling who wrote his comments to Dr. Sturtevant in a letter, December 21, 1964. Dr. Stirling has kindly granted permission to cite the letter, and all references to Stirling in the text derive from his letter.

52. Stevenson (1901–1902), 379; 381–82.

53. Stevenson (1901–1902), 608. Fenton's letter already referred to includes some of the Stevenson legends and sources of further data which unfortunately could not be consulted before the deadline date on the present paper. Like other people who recalled stories of her terrible temper, Fenton notes "Tilly's fights with Major Powell who used to fire her regularly and then she would threaten to invoke Congress on him and get herself restored to office. On one of these occasions, he got so mad he had a stroke and that finished him." Stirling's letter substantiates this account as he learned it from May S. Clark, who was present in Powell's office; ". . . Tilly stormed in the door, leaned over Powell's desk and shaking her finger in his face, shouted, 'Major Powell, you are a damned liar!' The major, face flushed, rose in his chair and fell back with the first of the strokes which later resulted in his death." Stirling substantiated another incident first mentioned to me by Fenton: once when Stevenson was asked to itemize an expense account, she filed under informants' fees, "One man, one night, one dollar." On another occasion, according to Stirling:

> *She included a case of Scotch in her expense account, which of course was turned down. She insisted that it was necessary in her work, since nothing else would induce the Indians to give out their more secret information. It was pointed out to her that it was illegal to give whiskey to Indians. She replied that it was only illegal to sell it to them. The item became a matter of pride and principle with her, and she insisted she would fight it through.*

Harry Dorsey, administrative assistant to the Secretary (who told me this story), finally settled the matter by paying her from the Smithsonian Institution private funds, but allowing her to think she had won her point, and that it had gone through the Government Accounting Office."

54. A. V. Kidder, Sr., personal correspondence with N.O.L. Stirling commenting on this paper, notes: "J. P. Harrington also told me the story of Tilly's Indian name. He said that the Indians told her it meant "Little Mother" and that she was quite proud of it: Actually, the literal translation of the name was 'Big broad buttocks like a mesa.' "

55. Tozzer (1933), 475–82. Unless otherwise cited, all biographical data on Zelia Nuttall are taken from this source which also includes a full listing of her bibliography. After the first draft of this paper was written I learned that Ross Parmenter was working on a full-length biography of Nuttall and so I discontinued research on her. I had intended to delete Nuttall from this account but Mr. Parmenter urged me to retain it as useful background material to his more specialized study of a phase of Zelia Nuttall's career which is included in this volume.

56. XXVII (1928), 40–43.

57. "Frances Densmore," *Science*, CXXV (1957), 1240. Hereinafter cited as "Densmore," *Science* (1957). Just as this article in honor of Densmore's ninetieth birthday went to press, news was received of her death.

58. Phyliss Ashmun, "Indian Music Expert Reveals Highlights of Fascinating Career," *Ashland Daily Press* (Ashland, Wisconsin), July 28, 1945. Hereinafter cited as Ashmun, 1945. Densmore was seventy-eight years old at the time of this interview and was engaged in a study of Indian music in the Upper Peninsula of Michigan for the University of Michigan.

59. Stirling letter, December 21, 1964. For further data on Densmore's work with the Bureau of American Ethnology, cf. "Densmore," *Science* (1957); Marquis, *Who Was Who*, III (Chicago, 1960), 222.

60. Ashmun, 1945.

61. Mabel Densmore, personal correspondence with N.O.L.

62. Frances Densmore, "Chippewa Music," Smithsonian Institution, Bureau of American Ethnology, *Bulletin 45* (1910), 3. The second volume of this work appeared as *Bulletin 53* (1913).

63. Frances Densmore, "The Music of the Filipinos," *American Anthropologist*, VIII (1906), 611–32.

64. "Densmore," *Science* (1957).

65. Ashmun, 1945.

66. A. A. Kroeber, "Elsie Clews Parsons" (obituary, Part II of two parts), *American Anthropologist*, XLV (1943), 252–55. The first three pages detail biographical data on birth, marriage, etc.

67. Leslie Spier, "Elsie Clews Parsons" (obituary, Part I), *American Anthropologist*, XLV (1943), 244–51. Hereinafter cited as Spier (1943). Assessment of Parson's sociological writing, 245–47.

68. Spier (1943), 245–50.

69. Gladys Reichard, "Elsie Clews Parsons," *Journal of American Folklore*," Vol. LVI (1943), 45–48. (Parsons' bibliography, 48–56.) Hereinafter cited as Reichard (1943). This entire issue of the *JAF* is a memorial in honor of Parsons.

70. Spier (1943), 244.

71. Reichard (1943), 48.

72. "Anthropology and Prediction," *American Anthropologist*, XLIV (1942), 337–44.

73. "Code of Ethics of The Society for Applied Anthropology" (Mimeograph, 7 pp. including discussion of Code by John W. Bennett, 1962, 2–7).

74. A. I. Hallowell, "The Beginnings of Anthropology in America," *Selected Papers from The American Anthropologist, 1888–1920,* ed. Frederica de Laguna (Evanston, 1960), pp. 1–90. Fletcher is noted here only for her archeological interests in her work with F. W. Putnam in raising money to purchase the Serpent Mound area and turning title over to the Ohio Archeological and Historical Society in 1900. See Hough (1923), 254–58 for further discussion of Fletcher's interest in archeology.

75. That women were not oblivious to the problems of physical anthropology may be seen in Alice Fletcher, "The Problems of The Unity or The Plurality and The Probable Place of Origin of The American Aborigines. (A Symposium.) Some Ethnological Aspects of the Problem," *American Anthropologist*, XVI (1912), 37–39.

## GLIMPSES OF A FRIENDSHIP

1. *American Anthropologist.* "The American Anthropological Association," Vol. 5, No. 1 (Jan.-March 1903). 178–92.

2. *American Anthropologist.* "Anthropologic Miscellanea," Vol. 13, No. 2 (April-June 1911). 344.

3. *American Anthropologist.* "Anthropological Notes," Vol. 18, No. 1 (Jan.-March 1916). 150.

4. *American Anthropologist.* "Proceedings of the American Anthropological Association for the Year Ending December 1928," Vol. 31, No. 2 (April-June 1929). 313–27.

5. American Association for the Advancement of Science. *Proceedings of the American Association for the Advancement of Science, Thirty-fifth Meeting Held at Buffalo, New York, August 1886.* F. W. Putnam (ed.) (Salem, 1887).

6. American Association for the Advancement of Science. *Proceedings of the American Association for the Advancement of Science, Fortieth Meeting Held at Washington, D.C., August 1891.* F. W. Putnam (ed.) (Salem, 1892).

7. American Association for the Advancement of Science. *Proceedings of the American Association for the Advancement of Science, Forty-ninth Meeting Held at New York, N.Y., June 1900.* L. O. Howard (ed.) (Easton, Pa., 1900).

8. Baerlein, Henry. *Mexico: The Land of Unrest* (Philadelphia, 1914), 103–09.

9. Bancroft, Hubert Howe. *The Book of the Fair* (Chicago and San Francisco, 1893). II, 629–63.

10. Batres, Leopoldo. *Memorandum Dirigido al Sr. Lic. D. Miguel Diaz Lombardo, Ministro de Instrucción Pública y Bellas Artes* (Barcelona, 1911).

11. Blom, Frans. Letter to R. P., February 2, 1962.

12. *Boas Anniversary Volume: Anthropological Papers Written in Honor of Franz Boas.* Berthold Laufer (ed.) (New York, 1906).

13. Boas, Franz. *Handbook of American Indian Languages, Bulletin 40, Part I, Bureau of American Ethnology.* (Washington, D. C., 1911). (Edits entire volume; contributes "Tsimshian," 283–422; "Kwakiutl," 423–558, and "Chinook," 558–678.)

14. Boas, Franz. *Curso de antropología general de F. Boas, Conferencias 1–8,* Escuela de Alto Estudios, Universidad Nacional. (Mexico, 1911-12).

15. Boas, Franz. "Summary of the Work of the International School of American Archaeology and Ethnology in Mexico, 1910–14," *American Anthropologist,* Vol. 17, No. 2 (April-June 1915). 384–89.

16. Boas, Franziska. Letters to R. P., February 1 and May 12 and 20, 1964.

17. Bulmer, Gillian. Letter to R. P., October 11, 1962.

18. Campbell, T. N. "George Charles Marius Engerrand, 1877–1961," *American Anthropologist*, Vol. 64, No. 5, Pt. 1 (October 1962). 1052–56.

19. Collier, Donald. Letter to R. P., June 21, 1962.

20. Conway, Marjorie. Letter to R. P., November 27, 1961.

21. Covarrubias, Miguel. *Indian Art of Mexico and Central America.* (New York, 1957). 14.

22. Duffus, R. L. "Franz Boas vs. Hitler," review of Boas' "Race and Democratic Society," *New York Times Book Review*, Section 7, February 10, 1946.

23. Dulles, John W. F. *Yesterday in Mexico.* (Austin, 1961).

24. Escuela Internacional de Arqueología y Etnología Americanas. *Año Escolar de 1910 a 1911: Informe del Presidente de la Junta Directiva.* (Mexico, 1912).

25. Escuela Internacional de Arqueología y Etnología Americanas. *Album de Colecciones Arqueológicas, Laminas 1–69: Seleccionadas y arregladas por Franz Boas.* (Mexico, 1911–12).

26. Escuela Internacional de Arqueología y Etnología Americanas. *Año Escolar de 1911 a 1912: Anexo al Informe del Presidente de la Junta Directiva, Exposicion de Trabajos.* (Mexico, 1912–13).

27. Escuela Internacional de Arqueología y Etnología Americanas. *Año Escolar de 1911 a 1912: Informe del Presidente de la Junta Directiva.* (Mexico, 1913).

28. Field Columbian Museum. *An Historical and Descriptive Account of the Field* Columbian Museum. Pub. 1, Vol. 1, No. 1. (Chicago, 1894).

29. Gamio, Manuel. "Los Monumentos Arqueologicos de las inmediaciones de Chalchihuites, Zacatecas," *Anales del Museo Nacional de Arqueología, Historia y Etnología.* Tomo II (Mexico, 1910).

30. Gamio, Manuel. *Texto para el Album de Colecciones Arqueológicas Seleccionadas y Arregladas por el Dr. Franz Blom.* (Mexico, 1921).

31. Gamio, Manuel. "Boas Sobre Cerámica y Estratigrafía," *American Anthropologist*, Vol. 61, No. 5, Pt. 2. Memoir 89: "The Anthropology of Franz Boas" (October, 1959). 117–18.

32. Godoy, José F. *Porfirio Diaz, President of Mexico, The Master Builder of a Great Commonwealth.* (New York and London, 1910). 75.

33. Hay, Clarence L. Personal communication, May 4, 1962.

34. Hay, Clarence L. Letter to R. P., July 2, 1962.

35. Herskovits, Melville J. *Franz Boas: The Science of Man in the Making.* (New York, 1953).

36. International Congress of Americanists. *Actas de la Novena Reunion, Huelva, 1892.* (Madrid, 1894).

37. International Congress of Americanists. *Verhandlungen des XVI Internationalen Amerikanisten-Kongresses, Wien 9, bis 14, September, 1908.* (Vienna and Liepzig, 1910).

38. International Congress of Americanists. *Reseña de la Segunda Sesion del XVII Congreso Internacional de Americanistas efectuada en la Ciudad de Mexico durante el mes de septiembre de 1910.* (Mexico, 1912).

39. International Congress of Americanists. *Proceedings of the XVIII Session, London, 1912.* (London, 1913).

40. International Congress of Americanists. *Proceedings of the Twenty-Third International Congress of Americanists, New York, 1928.* (New York, 1930).

41. Jacobs, Paula. Personal communication, February 8, 1964.

42. Kroeber, A. L. "Frederic Ward Putnam," *American Anthropologist*, Vol. 17, No. 4 (October–December 1915). 712–18.

43. Kutscher, Gerdt. "Los Estudios Americanos en Berlin," *Berlin, Piedra de Toque del Mundo Libre.* (Hamburg, 1959). 34–37.

44. Laughton, Nadine. Unpublished notes on Zelia Nuttall's relatives, January 22, 1961.

45. MacCurdy, George Grant. "Seventeenth International Congress of Americanists, Second Session — City of Mexico," American Anthropologist, Vol. 12, No. 4 (October-December 1910). 600–05.

46. MacCurdy, George Grant. "Duke de Loubat," *American Anthropologist*, Vol. 29, No. 2 (April–June 1927). 340.

47. Mason, J. Alden. "Franz Boas as an Archaeologist," *American Anthropologist*, Vol. 45, No. 3, Pt. 2. Memoir 61: "Franz Boas, 1858–1943." (July–September 1943). 58–66.

48. Mason, J. Alden. Letter to R. P., February 11, 1963.

49. Mason, J. Alden. "la quincena furiosa," *Ciencias Politicas y Sociales,* Año IX, No. 32 (Mexico, April–June 1963). 223–55.

50. McCown, Theodore D. "Alfred Louis Kroeber (1876–1960)," *Robert H. Lowie Museum of Anthropology, University of California, Annual Report for the year ending June 30, 1961.* (Berkeley, 1961). 29–37.

51. Miller, Thomas B. Personal communication, September 2, 1961.

52. Moore, Sally Falk. "The Department of Anthropology," *The Bicentennial History of Columbia University: The History of the Faculty of Political Science.* (New York, 1955). 147–60.

53. *New York Evening Post.* "A Toltec Teapot Tempest." (New York, Dec. 31, 1910).

54. *New York Evening Post.* "John Hay's Son, Refugee; Tells of Huerta's Attitude and Fight at Vera Cruz." (New York, May 4, 1914).

55. *New York Times.* "Calles Ousts an Official." (New York, June 9, 1925).

56. *New York Times.* "Boas of Columbia to Retire June 30." (New York, March 20, 1930).

57. *New York Times.* "Roland Dixon of Harvard Dies." (New York, December 21, 1934).

58. *New York Times.* "Prof. Franz Boas, Scientist, Dies, 84." (New York, December 22, 1942).

59. *New York Times.* "Ernst Boas Dead; Heart Specialist." (New York, March 10, 1959).

60. Noguera, Eduardo. *Guide Book to the National Museum of Archaeology, History and Ethnology.* Popular Library of Mexican Culture (Mexico, 1938). 5–7.

61. Nuttall, Dr. George H. F. "Zelia Nuttall, b. 1857 d. 1933." Unpublished notes, June 19, 1933.

62. Nuttall, Zelia. "The Terracotta Heads of Teotihuacan," *The American Journal of Archaeology and of the History of the Fine Arts.* Vol. 2, No. 2 (April–June 1886), 157–78 and Vol. 2, No. 3 (July–September 1886) 318–30. (Baltimore, 1886).

63. Nuttall, Zelia. "Preliminary Note of an Analysis of the Mexican Codices and Graven Inscriptions," *Proceedings of the American Association for the Advancement of Science, Thirty-fifth Meeting.* (Salem, 1887). 325–27.

64. Nuttall, Zelia. "Standard or Head-Dress?" *Archaeological and Ethnological Papers of the Peabody Museum,* Vol. 1, No. 1 (Cambridge, 1888). 1–52.

65. Nuttall, Zelia. "Relics of Ancient Mexican Civilization," *Proceedings of the American Association for the Advancement of Science, Fortieth Meeting.* (Salem, 1892). 355–57.

66. Nuttall, Zelia. Letter to Frederic Ward Putnam, April 16, 1892. Archives of Harvard University.

67. Nuttall, Zelia. "Ancient Mexican Featherwork at the Columbian Exposition at Madrid," *Report of the U.S. Commission to the Madrid Exposition,* Executive Documents of the House of Representatives for

the 3rd Session of the 53rd Congress 1894–95, Vol. 31, No. 100. (Washington, 1895). 329–37.

68. Nuttall, Zelia. "The Meaning of the Ancient Mexican Calendar Stone," *Proceedings of the American Association for the Advancement of Science, Forty-ninth Meeting.* (Easton, Pa. 1900), 320.

69. Nuttall, Zelia. *The Fundamental Principles of Old and New World Civilizations.* (Cambridge, 1901).

70. Nuttall, Zelia. "Introduction," *Codex Nuttall, Facsimile of An Ancient Mexican Codex.* (Cambridge, 1902).

71. Nuttall, Zelia. *The Book of the Life of the Ancient Mexicans: Part I, Introduction and Facsimile.* (Berkeley, 1903).

72. Nuttall, Zelia. "Some Unsolved Problems in Mexican Archaeology," *American Anthropologist,* Vol. 8, No. 1 (January–March 1906). 133–49.

73. Nuttall, Zelia. "The Astronomical Methods of the Ancient Mexicans," *Boas Anniversary Volume.* (New York, 1906). 290–98.

74. Nuttall, Zelia. "A Curious Survival in Mexico of the Use of the Purpura Shellfish for Dyeing," *Putnam Anniversary Volume.* (New York, 1909). 368–84.

75. Nuttall, Zelia. "The Island of Sacrificios," *American Anthropologist,* Vol. 12, No. 2 (April–June 1910). 257–95.

76. Nuttall, Zelia. "The Aztecs and their Predecessors in the Valley of Mexico," *Proceedings of the American Philosophical Society.* (Philadelphia, 1926) 245–55.

77. Nuttall, Zelia. "Sculptured Rebuses" (Abstract 64), *Abstract of Papers Presented at the 23rd Congress of Americanists.* (New York, 1928). 41.

78. Nuttall, Zelia. "Nouvelles lumières sur les civilisations américaines et le système du calendrier," *Atti del XXI Congresso Internazionale degli Americanisti. Roma Settembre 1926.* (Rome, 1928). I, 119–48.

79. Nuttall, Zelia. "Note on Some of the Jewels Contained in Tomb 7 at Monte Alban," *Bulletin of the Pan American Union.* Vol. 66, December 1932 (Washington, 1932). 896–98.

80. O'Shaughnessy, Edith. *A Diplomat's Wife in Mexico.* (New York, 1916).

81. Peabody Museum of American Archaeology and Ethnology. *Codex Nuttall, Facsimile of an Ancient Mexican Codex,* with an introduction by Zelia Nuttall. (Cambridge, Mass., 1902).

82. Peterson, Frederick. *Ancient Mexico.* (New York, 1959). 32.

83. Portilla, Miguel-Leon. "Manuel Gamio, 1883–1960," *American Anthropologist*, Vol. 64, No. 2 (April 1962). 356–66.

84. *Putnam Anniversary Volume: Anthropological Essays Presented to Frederic Ward Putnam in honor of his Seventieth Birthday, April 16, 1909, by His Friends and Associates.* Franz Boas (ed.) (New York, 1909).

85. Putnam, F. W. *Twentieth Annual Report*, Peabody Museum of American Archaeology and Ethnology in Connection with Harvard University. (Cambridge, 1886).

86. Putnam, F. W. *Twenty-sixth Annual Report*, Peabody Museum of American Archaeology and Ethnology, Harvard. (Cambridge, 1892).

87. Putnam, F. W. *Thirty-fifth Annual Report*, Peabody Museum of American Archaeology and Ethnology, Harvard. (Cambridge, 1901).

88. Romanell, Patrick. *Making of the Mexican Mind.* (Lincoln, Neb., 1952).

89. *Science*, "University and Educational News," n.s. Vol. XXXII, No. 828 (November 11, 1910). 662–63.

90. *Science*. "The International School of American Archaeology and Ethnology," n.s. Vol. XXXIII, No. 841 (February 10, 1911). 211.

91. *Science*. "Accounts of the Sessions of the Sections and Societies of the Fifth New York Meeting of the American Association for the Advancement of Science," n.s. Vol. LXIX, No. 1779 (February 1, 1929). 122–24.

92. Seler, Eduard. "Ancient Mexican Feather Ornaments," *Bureau of American Ethnology Bulletin No. 28.* (Washington, 1904). 57–74.

93. Seler, Eduard. "Basis and Object of Archaeological Research in Mexico and Adjoining Countries," *Science* (March 17, 1911). 397–402.

94. Seward, Julian H. "Alfred Louis Kroeber, 1876–1960," *American Anthropologist*, Vol. 63, No. 5, Part 1 (October 1961). 1038–59.

95. Tanner, J. M. "Boas' Contributions to Knowledge of Human Growth and Form," *American Anthropologist*, No. 5, Part 2. Memoir 89: "The Anthropology of Franz Boas." (October, 1959). 76–111.

96. Tozzer, Alfred M. "Report of the Director of the International School of American Archaeology and Ethnology in Mexico for 1913–14," *American Anthropologist*, Vol. 17, No. 2 (April–June 1915). 391–95.

97. Tozzer, Alfred M. "Zelia Nuttall," *American Anthropologist*, Vol. 35, No. 3 (July–September 1933). 475–82.

98. Tozzer, Alfred M. *Chichen Itza and its Cenote of Sacrifice.* Memoir of the Peabody Museum of Archaeology and Ethnology, Harvard University, Vol. XI. (Cambridge, 1957). 9.

99. University of Pennsylvania. "Collections and Publications," *Free Museum of Science and Art Bulletin*, Vol. 1, No. 1 (Philadelphia, May 1897).

100. Wake, Charles Staniland (ed.) *Memoirs of the International Congress of Anthropology.* (Chicago, 1894).

101. White, Leslie A. "The Ethnography and Ethnology of Franz Boas," *Bulletin of the Texas Memorial Museum, No. 6, April, 1963* (Austin, 1963).

102. *Who Was Who in America, Vol. I*, 1897–1942. (Chicago, 1943).

103. *Who Was Who in America, Vol. II*, 1943–1950. (Chicago, 1950).

104. World's Columbian Exposition, 1893. *Official Catalogue, Part XII, Anthropological Building, Midway Plaisance and Isolated Exhibits.* Revised Edition. (Chicago, 1893).

105. Yampolsky, Helene Boas. Letter to R. P., June 17, 1963.

106. Yampolsky, Helene Boas. Personal communication, June 24, 1963.

# FRANZ BOAS:
# ETHNOGRAPHER ON THE NORTHWEST COAST

1. Most of the information on which this study is based comes from more than 50,000 pages of diaries, letters and other manuscript materials written to and by Franz Boas. I warmly acknowledge the debt I owe to my wife and research assistant, Evelyn C. Rohner, who read and abstracted a large part of the Boas correspondence. Special recognition is also given to Dr. Hedy Parker for her steady efforts to translate more than five hundred pages of Boas' letters and diaries from handwritten German script. A great part of the information in this study comes from these translations. Some of the translations were not completed in time to be included in this article. I want to express my appreciation to the American Philosophical Society for permission to publish this material. Research for this article would not have been possible without a grant from the University of Connecticut Research Foundation and from the American Philosophical Society.

I want to thank Marius Barbeau, David Bidney, Franziska Boas, Helen Codere, Wilson Duff, Frederica de Laguna, Walter Goldschmidt, Erna Gunther, A. I. Hallowell, Harry Hawthorn, June Helm, Jules Henry, Gordon Hewes, E. Adamson Hoebel, Dell Hymes, Melville Jacobs, Seth

Leacock, Edwin Lemert, Paul Leser, Alexander Lesser, G. P. Murdock, Ronald Olson, Amelia Schultz, George Stocking, Wayne Suttles, Ruth Underhill, Arthur Vidich, Ruth Sawtell Wallis, Wilson Wallis, and Harry Wolcott for their excellent criticisms and comments on an earlier draft of this paper. I am gratified by the thought and consideration they put into their observations. Their assistance has helped add many new insights into the problem of Boas as an ethnographer.

The material regarding the way in which the Kwakiutl perceive Boas is based in part on taped and written interviews with several key informants during our periods of field research among the Kwakiutl from August, 1962, through August, 1963, and again during the summer of 1964. The remainder is based on Boas' correspondence with the Kwakiutl.

2. George Hunt, Boas' major Kwakiutl informant, was born in February, 1854, to a Scot father and Tlingit mother. He was raised among the Kwakiutl at Fort Rupert and learned Kwakwala, the native language of the Kwakiutl, as his first language. Boas met Hunt in Victoria in June, 1888, but the latter did not become Boas' major informant until after the World Columbian Exposition at Chicago in 1893.

Hunt sent 5,650 pages of manuscript materials to Boas from 1896 until Hunt's death on September 5, 1933. This figure offers only a minimal estimate, however, of the work that Hunt did for Boas because Hunt also sent an unknown number of pages of data to Boas from 1894 to 1896. Furthermore, Hunt had been working with Boas from time to time from 1888 to 1893 at which time Hunt brought a group of Indians to the Chicago Exposition. It was here that Boas trained Hunt in the rudiments of phonological transcription. Leslie White (1963:33) estimates that Hunt contributed over two-thirds of Boas' major works on the Kwakiutl. This must be taken as a conservative estimate.

3. In 1885 Boas worked as an assistant under Bastian in the Royal Museum of Ethnology in Berlin. Bastian, Curator of Ethnography there, wanted Boas to collect specimens for the museum.

4. When Boas began research in 1884 the committee consisted of Edward B. Tylor, chairman; George M. Dawson, director of the Geological Survey of Canada (Ottawa); General Sir J. H. Lefroy (London) who dropped from the committee in 1891; Daniel Wilson (Toronto) who dropped from the committee by 1894; R. G. Halburton (London), and George W. Bloxam (London), secretary of the committee, who was no longer participating by 1895. Cuthbert E. Peek (London) became

secretary in 1896. Horatio Hale (Ontario), editor of the committee, became a regular participating member in 1894.

5. Most of the interior of the province falls within the Plateau culture area rather than the Northwest Coast culture area where he was accustomed to working. Technically, because this article is concerned with Boas' field research on the Northwest Coast, consideration of his work in the interior of British Columbia should be excluded. To do so, however, would distort the story of Boas as an ethnographer. No clear conceptual or methodological distinction can be made between his work on the North Pacific Coast and his research in the interior of British Columbia.

6. His wish to take his family to Victoria did not materialize.

7. In one of his publications Boas (1896:232) wrote, "On one of my later visits I had received an Indian name, Heiltsakuls, 'the one who says the right thing.'" The translation of the name given in this source does not agree with the translation which he wrote to his wife and which is cited in the text of this paper. Furthermore, according to George Hunt's daughter (personal communication) the name which was given to Boas by George Hunt was really *hēíLaḵwaləts*.

8. A more complete description of this field trip is not included here because Boas summarized his major activities during the 1897 field trip in one of his publications (Boas 1898:8-11).

9. References to Hunt's lifetime work with Boas are impossible to include in this paper because of their extensiveness. They will be the point of focus in a later article which I plan to write.

10. Boas spent part of July in San Francisco before going into the field in 1914. His letters from British Columbia give few indications of his activities there, but they are filled with statements about his acute concern regarding the war in Europe and his apprehension about his mother's welfare in Germany. The day he arrived in Cranbrook, for example, he wrote to his wife: "I hope my work here will get ahead quickly so that I can get home soon. I don't feel like working at all. The terrible war drives me crazy" (Boas: 8/7/14).

11. Prior to going to British Columbia, Boas and his wife stayed for a week in Seattle with Leslie Spier and his wife, Erna Gunther. Here Boas formed a committee for the emergency Society to assist colleagues as a consequence of the war. They then visited Victoria where Boas continued his work with George Hunt. This was the first time in twenty-two years that Boas had been in Victoria.

12. I have anglicized the Kwakiutl term *nəᵉmī'mot* (which designates the Kwakiutl ambilateral descent groups) to *numimot* (Rohner n.d.:48-49). Boas used the term nememot (*nəᵉmī'mot*) for many years in his correspondence with George Hunt, but he did not use it in his major publication on Kwakiutl social organization (Boas: 1920).

Prior to leaving for British Columbia in 1923, for example, Boas wrote to Hunt: "I hope you received my letter in which I asked you to go to Bella Bella about the 10th of this month and to try to straighten out in the greatest possible detail the neᵉmemot of the Bella Bella and the neighborhood" (Boas: 10/8/23).

13. Boas addressed his letters to the Governor of British Columbia, but since British Columbia does not have a Governor I presume he meant Lieutenant-Governor.

14. These comments by Mrs. Johnson were tape-recorded in Fort Rupert on June, 1964. The taped portion of the interview, of which this is a part, has been transcribed and appears at the end of this essay.

15. I am indebted to Paul Leser for these comments on the attitude of European scholars toward field work before 1920.

REFERENCES CITED

Boas, Franz
1886–1933    Boas Family Papers. Unpublished letters and diaries in the Library of the American Philosophical Society, Philadelphia.

1896    "The Indians of British Columbia," *Bulletin of the American Geographical Society*, 28:229-243.

1898    "Operation of the [Jesup North Pacific] Expedition in 1897," *American Museum of Natural History*, Memoirs, Vol. 2.

1909    "The Kwakiutl of Vancouver Island," *American Museum of Natural History*, Memoirs, Vol. 8.

1920    "The Social Organization of the Kwakiutl," *American Anthropologist*, 22:111-26.

Cranmer, Daniel
1943    Correspondence with Franz Boas. Unpublished letters in the Library of the American Philosophical Society, Philadelphia.

Dawson, George M.
1894    Correspondence with Franz Boas. Unpublished Letters in

the Library of the American Philosophical Society, Philadelphia.

Fortes, Meyer
1953     "Social Anthropology," A. E. Heath (ed.), *Scientific Thought in the Twentieth Century*, New York: Frederick Ungar Publishing Company, pp. 329–56.

Goldenweiser, Alexander
1941     "Recent Trends in American Anthropology," *American Anthropologist*, 43:151-63.

Hale, Horatio
1888–1890 Correspondence with Franz Boas. Unpublished letters in the Library of the American Philosophical Society, Philadelphia.

Hunt, George
1930–1931 Correspondence with Franz Boas. Unpublished letters in the Library of the American Philosophical Society, Philadelphia.

Jacobs, Melville
1959     "Folklore," *The Anthropology of Franz Boas*, Walter Goldschmidt (ed.), American Anthropological Association, *Memoir*, 89.
1965     Personal Communication.

Johnson, Mrs. Tom
1964     Personal Communication (taped interview).

Lowie, Robert
1937     *The History of Ethnological Theory*, New York.

Rohner, Ronald P.
    *The People of Gilford: A Contemporary Kwakiutl Village*, National Museum of Canada, Bulletin (forthcoming).

Spier, Leslie
1943     "Franz Boas and Some of His Views," *Acta Americana*, 1:108-127.

White, Leslie
1963     *The Ethnography and Ethnology of Franz Boas*, Texas Memorial Museum Bulletin No. 6.